THE LAST
VOYAGEURS

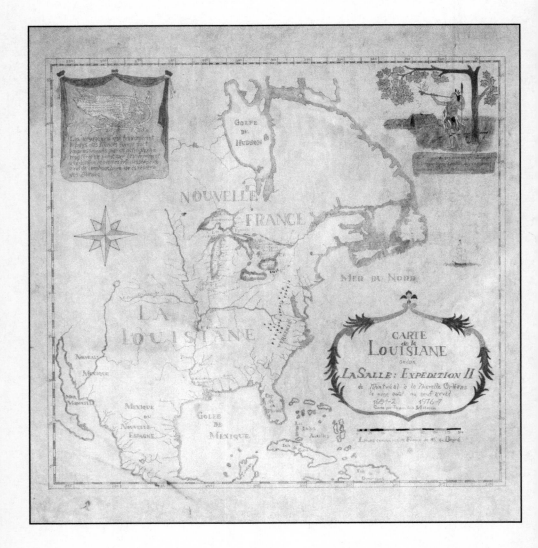

THE LAST VOYAGEURS

Retracing La Salle's Journey Across America:
Sixteen Teenagers on the Adventure of a Lifetime

LORRAINE BOISSONEAULT

PEGASUS BOOKS
NEW YORK LONDON

THE LAST VOYAGEURS

Pegasus Books LLC
80 Broad Street, 5th Floor
New York, NY 10004

Copyright © 2016 by Lorraine Boissoneault

First Pegasus Books edition April 2016

Interior design by Maria Fernandez

Library of Congress Cataloging-in-Publication Data is available.

ISBN: 978-1-60598-976-1

10 9 8 7 6 5 4 3 2 1

Printed in the United States of America
Distributed by W. W. Norton & Company

For Mom and Dad,
who taught me to make life an adventure

CONTENTS

PROLOGUE

Gary, Indiana
December 19, 1976

The travelers trudged across damp dirt roads in a jagged line,
some clumped together in groups of two or three, others
walking alone. Overhead the sky was clear blue, the occasional wispy cloud drifting by. But few of the men could see the
sky, or the icy lake beneath it that lay immediately to the north.
They were bent over with unwieldy fifty-pound loads balanced on
their backs. The weight of these loads, wooden chests filled with a
variety of shelter-building tools and other essential items, was borne
by a leather strap wrapped around the forehead. Some supported the
load with their hands, while others let their arms dangle limply at
their sides. The odd rock that appeared underfoot jabbed through
layers of wool and leather, bruising the heel and testing the strength
of the moccasins. What the men could see of their surroundings
provided little relief from the drudgery of the march.

When it was founded in 1901, U.S. Steel was the largest business
enterprise ever launched; after almost a century in operation, the
Gary Works facility was a formidable operation to behold. Close

to the horizon, smoke obscured the sky. Tall metal towers belched puffs of dirty white gas. Behemoth machines stretched into the distance: blast furnaces, annealing operations, temper mills, ladle metallurgy facilities. All were connected by an intricate system of railroad tracks and pipes. The air reeked of sulfur and chemicals. The stench burned like bile in the travelers' throats and seeped into their pores and fibrous wool clothing. For days to come, whenever they sweated they would catch the lingering smell of the steel mills.

It would have been an otherworldly sight to the French explorers these twenty-three men were impersonating. It was already stark and depressing to the modern travelers who had grown up with the knowledge of steel mills, who regularly used dozens of products made from metal. But for the Frenchmen who had covered the same ground three hundred years earlier, the industrial complex could have been a scene from Dante's *Inferno*. All that was missing were a few hundred doomed souls and the Devil himself.

Reid Lewis had never envisioned himself or his crew in Gary, Indiana, marching through U.S. Steel's largest manufacturing facility. He'd thought of his expedition as a crusade for the environment and the past. When their route had been determined months earlier, they'd planned to paddle their canoes across the southern shore of Lake Michigan, passing the industry and pollution at a distance. That plan had seemed feasible all the way up until the previous week. Then the weather got colder and the snow came down heavier and the ice along the shoreline grew thicker. Too many days were spent in warm auditoriums doing educational presentations instead of paddling across the unfrozen stretches of lake. It became impossible to safely launch the canoes, trapped as they were behind 8-foot-high palisades of ice.

The options before them had been limited. They could go immediately south on the Chicago River rather than taking the longer route they'd planned from the St. Joseph River to the Kankakee. Or they could follow the Des Plaines River to the Illinois. Finally, they could abandon their canoes and most of their equipment and start walking across northern Indiana and southern Michigan toward the St. Joseph River. The decision came down to a single question: What did René-Robert Cavelier, Sieur de La Salle do? He'd never gone down the Des Plaines, and although he had traveled the Chicago River, the journey Lewis and his men hoped to re-create had not followed that path. What La Salle *had* done on more than one occasion was abandon his canoes and nonessential gear when the winter became too fierce and froze all open water. He either built new canoes later or traded for them.

It was decided that the modern crew would walk. Walking was unappealing, especially considering the terrain they'd have to cover. But after nearly a week of indecision, any choice was better than more uncertainty. They sent their canoes and equipment ahead by truck since they couldn't very well rebuild or trade for the vessels—the faux birch-bark boats were among the few of their kind in the world.

They now found themselves plodding along the dirt and concrete roads as if on a death march. A midnight blue police car escorted them through the mill yard, its lights flashing. Some of the mill's operations had been halted for the group for safety reasons. One of the security guards told the travelers that this act of charity and goodwill would cost U.S. Steel somewhere around $30,000. If they'd had any other choice, they wouldn't be walking at all, but at least walking through the mill cut down on the number of miles they'd have to cover. When traveling on foot, every mile made a difference—the shorter the route, the better.

Workers at the mill stared at the strange men as they marched along with their wooden chests and canvas bags of gear. Some of the travelers wore colorful knitted hats and mittens while others had their sleeves rolled up to the elbow and covered their heads only with bandanas. One young man wearing a green headband had a black-powder musket perched on top of his bags. A few workers shouted questions to the group as its members walked by the red-hulled SS *Arthur M. Anderson*, a mammoth lake freighter that was famous for being the last vessel in touch with the doomed *Edmund Fitzgerald* before it sank in 1975. The bulwarks separating the lake from the shoreline were rimmed with ice, the mill's equipment covered in a thin layer of frost and snow.

On their first day of walking, the men covered thirteen miles and finished the trek at Marquette Park in Indiana. Exhaustion overtook everyone, dulling their relief at having survived the hike through hell. The crew's doctor was called upon to bandage blisters and examine sore feet. No one was accustomed to walking such distances carrying heavy loads. At least they didn't have too many more days of hiking ahead of them: with an average of thirteen miles a day, including a break for Christmas, they would reach the St. Joseph River within a week, on December 26. Locals said the head of the river was still unfrozen. If the men arrived on schedule, they could rapidly paddle from the St. Joseph to the Kankakee and the Illinois River before everything iced over.

As planned, the men reached the St. Joseph on December 26. The river was frozen.

Chapter One

MAKE NO LITTLE PLANS

**Montreal, New France
1600s**

Had the Biblical chroniclers begun their task several thousand years later, at the dawn of the Age of Exploration, the Genesis version of European history in North America might go something like this: *In the beginning there were cod. And man caught the cod and ate the cod, and saw that cod was good.*

However lofty the Europeans' later motivations for migrating to the New World might have been—religious freedom, king and country, a chance at a new life—what first drove them to make the voyage across an expansive ocean was their enormous appetite for both fish and profit. Cod made up 60 percent of all fish eaten in Europe and could be cooked fresh, or salted, or preserved with lye, as in the traditional Nordic dish lutefisk. The abundance of the fish on the western side of the North Atlantic was a marked contrast to the waters around Europe. When Basque fishing fleets discovered the huge stock around the year 1000, they kept their voyages across the Atlantic secret. For hundreds of years they controlled the market. But the secret didn't last.[1] By 1550, fishermen of multiple European nations were taking advantage of the bounty overseas, and they soon made another new discovery: the indigenous people of the continent, who the Europeans encountered when they set up fish-drying racks on the shores of North America. The Native Americans were curious and eager to trade, and they possessed something that proved to be immensely valuable to the men who came across the ocean: beaver furs.

And with the cod came the beaver, and man used beaver skin to cover himself, and knew that beaver was good.

Beaver skins were highly valued because the fur was soft yet waterproof. When the skins were turned into felt they could be used to make the stylish men's hats that became popular across Europe starting in the mid-1500s. On that continent the animals had been hunted almost to extinction for their pelts, and by the 1600s lived almost exclusively in Russia. This new source of furs on the other side of the Atlantic offered a lucrative opportunity for expansion into the New World. Sailors and merchants from across Europe traversed the ocean for the sake of their stomachs, then stayed to pad their wallets. The French were among those Europeans coming to the New World, and navigator Samuel de Champlain created a permanent French claim to the region by founding Quebec City in 1608. Later he traveled west to explore the Great Lakes, or the "sweet seas," as he called them.[2]

While Champlain tromped across the interior of the continent at the beginning of the 17th century, the private French trading group Compagnie des Cent-Associés held a monopoly over the fur trade. Most Frenchmen avoided the difficult work of trapping beavers themselves; they relied on Native Americans to capture the beavers, then traded guns, pots and pans, cloth, and other goods for the furs. Most prized among the types of furs on offer were *castor gras*, greasy beaver skins. This variety of pelt was created by the natives, who wore the coarse beaver fur directly against their skin for up to a year. The garment absorbed body oils and the rough outer hairs were rubbed away, leaving the soft undercoat exposed and ready for the felting process.

The arrival of Europeans caused no small amount of upheaval in native communities. By the early 1600s, Native Americans had been trading for European goods for three-quarters of a century. The race to acquire guns, fabrics, and cooking utensils exacerbated conflicts that had long been brewing between different Native American nations. The Iroquois Confederacy and several tribes that belonged to the Algonquian language group, all of whom lived in the Northeast and around the Great Lakes, were engaged in a bloody conflict over land and resources, which would later be called the Beaver Wars. Although the Europeans may not have understood the nature of the conflict—or realized that they were one of the main causes of it—they were quick to use it to their advantage.

In 1603, Champlain allied himself against the Iroquois because members of other tribes, such as the Huron, were willing to trade with the French, whereas the Iroquois' warfare interfered with the trade. In the coming years, the Iroquois began attacking French settlements directly. During the early years of his rule, which began in 1643, King Louis XIV had maintained an "out of sight, out of mind" policy when it came to governing the colony, but as the clashes continued to escalate in frequency and severity, he knew the time had come for intervention. In 1663, he made New France a royal province. The territory would eventually stretch across modern-day eastern Canada to the Great Lakes and down the Mississippi River. In 1665, King Louis sent a 1,250-man regiment to Quebec to defend the colonists. A local government was established and the power was divided between three leaders: a governor who dealt with military and diplomatic affairs, an intendant for economic issues, and a bishop for spiritual matters. A council of colonists advised the governor and intendant.

In addition to sending more men to the burgeoning colony, King Louis's minister of finances Jean-Baptiste Colbert initiated a recruitment program called *filles du roi* (King's Daughters) so that the men could have suitable European wives and begin the business of repopulating the "savage wilderness." Although six hundred girls emigrated between 1663 and 1673, their arrival only seemed to cause more problems. Sometimes double and triple marriages were performed, and in other cases no one would marry the women, leaving them to be cared for by the community.[3]

After more than a century of Europeans jostling for power and territory in North America, the number of players had been reduced but the stakes were much higher. England seized control of New Netherlands (a territory along the East Coast that included modern-day New York City) in 1664, effectively sealing the Dutch out of the new territory. By that point warriors in the Iroquois Confederacy had chased all the other Northeastern tribes hundreds of miles away from their homes, resulting in a mass migration that forced most tribes to resettle west of the Great Lakes. All this had been done in an attempt to monopolize trade with the Europeans, and it had worked with the English and the Dutch—but the French remained steadfast in their refusal to trade with the Iroquois. With the British and French vying for control of the St. Lawrence River and the Iroquois struggling to maintain their grasp on the region, it seemed as if any outcome were possible.

It was into this world of foreign peoples and complicated politics that René-Robert Cavelier, Sieur de La Salle arrived in 1667 at the age of 23. The population of French citizens in North America was around four thousand. Prior to coming to New France, La Salle had spent years studying under the Jesuits. Because he planned to become a priest he had renounced his claim to any land or wealth he might otherwise have inherited from his family in Rouen, Normandy. But after repeatedly requesting and being denied the opportunity to travel abroad as a missionary and teacher, La Salle left the Jesuits with the knowledge that there was nothing for him in France. His older brother, Jean, was a Sulpician priest who lived on the other side of the Atlantic in New France. La Salle decided to use his brother's connections as a chance for a new adventure and traveled to reunite with him in 1667.

He was granted a *seigneurie* from the Sulpicians on the western side of the Island of Montreal later called La Chine, a landholding that came with a number of responsibilities, including constructing homes and a farm and managing the people who lived on it. La Salle spent the next several years learning the languages of local tribes and developing his property. But a life of administrative duties and overseeing a seigneurie wasn't enough to satisfy La Salle. He wanted to see more of this new world.

⚬—⚬—⚬

Green Bay, Wisconsin
September 18, 1973

"I was taught that our country was developed from the east to the west by the covered wagon," said Reid Lewis from behind a tall podium, his face peeking over the top and his voice amplified by a foam-covered microphone. He spoke with a French accent and the white feather in his hat fluttered in the wind. "If they tell you that, you say, '*Excusez-moi*, that is not so.' Because our part of the country was developed from the north to the south, not by the covered wagon, but by the canoe. And it was the French that did that." He paused to look out at the audience of children and adults sitting and standing in the grass. "And you know something else," he added, "they will tell you democracy was born in the east, perhaps in Philadelphia. If they tell you that, you say, 'Excusez-moi, that is not so.' Democracy began in my state of Illinois because the French men and women voted. And you did not have to be rich. While meantime out East only the men could vote and they had to be rich to vote. So you see, we have very much to be proud of."

Lewis was at the end of a months-long canoe journey down Lake Michigan and half of the Mississippi River, then back up it again. Given another option, maybe he wouldn't have paddled back up the Mississippi. The river had a crushingly powerful current that constantly pushed against the canoes, and the oppressive summer heat made it feel as if they were sitting in a sauna all day long. But that was the beauty of historical reenactments—the choice was out of his hands. The route had been determined long before Lewis came along to paddle it. It was the passage followed by Louis Jolliet, a French explorer who was the first European to paddle on the Mississippi River three hundred years earlier and the man Lewis was supposed to be impersonating. Jolliet was the reason why Lewis was dressed in a blue shirt with a ruffled collar, the reason why he adopted a French accent whenever he spoke in front of a crowd, and the reason why he found himself on this expedition. Well, technically, Ralph Frese, master canoe builder and amateur historian, was the reason Lewis was on the expedition. Frese had recruited Lewis to lead the group of seven men down the river. But that was just semantics. The initiative began with Jolliet and Jacques Marquette, the Jesuit priest who accompanied the explorer. And now it was ending with them (or rather with modern American men pretending to be them).

Lewis returned to his home in Elgin, a suburb of Chicago, after his summer reenactment. It was time to get back to the business of living like a 20th-century man. He resumed teaching French to high school students, going on dates with his girlfriend, Jan, and spending as much time as possible outdoors. Frequently he thought back on the Jolliet-Marquette reenactment voyage. It had been physically difficult but mentally invigorating to momentarily escape the suffocating grasp of modernity. Now he was back to seeing all the ways in which the world seemed to be falling apart. The Civil Rights movement had ostensibly ended with the Civil Rights Act of 1968, but there were plenty of unresolved questions on the issue of race; the Vietnam War was still chewing soldiers up and bringing them back with injuries both bodily and spiritual; the Watergate scandal continued to unfold and now Vice President Spiro Agnew was resigning; and the Cold War with the Soviet Union loomed over everyone. Somewhere along the way it seemed to Lewis that society became much more complicated and citizens were caught up in numerous forms of social strife. Who could be sure of what choices would result in a better future?

But maybe there was a way to get people refocused on action and daring. The idea came to Lewis in the shower, of all places. Maybe the key to solving the problems of the future was to look into the country's past, like some kind of reverse fortune-telling. What if he attempted something even bigger than the Jolliet-Marquette voyage, with more participants, and the whole nation watching? The crew could test themselves against the elements, study the environment of the rivers and lakes they traveled across, and talk with communities along their route. They'd prove that same spirit of adventure and determination on which America was founded was still thriving, and that it could be harnessed to confront all the problems the country faced.

And there'd never been a better time for it—the entire country was gearing up for a celebration of the American Revolution bicentennial.

———

"To recall [July 4, 1776] is not, I hope, to indulge in chauvinism," wrote journalist Bill Moyers in *Newsweek* in July 1975.[4] His fear wasn't unreasonable. The anniversary had been on people's minds since the late sixties, and no one could decide how best to commemorate the birth of the nation. On July 4, 1966, the federal government created the American Revolution Bicentennial Commission to oversee bicentennial festivities. Almost as soon as the commission was born, it began experiencing existential quandaries. What should the bicentennial be? A celebration or a somber remembrance of the past? A unified undertaking or a series of events spread across the country? Public figures and government officials weighed in with their opinions. John Rockefeller III announced, "If we allow the birthday-party concept to prevail, we will have missed a once-in-a-century opportunity to stimulate a sense of renewal and rededication, even an American renaissance."[5]

While communities around the country began planning pageants and writing songs, the bicentennial commission floundered under its identity crisis. When it submitted a first report to President Nixon in 1970, it came under attack for its ineptitude and for recruiting corporate businessmen who wanted to use the bicentennial to sell things. Some critics were beginning to label it the "buy-centennial" for all the kitschy memorabilia that were popping up—mugs in gas stations, red-white-and-blue toilet seats, children's lunch boxes, buttons bearing George Washington's face and Paul

Revere's silhouette.[6] By 1973 the commission was replaced by a new board, the American Revolution Bicentennial Administration (ARBA), and it was decided that there would be no one national celebration. The ARBA would coordinate with towns and cities around the country that wanted to host events.

Preparations began well in advance of the two-hundredth anniversary, with some activities starting a year early. The American Freedom Train, a twenty-four-car museum on wheels carrying documents and artifacts, set off on its journey in 1975, with plans to stop at eighty cities around the country. The city of Chicago was organizing a massive bicentennial International Trade Exposition to be held at Navy Pier on Lake Michigan. Attendants would include representatives from Japan, Spain, Yugoslavia, Luxembourg, South Korea, West Germany, Pakistan, Morocco, and many others. The Watershed Heritage Project set about training thousands of students around the country to monitor water quality and other environmental factors in hopes of cleaning up the nation's waterways. More than four thousand bicyclists had agreed to ride across the nation on a "bike-centennial" journey from Jamestown, Virginia, to Astoria, Oregon. New York City was gearing up to host some of the world's most famous tall ships for an aquatic parade on the Fourth of July. And then there were the nearly twenty million elementary and junior high school students who sent letters to one another to replicate the colonial "Committees of Correspondence," in which colonists protested British rule.[7]

Ambitious individuals were just as eager to join the furor. Robert Cowles, Jr., a 23-year-old from Virginia and a fifth-generation direct descendant of Thomas Jefferson, grew out his wavy red hair and created an hour-long live performance called "An Interview with Thomas Jefferson." His profile, demeanor, and knowledge of his ancestor's history made him undeniably appealing—it was like watching one of the Founding Fathers come back to life to see what the country had become. Dan Ambrose, another young man fascinated with his country's history, walked six hundred miles across the Camino Real in a wool habit accompanied only by a donkey named Holley. His 1975 trip brought him in contact with twenty Jesuit and Franciscan missions along the dusty California route.

Amid the plans happening around the country, Reid Lewis busied himself with the early stages of creating a reenactment that would outdo all other reenactments. First he needed to pick an explorer—a French one, since his expertise was in French language and history. Preferably an explorer whose journeys took him across the central part of the country, through the Midwestern states and Lewis's home of Illinois. This was the regional history that was most often overlooked by those living along the coasts, Lewis thought. Finally, planning the voyage would be much easier, not to mention more historically accurate, if there were a lot of written records about this explorer.

After some deliberation, Lewis settled on René-Robert Cavelier, Sieur de La Salle, the first European to travel to the mouth of the Mississippi River. La Salle's was a lengthy voyage that passed through the heart of the country and, despite some disagreements between historians on the smaller details, there were ample written records about La Salle's life and successful expedition.

Lewis decided to call his grand scheme La Salle: Expedition II. A simple, memorable name for what would be the most ambitious educational project he'd ever attempted: a 3,300-mile canoe journey across North America—from Montreal to the Gulf of Mexico—completed by twenty-three men all looking, sounding, and behaving like the French voyageurs who made the same journey almost three hundred years earlier. Those voyageurs were the men who paddled the canoes and carried furs during overland portages, the Europeans who peeled back the mysterious interior of North America and were among the first to have contact with native tribes. In Lewis's version of events, the crew of voyageurs would be comprised mostly of recently graduated high school students. They'd use the journey to create educational material for their peers on subjects like hydrology, history, and ecology, all while giving performances for communities along their route. Would it require an epic amount of planning, paperwork, and fund-raising? Yes. Would there be unforeseen obstacles to contend with? Undoubtedly. But once he got the idea in his head, Lewis couldn't let it go. He was an ambitious man, driven to succeed, the kind of person who'd become director of a summer school in France during his first year of teaching. He figured he was ready for this next great challenge, regardless of what other people might say.

But before he could convince anyone that his plan wasn't some half-baked bicentennial folly, he knew he'd need to explain why. Why go to all the trouble of dragging twenty-three men, sixteen of whom would still be teenagers, across two countries for eight months? Why the costumes, the canoes, the research projects?

Lewis had several points to make when he gave his response, and his answers lay at the heart of what drove him to bring the trip to fruition. First, people had been lamenting "the youth of today" for as long as he'd been a teacher. Adults routinely deplored modern teenagers' behavior, saying they were lazy or reckless or couldn't be trusted with important tasks. Lewis believed that if he gave students the right instructions and had a little faith, they'd surprise him. Youth was not synonymous with bad behavior. Next, he liked to point out that most people were celebrating the bicentennial of the American Revolution with events featuring British history on the East Coast, but Frenchmen had been the ones to explore the continent long before American settlers in the British-controlled territories traveled west. All that history had been forgotten or relegated to a few short lines in history textbooks, Reid believed, and it deserved a prominent place in the national narrative.

Finally, Lewis felt the country needed to be resuscitated from its stupor. The last two decades had induced a crisis of national identity. Lewis thought the time had come to rejuvenate the nation's zeitgeist. He wanted to inject it with the same spirit of discovery and curiosity that marked the European Age of Exploration. What better way to do that than to prove, with the entire nation watching, that modern man was just as capable of great feats as his forebears? Paddling down the major waterways of North America might not change anyone's stance toward the Soviet Union or desegregation, but maybe it would motivate people to do more than sit idly by and wait for the world—and their own lives—to magically fix themselves.

As for the costumes, well, they couldn't very well interpret the 17th century dressed in bell-bottoms and T-shirts. If they were going to do the thing, they'd do it right.

For all his charisma and confidence, Lewis knew he couldn't achieve a voyage of this magnitude alone. He'd need other adults to help him, men who possessed skills he didn't have, who could be counted on in life-or-death situations, and who would help him choose the teenage crew members. To start with, Lewis recruited his older brother, Ken. It was more than nepotism that spurred Lewis to call on his brother for assistance: Ken was smart, industrious, and one of Reid's most trusted friends.

When they were boys, Ken was always teaching Reid new things, though they were less than two years apart. One winter Ken had learned all about making cheese and used buckets of snow to teach Reid about cutting the curd and separating the whey. Later, when Ken started studying French, Reid decided he needed to learn the same language. Ken shared what he learned throughout his academic career and, later in life, from books he read for recreation. These lessons never felt patronizing. Reid looked up to his brother and enjoyed spending time with him, and the two had stayed close into adulthood.

This closeness was probably aided by the fact that they had such different personalities and careers; it rarely felt as if they were competing with each other. Reid liked being in charge of things and enjoyed the spotlight. He had a gift for conjuring up grand schemes and believing so strongly in their achievability that everyone else felt compelled to share in the vision. Ken wasn't the type to come up with a master plan. Instead, he thought of himself as the perfect follower. He'd proved just how well he could work with a team during the Jolliet-Marquette expedition, having supported Reid as leader of that voyage in 1973. He'd created an educational musical presentation for the last trip and planned to do so again for La Salle: Expedition II. He even offered to learn about accounting so that he could keep the books for the expedition. For his role, he chose the name Antoine Brossard from among a list of twenty-three known crew members of the original expedition.

For the remainder of adult spots on the crew, Lewis hoped to recruit teachers from his current and former school districts. He'd begun his teaching career in Crown Point, Indiana, and since moving to Illinois taught exclusively in Elgin. Elgin had two high schools, Larkin High School, where Lewis taught, and Elgin High School. He planned to recruit teachers and students from both schools and circulated memos at the start of the 1974 school year. The memos for the teachers described the goals of the trip, some of the research projects he wanted to undertake, and what kind of involvement would be required of them over the next several years. As for the students, Lewis asked that a small subset (only boys currently in their junior year of high school) attend a presentation he gave in Elgin and Larkin high schools. If they were interested, they could submit a short application and come to a subsequent informational meeting.

But Lewis wasn't content to wait for applications to come to him from the teachers. They would be his main source of support before and during the expedition, leading research projects and helping the students properly prepare for the physical and mental trials ahead of them. In addition to sending announcements, Lewis reached out to several teachers he judged would be valuable assets on the expedition. The first was Dick Stillwagon, a biology teacher at Crown Point High School in Indiana.

Lewis and Stillwagon had taught in the same school in the sixties. They became close friends outside of work, taking martial arts classes together and singing with a folk group. Lewis knew Stillwagon's skills in canoeing and first aid would be invaluable along the route, and he'd asked Stillwagon to join the crew shortly after the idea first came to him. Despite being married and having four kids, Stillwagon agreed to play the role of 17th-century surgeon Jean Michel and lead the fitness and health projects. He was also charged with developing a workout regimen to prepare the crew members for the expedition. Stillwagon knew it would be hard to spend so long away from his wife, Rowena, and their sons and daughters, but he'd been looking for an escape from classroom teaching for years. This was the perfect chance.

John Fialko was another teacher Lewis had worked with, this time at Larkin High School. He'd always admired Fialko and knew he could be counted on. Lewis liked to call him "General"—Fialko taught shop and metalworking and the sign on his classroom door said GENERAL METALS. Like Lewis, Fialko was slight in stature, had a deep respect for the people of the past, and was passionate about the outdoors. But the men also had one significant difference: Fialko was introverted and didn't enjoy spending time in front of the public. That he felt more comfortable doing things with a few people or by himself was one of two concerns they discussed about Fialko's joining the trip. The second concern was that he didn't swim. Privately, he was apprehensive about the scope of the project and suspected Lewis might have bitten off more than he could chew. But all the same, he felt that he needed a change from work. And he'd always wondered: If you took a person from the 20th century and tossed him back in time a few hundred years, would he survive? The expedition Lewis proposed might be Fialko's best opportunity to answer that question. Fialko was given the name of La Salle's armorer, Pierre Prudhomme. He took charge of the musket building and canoe construction projects.

The final two teachers to join Lewis's crew were Ron Hobart and Terry Cox. Both were in their twenties, the youngest adult crew members. Cox taught history at a high school in Downers Grove, Illinois, where Lewis had given a presentation on the Jolliet-Marquette expedition. But Cox had actually heard of Lewis before then; Lewis had taught French at Crown Point High School during Cox's own senior year there. Years later, after Lewis gave a presentation to Cox's history class at Downers Grove, Lewis mentioned he was planning an even larger expedition and asked if Cox might be interested in joining as the leader of the history project. Cox told him he'd give it some serious consideration.

Cox was intrigued by the physical challenge of the expedition. Could he force his body to provide the power needed to carry him across the country? It was the ultimate test of machismo. But the more he learned about La Salle, the more excited he became for the historical component. Across the country, people were pursuing a number of unusual projects to celebrate the bicentennial, from re-creating Paul Revere's night ride to traveling west in covered wagons. La Salle: Expedition II was much larger in scope than anything else he'd heard about. It was something to take pride in. Although his wife, Pam, laughed when she first learned he was considering it—he'd just had two knee surgeries and this wasn't going to be a summer hike through the woods—she supported him and the expedition wholeheartedly. Cox accepted the position and his new name, Andre Baboeuf. They couldn't find anything written about Baboeuf, so Cox came up with his own backstory for the character. Pam found a bear claw for him to wear on a thong around his neck since he wouldn't be allowed to wear a wedding band during the expedition, given that men of the period wouldn't have worn them. The claw inspired his "Baboeuf and the Bear" tale, in which the French voyageur is attacked by an angry black bear and manages to wrestle the beast to the ground and bite one of its claws off before escaping unscathed. He was never able to finish the story without his audience exploding in laughter.

Ron Hobart taught middle school science in Elgin, a combination of earth science, physics, and chemistry. He first learned about the expedition in a school memo all teachers received at the start of the day. Like the other adult crew members, Hobart had often wondered what it would have been like to grow up in a different era. After meeting with Lewis, Hobart was invited to a group meeting where interested students could ask questions about the expedition. At the meeting, Hobart was surprised to be announced as "the newest crew member." Surprised, but not bothered. If Lewis wanted him for the trip, he was in. He took his place as head of the science project and the group's navigator, as well as the name Louis Baron.

Even with an efficient and motivated crew of adults, Lewis knew the expedition would need land support. They needed a liaison team that would work with communities in advance to schedule presentations and organize approved campsites for the men. The liaison team would have to start corresponding with these communities as soon as possible, sending hundreds of letters and making phone calls and getting towns excited to host the reenactors. They would follow the voyageurs in vans, carrying sound equipment, extra food for the men, and winter clothing. Lewis envisioned a leader or two to head the liaison team, plus a photojournalist who could take pictures and write about the journey for local newspapers, an alternate who would swap into the crew if someone fell ill or was injured, and a couple of teenagers who were willing to support the adult leaders. The group could start by operating out of the expedition's headquarters, La Salle National Bank on La Salle Street in downtown Chicago. When Lewis had approached the head of the bank with his idea for the expedition, the bank offered to cover all the secretarial costs of the expedition and give them an office to operate out of. This would be the expedition's base camp for the next year, and members of the liaison team would undoubtedly spend much of their time there—just as soon as Lewis found someone willing to lead the group.

Together the small crew set about crafting a world that had existed centuries earlier. They began in the autumn of 1974, with only two years to plan and prepare, a terribly short period of time considering how much there was to do if they truly wanted to resurrect the past. They'd have to work furiously and ceaselessly, spurred, perhaps, by the patriotic sentiments shared by their countrymen and even foreign visitors. As Argentinian writer Jorge Luis Borges said during a trip to the United States before its bicentennial,

"The United States was a country of great individuals—Whitman, Thoreau, Emerson, Poe—the people who really set your country apart. But America seems to be drifting away from the great ghosts who were so important to mankind . . . America is still the best hope. But the Americans themselves will have to be the best hope, too."[8] Reid Lewis was ready to accept that challenge.

How does one explain a man such as Reid Lewis? Like René-Robert Cavelier, Sieur de La Salle, Lewis was consumed by an idea, incapable of accepting defeat, tenacious, and exacting. Unlike the French explorer, Lewis lived in a world of ever more astonishing technology, a world of democratic governments, rapidly changing social norms, and no more *terra incognita*. That last fact didn't bother Lewis. His mission wasn't to discover new land but to remind people of the history of this land, to reinvigorate them to great endeavors.

At 34 years old, Lewis was thin and strong, with ropy muscle earned over the course of years spent canoeing for reenactments and for fun. His wavy brown hair was thinning at the top of his head. He planned to grow a mustache and wear a black wig during his appearances as La Salle. Lewis was charismatic and personable, equally comfortable in front of a classroom or a camera. He had a gift for drawing others into his vision, no matter how wild it seemed. He recognized that he asked a lot of other people and sometimes pushed them beyond a point of comfort. He demanded that much and more of himself. And when people weren't living up to his expectations, it was frustrating. Sometimes during the preparation process for the voyage he wondered if everyone felt the same level of dedication as he did, or if his expectations were simply too high.

Lewis hadn't planned on becoming a professional reenactor when he entered college. He hardly knew what he wanted to do. At one point he'd entertained the idea of being a farmer, but that idea never progressed beyond a daydream. He knew he didn't want to be a lawyer like his father, and he liked being outside. His real passion had always been learning about France. French language, culture, history, food—all of it was equally fascinating. The more he learned, the more his enthusiasm for the subject grew.

The obsession began with his roots: his grandfather, Emile Henri, became an orphan when his family immigrated to the United States from France in the 1800s and his parents died shortly after their arrival. He was adopted by the Lewis family and stayed in Illinois, eventually passing on part of his name to his grandson Reid Henri Lewis. On a family trip to France during Reid's high school years, the Lewises visited Fresse, the village in the Vosges Mountains where Emile's parents had lived. They found a birth record for Emile and discovered distant cousins still living in the same town. It was something of an epiphany for Reid, to see that familial connection in flesh and blood. When he entered college, that experience was part of what led him to study history and the French language.

By itself, successfully tracing his lineage back to Europe wasn't enough to explain Lewis's decision to be a reenactor. Plenty of people become absorbed in uncovering the secrets of their genealogy without ever wanting to *live* the way their ancestors did. For Lewis, it was some combination of upbringing and inherent personality. Adventure had been an essential part of his childhood. The Lewis family traveled extensively across the country and Reid's parents never revealed the destination to their two boys. Once, the family climbed aboard an airplane on the runway to see what the inside looked like—before the days of airport security, family and friends could board the plane to see their loved ones off. The plane was equipped with seatbelts, a novelty that their car didn't have. When the captain announced over the speaker that they'd be departing soon for Cuba and anyone without a ticket should exit the plane, Reid's father held a finger up to his lips and said, "Let's just stay here." Only later did Reid find out that they'd purchased tickets in advance; Cuba had been their destination all along.

From childhood adventures with his family, Lewis moved on to larger undertakings as an adult. He traveled extensively, including a stint at the Sorbonne to study French. He volunteered to join a team of shipwreck divers who traveled to Ecuador in search of the treasure of Sir Francis Drake's ship *Golden Hind*, though they never discovered anything. For someone who loved travel and history, the world was full of potential. Stories of people who lived centuries earlier were etched in the surface of the earth, visible if you took the time to look for them.

Teaching was never the career path Lewis had envisioned for himself, but it suited his personality. He made the decision to head to the classroom based on his experiences in Boy Scouts and his love of sharing knowledge with others. He knew he'd have the opportunity to expose kids to a new language and to his personal brand of stick-to-it-iveness, which he hoped would serve them throughout their lives even if they forgot how to conjugate French verbs. He spread his fondness for history and the outdoors to his students by encouraging them to sew costumes on weekends and get permission from parents to go on canoe trips down the Mississippi for miniature reenactments. The students, who tired quickly but loved the trips nonetheless, paddled up to Fort de Chartres near Prairie du Rocher, Illinois, belting out songs in French. Lewis was an enthusiastic teacher with a dramatic flair, and he was convinced that school could be every bit as exciting as any hobby.

Lewis might be best summarized by one of his favorite inspirational quotes, originally voiced by the Chicago architect Daniel Burnham: "Make no little plans; they have no magic to stir men's blood and probably themselves will not be realized. Make big plans; aim high in hope and work, remembering that a noble, logical diagram once recorded will not die, but long after we are gone be a living thing, asserting itself with ever-growing insistence."

Chapter Two

✴

RECONSTRUCTING THE PAST

Quebec, New France
September 15, 1678

During his first ten years in New France, La Salle did everything he could to become an explorer in the truest sense of the word. He wanted to reach a new frontier, to leave his mark on the history of the continent. Motivated by his own desire for prestige and economic prosperity, La Salle initially endeavored to find a passage across the continent to the Pacific. After selling his property in 1669 to finance his voyages, La Salle departed down the Ohio River. He undertook multiple voyages along that river, but they each came to nothing. In the meantime, Louis Jolliet and Jacques Marquette discovered the Mississippi River in 1673.

Although La Salle's attempts to find a water route to the Pacific were all abortive, they did teach him more about diplomacy and

22

the languages and cultural traditions of various Native American tribes. The French colony in New France was small, and La Salle's attempted explorations and newfound skills didn't go unnoticed. He earned enough of a reputation that in 1673 the governor of New France, Louis de Buade, Comte de Frontenac, included him as a translator and emissary on a mission to negotiate with local Iroquois chiefs at the mouth of the Cataraqui River (near modern-day Kingston, Ontario). After the successful conclusion of the discussions with the Iroquois, La Salle oversaw the construction of a fort at the opening of Lake Ontario, which he named for the French governor. Since neither Frontenac nor La Salle had explicit permission from King Louis to build the fort, La Salle returned to France in 1674 to argue for its necessity.

While in France, La Salle explained why Fort Frontenac was so valuable: it helped the French maintain an upper hand against the Iroquois. He stated his case so eloquently that he was given control of Fort Frontenac and awarded the rank of nobility, complete with his own coat of arms (a greyhound on a sable field under a golden six-pointed star).[1] La Salle returned to the North American colony in 1675, armed with loans from his family to fortify the fort. For several more years he worked from Fort Frontenac and managed fur trade from the fort, helping to increase his fortune. He also further developed his plan to travel deeper into the heart of the continent. Then, in 1677, he returned to France to meet with King Louis and his minister of finance, Jean-Baptiste Colbert, who was charged with overseeing affairs in the colony. It was a voyage that marked a pivotal moment in La Salle's career.

Presenting his case to the French court, La Salle explained that he wanted to explore the Mississippi in order to expand trade into a more fertile climate. Not only would the French maintain their control of the St. Lawrence, they'd also have a warm-water port, which might help them stave off the British. Colbert began his tenure as manager of the colony with the goal of keeping the territory as small as possible. His rationale was that the colonists needed to create strong cities with cultivated land before spreading out to the interior of the country, which might have sounded feasible from his perspective in France but was absolutely ignored in North America. But the idea of having a warm-water port proved irresistible. Colbert wanted to exploit Canada's bound-less natural resources, but as it was, the St. Lawrence was too arduous a waterway for trade on a large scale: for half the year the channel was blocked with ice, and even when the route was clear, contrary winds often delayed ships for days from entering the St. Lawrence. The entrance had such a notorious reputation, it came to be known as "Cape Torment."[2]

With the urging of Colbert, King Louis was convinced. He granted La Salle letters of patent permitting the explorer to travel the Mississippi and build whatever forts he deemed necessary for the completion of his mission. Additionally, La Salle would have a monopoly on the fur trade that resulted from whatever territories he discovered on his voyage. There were two stipulations: La Salle would have to fund the mission on his own, and he would have only five years to finish the enterprise, after which he would no longer have a trade monopoly or the right to explore.[3]

For much of history, exploration has been the privilege and the burden of wealthy aristocratic men—or of poorer men who convince rich ones to sponsor their voyages. La Salle belonged decidedly to the latter category and struggled to finance his travels. It didn't help that currency in New France flew straight back to Europe almost as soon as it arrived—any coins that made it across the ocean were usually sent back as remittances by the importers. Colonists were forced to be creative when they wanted to spend locally. Beaver skins, moose hides, and even playing cards with their corners cut off were substituted for official French currency.[4]

Since he knew he couldn't expect to raise much money in the colony, La Salle spent several months in France raising the money necessary to fund his expedition. During this period he met an Italian soldier named Henri de Tonty. The two quickly became friends, and La Salle decided that the Italian's experience in military affairs would make him a valuable second-in-command. The Sicilian was known as "Iron Fist" for the prosthetic metal hand he wore on his right arm to replace the hand he lost to a grenade while fighting in Sicily.[5] Together, La Salle and Tonty set sail for New France in the late summer of 1678. It was the beginning of their goal to travel to the ends of the great Mississippi and find out what lands lay beyond the known world.

Elgin, Illinois
1975

Reid Lewis stood in front of a chalkboard facing his audience as he described the various parts of a 17th-century musket. A drawing of the gun on the board was labeled with the French names for the flintlock mechanism: *bassinet, batterie, couvre-bassinet*. It would've been a strange enough lesson in a regular high school French classroom, where students are usually taught strings of verbs and useful nouns and the occasional colloquialism. But Lewis wasn't just teaching his students the words for the parts of a French musket—he expected them to build the guns as well.

Although Lewis still dressed like a high school teacher (today it was a red turtleneck sweater and a brown tweed jacket, his fingertips dusted white with chalk) and spent much of his time in classrooms with teenagers, he hadn't been working as a salaried member of the staff at Larkin High School for a year. That's not to say he'd given up on education. His methods simply didn't follow the standard practice of having kids sit down, shut up, and absorb knowledge, and many of his lessons weren't taught in a classroom. Lewis preferred a more hands-on approach, such as taking a group of teenage boys out into the wilds of Wisconsin at Kettle Moraine State Forest in the middle of winter to teach them about cold weather camping and test their stamina. He had them pitch tents and go to sleep, then abruptly woke them all up at 2 A.M., telling them to pack their gear and sprint out of the forest. Not everyone had appreciated the test. One participant was so frustrated that he swung his backpack into a tree and broke the pack's frame. It was an unfortunate reaction, but the lesson was meant to uncover that sort of behavior. Lewis needed to see how the teenagers who expressed interest in the expedition would function in difficult outdoor experiences. Those who couldn't cope with unpredictability on weekend trips would probably cave under the pressure of a yearlong out-of-classroom experience.

The response to Lewis's initial presentation about La Salle: Expedition II in the two Elgin high schools had been gratifying and tumultuous. He needed sixteen students and more than sixty had turned up with their parents at the first informational meeting.

"We'll begin with historical research, because we want this expedition to be as authentic as humanly possible in the 20th century," he'd told the assembled group that fall night in 1974. It was a Wednesday at the beginning of the school year, and the Elgin High School library was packed. "The people with whom we come in contact will expect us to be authorities on the subject we're portraying; and if we aren't, we're letting them down and letting down one of the basic principles of the expedition. During the two years of preparation, the research will be going on constantly. As we get information we'll use it for our projects. In all, we'll have nineteen interdisciplinary projects. These will be the expedition's legacy."

Lewis's interrelated projects were the cornerstone of what he hoped would eventually become an entire educational unit. During the twenty-month preparatory period before the expedition and then during the expedition itself, the students and adult leaders would each be assigned several areas, including: mapping the 1976 route using 17th-century techniques; creating authentic clothing; learning voyageur paddling songs; a physiological study of how the crew members changed over the course of the voyage; voyageur eating habits; canoe construction; musket construction; language studies (French and some Latin); dramatic presentations; studying the journals of early explorers; sketching; photography; physical conditioning; background reading on related topics; general historic research; religious history of New France; scientific projects such as meteorology, natural observations, and astronomy; political history; and student radio productions. Each of the projects had an adult director, plus a professional adviser from the community, who would volunteer his or her time to help with the students' research. If all the materials were successfully compiled at the end of the expedition, they could be turned into lesson plans, studies, and teaching aids—or so Lewis hoped.

It was an impressive vision, and an overwhelming one for about half of the sixty teenagers who'd submitted applications. Some didn't want to give up their social lives, others balked at the idea of spending countless hours poring through scholarly research (including all seventy-one volumes of *The Jesuit Relations*). But even with the early wave of dropouts, more than thirty remained. Cutting the group down to sixteen, plus a few alternates, was a daunting task. Making the task more difficult were the age and temperament of his recruits. Lewis wanted young men who were capable and mature, who had a variety of academic backgrounds and could be counted on in a crisis. But he was choosing from a pool of 15- to 17-year-olds, a demographic notorious for undergoing drastic changes over the course of a few months or even a few weeks. Who was to say they wouldn't lose interest halfway through the trip?

—

"Let's say we've been gone just maybe a week; we just got to Lake Ontario, paddling the St. Lawrence. And you've already discovered that one member of your crew is not pulling his share of the load. How would you handle that?"

"I would talk to them," Chuck Campbell said in a quiet voice to the panel of adults in front of him. He was a shy kid, small and soft-spoken. He had outdoors experience from being in the Boy Scouts and described himself as a "willing worker" and an "interesting conversationalist." At the end of his answer, the adults simply said, "Okay." Without giving any positive or negative sign, they moved to the next question.

"Later on in the trip, you're tired, we get in real late one night and it's been a particularly bad day on the lake," the question began. "And when you're setting up camp you find out one of the guys in your canoe has a sleeping bag that's just drenched all the way through. And everybody is so tired and it's so late, you've got to get up early in the morning to leave, he doesn't want to spend the time staying up and letting it dry out. What's your reaction to that?"

One after another the questions came. Some were variations on the first two, others were about the group's research projects and budget. The exercise was an attempt to gauge how Campbell might react to the hardships that would inevitably arise on the expedition—and how well prepared he was to deal with the media.

If everything went as planned, the expedition would be followed by reporters every step of the way. Each of the adults had evaluation forms to rate every student's capacity for leadership, commitment, attitude, dependability, and so on. The evaluation criteria were as close to exhaustive as Lewis could make them. He knew picking the right crew was the difference between making it all the way to the Gulf of Mexico and having a blowup before they reached the Great Lakes. What made the process tricky was the gap between theory and practice: answering questions in a classroom is nothing like being stuck outside in the rain with boiled beans for dinner and a horde of journalists poking microphones in your face.

At the end of the interview session, Lewis asked Campbell to leave the classroom, then come back as if he were a voyageur just arriving after a day on the water, with an audience on shore eager to hear about the trip. Campbell was to conclude the impromptu skit with a verse of the French drinking song, "Chevalier de la Table Ronde."

Campbell left the classroom and closed the door behind him. When he came back, any nerves he'd felt during the interview seemed to have disappeared. His voice was confident as he described life on the river. Then, without hesitation, he broke into song. The adults cheered and clapped. Full marks for dramatization.

In addition to interviews meant to illuminate their character and show their level of comfort in front of the media, students had to prove their dedication to the expedition in other ways: learning the history of French explorers in North America, memorizing pages upon pages of relevant French vocabulary (*la cordelle* for tow rope; *l'hache* for ax; *la pagaie* for paddle), and contributing to the interdisciplinary projects. They did all this work in addition to their regular schoolwork, extracurricular commitments, and jobs, without knowing if they'd make the cut. There was a small scholarship promised for those who made it through the selection process and completed the voyage, but the overwhelming incentive for most of those going through the application process was the expedition itself. Many called it a once-in-a-lifetime opportunity. The chance to participate in something so vast in scope was worth all the extra work. Fortunately, the adults didn't take long to make their final decision. By early 1975 they'd winnowed away the remaining applicants to a crew of sixteen, a number that included Campbell. He was thrilled and his parents were somewhat relieved; their son had originally planned on spending the months following graduation doing a solo hike of the Appalachian Trail. At least now he wouldn't be alone.

Meanwhile, other pieces of the expedition were falling into place. Lewis enlisted the help of experts from Chicagoland and beyond to act as advisers, including famed Chicago weather forecaster Harry Volkman, Indiana Mental Health Department psychologist Will Kennedy, and Peter van Handel, a sports physiologist from the Ball State University Human Performance Lab. Lewis also found a priest who was the perfect replica of the priest who had accompanied La Salle: Father Loran Fuchs was a member of the Recollect Order (a French branch of the Franciscans) who had spent years canoeing in the Boundary Waters near Canada and was fit enough to make the journey. The priest agreed to join the expedition and play the role of Pere Zenobe Membre.

As it came together, the expedition, like dozens of other projects celebrating the country's bicentennial, was starting to get more press attention—so much so that people began approaching Lewis with ideas for the reenactment. One such man was Joel Knecht, who had expertise in Native American history and 17th-century clothing. The blond-haired, blue-eyed teacher from Connecticut was knowledgeable and enthusiastic. He had plans to help the expedition develop authentic attire, which was a subject Lewis and the other teachers knew little about. After debating the merits of adding another person, Lewis welcomed Knecht to the crew.

Lewis also found the perfect person to head the liaison team: his wife, Jan. The newlyweds had been dating while Reid was on the Jolliet-Marquette expedition, so Jan knew the lengths her husband was willing to go to accomplish a historic reenactment. Reid liked to joke that when they got engaged, he and La Salle came in the same package. He believed in this second expedition so much that she couldn't help but believe in it, too. She wanted to make his dream come true. If that meant figuring out the logistics and doing publicity work while receiving none of the fame and acclaim showered on the crew, so be it. Though it did sometimes feel like she was drowning under a mountain of paperwork.

Thankfully, she had her best friend, Marlena Scavuzzo, to help with all the secretarial work. Marlena joined when Jan asked her because she thought the trip sounded exciting, like something out of an adventurous romance novel. The two friends had met when they were both studying to be high school English teachers at Western Illinois University and stayed close even after going to work in different schools. If there was anyone Jan could rely on to be a brick and accept her bossiness, it was Marlena. She was relieved she'd have her best friend with her on the expedition, because accomplishing everything on her own would've been impossible.

At the beginning of 1976 two more women joined the liaison team as well. Cathy Palmer, a senior graduating that summer from Elgin High School, had originally wanted to be part of the crew. When she learned that only male applicants were allowed (a strict rule meant to reflect the original voyage's demographics), she and a friend fumed but let the matter drop. A year later during study hall she saw George LeSieutre, one of the crew members, sewing leather moccasins. She was intrigued. She asked what he was doing, and he reminded her of the expedition she'd heard about a year ago. This time she decided she wanted to be part of it, even if she wasn't going to be paddling in the canoes with the men. She applied to join the liaison team and was accepted.

Sharon Baumgartner had already graduated and started taking classes at Elgin Community College when most of the other crew members were finishing their senior year of high school. But she heard about the voyage all the same because she was dating Marc Lieberman, one of the members of the expedition. She slowly got pulled into the liaison team, though no one really outlined what she and Palmer would need to do in advance. For all the training the crew members underwent, the leaders of the liaison team didn't share much with their younger counterparts about how they should prepare. The older women never discussed their letter-writing campaign with the new recruits, perhaps because they felt it wasn't the girls' responsibility. All Palmer and Baumgartner knew was that there would be some publicity work and they'd drive around the country following the crew. They'd pick up mail from prearranged drop sites, do laundry for the men, carry the bags of dried peas and beans that wouldn't fit in the boats, and set up the sound equipment for performances. It would be an adventure of sorts, even if it meant doing lots of work.

Despite how well everything was progressing, Lewis continued to have too many things to do and not enough time to do them. He'd already quit his job as a teacher at the end of the 1974 school year. Now he started sleeping less and dedicating all his time, including weekends, to the expedition. No matter how much he planned and how comprehensively he explained his detailed strategy for the voyage, there were always complications arising and detractors pointing out various impossibilities.

Of the ongoing issues, fund-raising remained the most challenging. From the start, Lewis had known the expedition would be a costly undertaking. All the teachers he brought onto the expedition would need salaries, and the average yearly income for a teacher at the time was $12,000.[6] He also planned on paying the two heads of the liaison team, the photojournalist who would travel with the crew and publish stories and photos of them in newspapers along their route, and potentially a film crew that would make a video of the expedition. The crew members would need food, health insurance, and materials to make their clothing and tools (leather, wool, wood, and metal). He wanted two vans for the liaison team and enough money to cover the cost of their accommodations over the course of the journey. All in all, Lewis anticipated the trip costing $595,000 (close to $2.5 million in today's currency), an amount that seemed impossibly large, despite the number of in-kind donations offered to him by various public and private groups.

Lewis wasn't going to raise those kinds of funds through bake sales and car washes—he needed a professional to assist him. He worked with two separate fund-raising groups for several months, but neither raised much money. Their explanation for the lack of results was that the expedition didn't have a natural constituency, unlike a cause such as a hospital or new school. So Lewis turned to grant writing and donations from states, Canadian provinces, and individuals. He took out around $30,000 in personal loans, sold his car, and poured his savings into the project. He recruited the other adult crew members to undertake fund-raising efforts of their own in different parts of the Midwest, though they struggled with how to approach the problem. Some of the parents of the teenage crew members did their own work to raise money. Ken Lewis learned fund accounting so that they could trace the individual dollar from the donor to what it was spent on. He knew it would be a scandal if they misused the donations and grants, so he spent innumerable long days recording each of the incoming donations by hand in ledger books.

Despite the many hurdles the expedition had to overcome, the teenage crew members never seemed too concerned by the possibility of failure. As long as they stayed committed to the vision, Lewis felt confident the crew would pull through, regardless of their critics and the monetary difficulties. The young men who had any doubts about the success of the expedition had already removed themselves from the running. The ones who remained were firm in their commitment to the expedition. They were enthralled by the scope of the challenge. It sounded like an adventure on a Homeric scale, a last chance to live in the wild before fully submitting to the strictures of adulthood. No one could call them frivolous, either, because they planned to educate their countrymen on a little-known but essential piece of North American history. As Lewis liked to say, "We're not doing this to indulge ourselves." Really, it was almost a patriotic duty.

On the corner of Irving Park Road and Narragansett Avenue in Chicago, a half dozen people worked in a large square building that had once housed a blacksmith's forge. Instead of the melodic pinging of metal being hammered into new shapes, the smithy now emitted the rasp of knives shaving curls of wood and the occasional thunk of an ax splitting logs. Inside the shop the air was thick with dust and the sickly perfume of drying fiberglass. Teenage boys came in and out of the workshop on different days, eager to help construct the canoes that would soon be carrying them down the St. Lawrence. Leading them in their efforts were metals teacher John Fialko and Ralph Frese, owner of Chicagoland Canoe Base, where the work was completed.

Frese had developed the design for the replica birch-bark canoes and built two on his own several years earlier. Those first two were used in the Jolliet-Marquette expedition. He based his boats on historical models and used traditional tools and techniques: no power tools, no glue, no nails. The sleek crafts were perfect imitations of Algonquian birch-bark canoes, but for one crucial detail: the birch-bark hull. Birch bark is a strong but high-maintenance building material that can be torn on sharp rocks and requires regular patching. Given the expedition's tight schedule and the long distance to be covered, it seemed like too much of a gamble to see if the canoes could survive such a journey. Plus, no one knew how birch bark would react to the pollution-infused waterways near Chicago. Instead, Frese developed a fiberglass hull, screen-printed to look just like birch bark. The layers of fiberglass cloth had an accumulated thickness of one eighth of an inch. Frese called his creation "Chicago bark."

To give the hull its shape, inner and outer gunwales (the upper edges of the boat) were attached at the top of each side of the hull and lashed together. Then, one-hundred rib planks cut from logs bought off a farm in southern Wisconsin had to be steamed into a U shape. The process of cutting a rib piece down to the proper size with a drawknife took about twenty-five minutes, and there were six hundred ribs to make for all the canoes. Each of the ribs had to be slid into its spot, and then the thwarts were placed above them, crosswise between the gunwales. Finally, the bow and stern pieces were gently inserted and the boat was turned upside down so that all the seams could be smeared with spruce resin gum. The entire process took somewhere between eight hundred and one thousand man-hours, but the finished product was a stunning vessel that looked almost ghostly in its effortless movement through the water. The first boat, christened the *Montreal*, was completed on February 2, 1976. The last one wouldn't be finished until barely a week before the group was set to depart from Illinois in July. Together, the fleet of six boats cost $25,000—Frese had been generous enough to give them one of the canoes for free.

Frese was an invaluable ally in the construction of the canoes, and in some ways, he was also the person who had pushed Lewis onto the path on which he found himself. Frese, a fourth-generation blacksmith, was fiercely proud of the history of the Midwest and had done all he could to educate people about it. He was especially interested in the 17th and early 18th centuries, the era of French exploration in the region. Before Lewis ever had the inkling of an idea to take students on canoe reenactments, Frese was organizing anniversary celebrations of famous events at places like Starved Rock State Park. When Frese had the idea for the three hundredth anniversary Jolliet-Marquette expedition and recruited Lewis to play a leading role, he had unwittingly infected the younger man with the reenactment bug.

All around the country, living history was in vogue. Places that purported to offer authentic glimpses into the past, like Pioneer Village in Salem, Massachusetts; Colonial Williamsburg in Virginia; and the Pleasant Hill Shaker community in Harrodsburg, Kentucky, were rising in prevalence and popularity. The American Revolution Bicentennial only fanned the flames of immersive nostalgia, sending hordes of people to museums, filling gas stations with commemorative mugs, and network television running "Bicentennial minutes" segments in which politicians and celebrities described a snippet of American history. The history fever even spread to pop culture, with shows like *All in the Family* and *The Carol Burnett Show* lampooning the Bicentennial minutes. It had never been cooler to show interest in—and even dress up as—a bunch of dead white guys.

○━━━○

"It was only by luck that La Salle's men finished the trip at all. They could've all been killed instead," Naval instructor Tom Kirkpatrick told the group of young men assembled before him at the Glenview Naval Air Station.[7] The statement was equal parts introduction and admonishment. Kirkpatrick was there to teach the men about surviving outdoors in the winter, but he also seemed doubtful about the expedition's ability to travel safely, regardless of how well they were trained. They could learn all about the dangers of hypothermia, how to stay warm with a severe windchill, and the body's physiological response to being plunged into cold water, but none of that mattered if they were wearing leather moccasins and nothing but a few layers of wool shirts. That was Kirkpatrick's real concern: the expedition's strict adherence to authenticity.

"Couldn't you make those things bigger?" Kirkpatrick asked as he inspected the group's moccasins. "That way you could slip them on over snowmobiling boots. Then you'd keep your feet warm and dry."

"If we went around wearing gunboats like that, people would laugh at us," Father Loran Fuchs answered.

Father Loran's response was representative of the other crew members' feelings on the matter. Authenticity was held up as the pinnacle to which everyone should strive. But the concept was a vague, slippery one. How do you re-create a perfect imitation of the 17th century when you live in the 20th? Lewis built a few loopholes into the expedition's parameters to account for the time discrepancy. They would be permitted to brush their teeth every day and

37

wear contact lenses if vision correction was necessary, though the anachronistic bottles of contact cleaning solution would need to be hidden. Anyone who wanted to read could pack books, despite the fact that most voyageurs were illiterate. And since La Salle and his men survived on food given by generous Native American hosts along the route, Lewis would let the crew eat any kind of food hospitable communities along the way gave and receive care packages from home, most of which would contain comestibles that wouldn't have existed or been available to the voyageurs. The men would also carry water in their boats instead of drinking out of the rivers and lakes.

Everything else would be re-created as accurately as knowledge allowed: clothes would be hand-sewn and colored with natural dyes; crew members would use French vocabulary and their French names in front of audiences; and food cooked in camp would be limited to oatmeal, cornmeal, peas, beans, and whatever fruits and vegetables communities donated to them. If Lewis had learned anything about reenactments during the Jolliet-Marquette expedition, it was that audiences noticed the details. On several occasions, people had looked askance at the men when they ate peanut butter and jelly sandwiches for lunch. Lewis wouldn't make the same mistake twice. It didn't matter that perfect authenticity was impossible. If they didn't at least try, how could La Salle: Expedition II say they'd achieved something only one other group of people had ever achieved in known human history? How could they bring the past to life without the proper accoutrements? How could they hope to understand the voyageurs' mentality if they didn't wear the same scratchy wool clothes and eat the same tasteless food?

All these questions may sound ludicrous, and they don't have any real answers. Wearing wool clothing and eating bean soup for dinner was no more likely to give them insight into the worldview of a 17th-century man than taking tea in the White House would illuminate the mysteries of the American presidency. Bridging the gap between three hundred years of elapsed time wasn't possible, especially in an era of accelerated technological and social change. The voyageurs who traveled into the continent's interior would sometimes go for months without seeing another European or meeting someone who spoke their language. They had never been vaccinated against any kind of disease, they had no reliable maps to consult, and for every tribe they met their chance of being warmly welcomed was matched by the likelihood of being attacked.

For most modern people, that level of ongoing apprehension is unfathomable, as are the hardships the voyageurs underwent and the standards of living they experienced. Although he would never frame it in such terms, Lewis's real achievement would be to produce the *illusion* of authenticity. Like a magician, his trick would only succeed if the audience was adequately impressed by the depth of the performance and ignored the strings holding it together. The entire undertaking placed an enormous burden on the crew members: look like rough voyageurs, but behave like civilized young men. No raiding villages, no sleeping with local wenches, no brawling to settle disagreements. As for boozing, there would doubtless be opportunities to drink on the expedition, and the legal age in Canada was 18. Across the United States it was more complicated since every state had its own laws. Just to be safe, all the parents were asked to sign a permission form stating their sons could drink, provided they behaved themselves.

To help with the ban on physical altercations, Lewis worked with psychologist Will Kennedy to develop a team-building seminar. The group spent a weekend at Camp Edwards, an idyllic location in the Wisconsin woods. Surrounded by towering pines and snowdrifts, the group enjoyed indoor heating as it went through exercises on how to talk through problems and address conflict before it erupted. The key, Kennedy told them, was to go straight to the person and be honest without being combative. Gossiping about someone behind his back would only add tension rather than diffusing hard feelings. And most important, Kennedy said, was that you understand and accept yourself.

"You cannot do a trip like this unless you can live with yourself," he told them. A few scribbled the phrase down in their binders, even though being able to live with others seemed like it would be the more challenging ordeal. Just working on preparations with other people was already becoming somewhat problematic. Lewis was getting reports from the other teachers that Knecht, the director of the clothing project, was undermining Lewis's leadership and credibility with the students. Plus, Knecht hadn't kept up with the workload he'd been assigned. If the situation didn't improve, Lewis would have to take action. For now, his attention was focused on two more-pressing concerns.

The first was the Chicago Flower and Garden Show. The annual event held on Navy Pier at the end of March celebrated all things green, and Lewis had secured a spot for the expedition by creating a presentation called "La Salle Expedition II: Planting the Lily of France." It was a loose interpretation of the exposition's theme, but had been enough to gain the men entry. They needed a finished canoe to display, as well as members of the team in their outfits to answer questions, sing paddling songs, and demonstrate the finger weaving process they used to make their sashes. If the show were a success, it would help invigorate the community. It also had the possibility of securing more funds for the expedition, an area in which Lewis was struggling.

Despite his continued efforts, fund-raising still ate up too much of his time with too few results. He regularly traveled to meet potential donors in person, because it made a stronger impression if they could see him in costume and look at pictures of the work being done. As one donor told him, "The problem with your expedition is that nobody believes it until they see it." All the time away from the group was diminishing Lewis's credibility with his crew. "We had almost a headless monster on our hands," Lewis said much later of the power vacuum caused by the fund-raising debacle. He wasn't around for group activities nearly as often as he would have liked to have been, and sometimes it seemed like he didn't have the opportunity to develop as close of a relationship with the students as he'd have liked. "Everyone started doing things pretty much on their own and that became pretty much the tenor of the expedition."

That dynamic came to its climax in a confrontation with Knecht, who had continued to chip away at Lewis's reputation when the leader wasn't around. His antiauthority stance was appealing to the teenagers; he'd been suggesting that Lewis wasn't such a great person to lead them after all, that maybe he should be replaced by one of the other adults. Lewis knew that if he didn't remove Knecht from the expedition, he'd be faced with a rebellious crew during the trip. Finally, reluctantly, Lewis went to Knecht's apartment to tell the man he wasn't going to be part of the crew. Lewis brought Ron Hobart with him in case the situation went south. That bit of foresight turned out to be fortuitous when Knecht tried to hit Lewis after being informed he wouldn't be joining the group on the expedition. But neither Hobart nor Lewis knew what to do when Knecht pulled out a gun from a desk drawer.

Darting forward, Lewis was able to get behind Knecht and grab the gun. He couldn't be sure whether it was an actual pistol or a starting gun (used at sporting events), but he wasn't about to test it out. Lewis and Hobart called the police but didn't press any charges. All three men agreed the situation had gotten out of hand. It was an emotional issue. No one was hurt and no one wanted to part with animosity. Lewis was simply relieved that he'd taken Knecht off the crew before it was too late and that he hadn't been injured and forced to postpone the expedition.

⸻

"Gauche, deux, trois, quatre. Droit, deux, trois, quatre." The repetitive chant wove through the patter of rain and drew the attention of motorists around Elgin as twenty-three men marched slowly down the sidewalk. It was a dreary, humid Tuesday morning in late June, and cars rumbled by at a quick clip as the men on foot hefted their heavy loads down the concrete path.[8] Wearing thin leather moccasins, the men chafed at their wool and canvas clothing, which itched despite being clean and new. Those carrying the four finished canoes also struggled to find a tolerably uncomfortable position to rest the sharp edges of the overturned boat on their shoulders. They tried to split the weight between four men, with two on either side bracing the gunwale somewhere between the neck and the shoulder, but even with the weight distributed between so many people, it was a painful task. They didn't want the gunwale to come down on bone, but it dug painfully into the muscle between the clavicle and the scapula if it wasn't braced on the sides with their arms. For the men who had been assigned to carry gear rather than canoes, it was equally challenging to find a way to transport the wooden chests and cast-iron cooking pots. Their shape just didn't settle easily against the spine. It was nothing like wearing a backpack, with padded shoulder straps and an accommodating form. All in all, it wasn't the most enjoyable way to spend a summer morning after school let out.

The practice portage (a term for crossing land between bodies of water with one's canoe and gear) was only a few miles long, but the unfamiliar weight of the gear and the slick streets and the stink of exhaust from cars that drove by made it feel much longer. They'd started the day at Camp WaDeDoDa, Cox's name for the building where the group did much of its metal and woodworking outside Larkin High School. The overland trek would end in South Elgin. There, they planned to put the finished canoes into the Fox River and paddle to the National Street Bridge. As they marched, keeping rhythm with French commands, a photographer from the *Daily Herald* snapped photos. Drivers slowed down to watch the line of men. At one point, the group passed a garbage truck and one of the collectors stopped his work to gawk.

Despite the misery of the portage, it was thrilling to elicit such reactions. To the men participating in the expedition and their family members, who had spent the past eighteen months helping sew clothes and knit socks and hats and scarves, it felt like the voyage was held together by shoestrings and force of will. Nothing was completely finished, including the crew itself. Only recently Lewis had been forced to find suitable alternate crew members. Originally he'd hoped to have two students travel with the four women of the liaison team, ready to jump in and fill a crew member's place if any fell ill or were injured. But after several teenagers quit during the training and the original alternates were pulled in to join the permanent crew, he needed new people to fill the positions. Lewis ended up looking outside Elgin. He chose a teenager from Evanston named Sid Bardwell who agreed to travel with the liaison team and take the name Castor Blanc or Nika, the Native American guide La Salle traveled with. Bardwell would sub in and out of the canoes whenever anyone got sick or injured, and would otherwise travel by car to help with advance publicity and setting up the sound equipment for the crew's presentations.

For all its moving parts and unsolved problems, the expedition looked like a fait accompli to outsiders. Members of the Elgin community had secured a float for the men to appear in the Fourth of July parade, planned a dinner with Mayor Richard Verbic to be hosted by the Junior Women's League on July 10, and organized a send-off breakfast for the voyageurs on August 3. Letters from supporters had been pouring into the La Salle: Expedition II headquarters. The crew received endorsements from Canadian Prime Minister Pierre Trudeau, Philippe Cousteau (filmmaker and son of Jacques Cousteau), and famed mountaineer Edmund Hillary. In 1953, along with Tenzing Norgay, Hillary was the first to reach the summit of Mount Everest, and he offered a few words of advice to the men preparing to go on their own quest: "The principles of expedition organizing are the same whether you are in the Himalayas or on the great rivers of America . . . careful planning, good equipment and a fit team, determination and enthusiasm, and the resolution to enjoy every moment of the experience."

Lewis was certain they were on track to have everything that Hillary advised. During the month of July, crew members worked frantically to complete any unfinished tasks before their departure. Lewis had to appear in costume for numerous events, write more grant applications, oversee the final stages of canoe construction for the last canoes, make last-minute changes to the schedule, buy vans for the liaison team to drive, and teach them to drive stick-shift since he couldn't afford to buy automatic vehicles. The four women spent an afternoon in a parking lot trying to get the vans in and out of first gear, without much success given the limited space. It looked like driving was going to be a trial by fire as soon as they hit the highway to Canada. The crew members did a canoe capsizing drill dressed in their full voyageur ensemble to make sure everyone understood how to right an overturned boat and climb back into it from the water. During another practice drill, they wore the voyageur clothing along with life preservers and jumped into a pool. The life vests functioned as well as advertised, easily providing buoyancy despite the weight of the sodden wool clothes. The life vests would be worn underneath the men's clothes during foul weather as a precaution.

A few weeks before the departure, each man got his camp duty assignments. The six-boat expedition was comprised of three modules: red, gold, and green. Two of the modules each included eight men (four men per boat), and the third module had seven men (four men in one boat and three men in the other). Each module would have a cook, a fire starter, woodchoppers, shelter builders, and a quartermaster (to organize gear). Whenever someone finished his main job, he'd be expected to do anything else that needed to be done. In addition to sharing meals and dividing up chores, the men in each module would also sleep in a large tent erected by using one of the canoes. On land, they'd take care of all the cooking and cleaning; on the water, the eight (or seven) men in each module would keep an eye on one another and make sure they didn't get separated from the rest of the group. The use of modules wasn't inspired by anything Lewis had read about in a history book; it just seemed like the best way to delegate. Lewis was a firm believer in the divide-and-conquer method of organization. Giving everyone tasks that suited their skill sets would free up his time to do more public relations work and big-picture planning.

While the members of the expedition went through all the items on their list of things-to-do-before-leaving-this-century, the rest of America reveled in its country's two hundredth birthday. The longest, widest, heaviest American flag ever made was unfurled from the Verrazano-Narrows Bridge in New York City. It was larger than half a football field, weighed around one and a half tons, and cost $45,000 to make. In Philadelphia, the biggest birthday cake ever baked towered over crowds, a five-story splendor of sugar and flour. The cake could serve 200,000 people. Half a million people gathered beneath the Gateway Arch in St. Louis, a five-hour parade wound its way through Philadelphia, and New York City executed a fireworks display that incorporated Ellis Island, Governor's Island, the Statue of Liberty, and all of New York Harbor.

"If to cynics the bombardment seems excessive—jingoistic and ingenuous at best, at worst grossly exploitative—Americans should nonetheless take heart from it," claimed *Time* magazine. "Only five years ago, in protest against the U.S. involvement in Indochina, the flag was being burned, burlesqued and spat upon. Today many of the selfsame Americans who chose then to disown their flag are hoisting it high. In a republic, the flag—not a royal family or the trophies of empire—represents in graphic form the experiences and beliefs of its people."[9]

Ironically enough, Lewis's canoe would be carrying the flag of King Louis, a white banner patterned with golden fleur-de-lys. He didn't see it as problematic. After all, French exploration conducted in the name of King Louis was part of what led to the birth of the United States.

The morning of August 3 arrived hot and sunny. A crowd of three hundred people stood on the banks of the Fox River near the Hemmens Cultural Center in Elgin. The canoes came down the river in a close formation, surprising a flock of mallard ducks that had been floating on the calm water. The sound of paddles pulling through the water was masked by the men's voices as they sang "Vent Frais," hitting the gunwales of the canoes with the shafts of their paddles in time to the music. As they approached the shore, the six canoes swung effortlessly around to face their audience and fired off a musket salute. The crew members were exhilarated to be on the water, in their clothes, in the boats they'd built, after two years of practicing and sewing and building. The crowd cheered as the paddlers pushed their boats onto the muddy shore and hopped out to carry the canoes uphill to the concrete stairs of the Hemmens Center. One by one the boats were lined up, with just enough space between each for a person to wiggle through. Kids in football jerseys and bucket hats reverently touched the wooden gunwales and watched the strangely dressed young men wander around talking to family and friends. The group performed another paddling song, "C'est L'aviron," before heading inside to enjoy their farewell breakfast.

At the end of the meal, everyone gathered outside for hugs, well wishes, and tears. This was the crew members' last chance to spend time with family members and enjoy the comforts of life indoors before embarking on their journey. When they returned to Elgin again, they'd be halfway through their journey and winter would be upon them. After the festivities at the cultural center ended, the men loaded the canoes up on trailers to be carted to the St. Lawrence, packed their gear into the cars and vans, said their final good-byes, and started the fourteen-hour drive to Montreal.

Ready or not, they were going.

Chapter Three

THE LIFE OF A VOYAGEUR

Montreal, New France
August 11, 1681

On the day that would mark the start of La Salle's successful voyage down the Mississippi River, he signed his life away to his cousin. For the past three years, La Salle had relied on credit and loans from relatives to pay his travel expenses. He'd planned to pay off his debts and eventually turn a profit by selling furs he collected along the way. But every one of his financial ventures had sunk, some of them literally, leaving him little with which to persuade investors to give him more money. Fortunately, he still had the support of Governor Frontenac, and he'd been given loans from his cousin Francois du Plet when creditors came after his property on Lake Ontario.[1] In gratitude for his cousin's support, La Salle made his will out to du Plet. He had no way of knowing whether the upcoming expedition would finally lead to fame and fortune—based on his experiences over the last three years, he had good reason to doubt a positive outcome.

When La Salle first returned from France in 1678, his immediate goal had been the construction of a ship. The *Griffon*, a forty-foot vessel, became the first of its type to ply the Great Lakes. Before it was completed, La Salle sent men ahead to the northern tip of modern-day Michigan. But when he arrived with the ship and the rest of his crew in 1679, he learned that the men who had been sent ahead had all deserted for fear that La Salle's mission would lead them to their deaths. After loading the *Griffon* with items to trade and sending it back east, expecting it would soon return with more supplies, La Salle sent Henri de Tonty to chase after the deserters while he and the rest of the men trudged through the snow to the St. Joseph River, more than three hundred miles to the south. La Salle instructed the voyageurs to construct a fort while they awaited Tonty's return, since they would need shelter if they hoped to survive the frigid winter.

It took three months for Tonty to return with the men he'd found. By that time, supplies were dwindling, and it was becoming apparent that the *Griffon* wasn't coming back. Whether a storm or sabotage was to blame for its disappearance was unclear. What La Salle did know was that between the cost of the ship itself and the furs it was carrying, he'd lost 52,000 livres (nearly $4 million in today's currency).[2] With his voyageurs facing starvation, La Salle and a few men returned to Montreal by foot (nearly eight hundred miles) in March 1680 to resupply the outfit. He placed Tonty in charge of the men who stayed at Fort Crevecoeur (a name that translates to "heartbreak"). Shortly after La Salle left, most of his remaining men left as well. Tonty returned to the fort one day after surveying the area and found it ransacked and deserted. The only explanation for the voyageurs' departure was a note that read *Nous sommes tous sauvages*, meaning, "We are all savages."[3] To top it off, when La Salle finally arrived in Montreal he learned that another ship coming from France and carrying about 20,000 livres worth of supplies for him had wrecked.[4] The Frenchman had lost all his money and half his men.

Upon returning to Fort Crevecoeur with more men in the late fall of 1680, having received word from Tonty that those left behind had deserted, La Salle discovered a massacre had taken place at one of the Illinois villages. For all La Salle knew, Tonty's body could have been among the charred corpses he encountered in the area. Tonty, who had been injured but survived the conflict, fled to a Jesuit mission in northern Michigan and received information about La Salle that wasn't much more encouraging. "We tried to pass the time as best we could," Tonty wrote. "We were informed, however, by many Ottawa braves that M. de la Salle was dead, and they gave us proofs pertinent to make us believe it to be true."[5] Throughout the year neither man knew if the other had survived the Native American wars that erupted across the eastern half of the continent.

When La Salle got word that Tonty was still alive in early 1681, he returned to Montreal and once more began the process of recruiting men for the expedition. This would likely be his last chance to prove the value of the Mississippi River. After all, the king of France had only given him five years to explore the territory and hold a monopoly over trade in the regions he discovered. Those five years would be up in May 1682.

Montreal, Canada
August 11, 1976

He wore his red jacket with gold brocade cuffs and a black felt hat with a wispy feather spilling down the side. Nothing like getting decked out in French court finery to celebrate a momentous occa-sion. The August day was humid and gray. The flag of Quebec, royal blue with a white cross and four white fleur de lys—one for each field of blue—fluttered in the wind. René-Robert Cavelier, Sieur de La Salle, grasped the pen to sign his will. All his property would be transferred to his cousin on the event of his death. Death seemed quite likely in the coming months. It often is when you try something absurd.

The scene was almost storybook perfect. The assembled men could have passed for actors in a high-budget period film, as long as you ignored the crowd of people dressed in waist-high denim jeans and plastic sunglasses. And the microphones on stage. And the fact that *this* Robert Cavelier's first language had been English, not French. But for an American playing a Frenchman, Reid Lewis spoke the language impeccably.

Colin Crevel, né Bob Kulick, surveyed the crowd. At six feet two inches and only 155 pounds, Kulick was one of the skinnier guys on the crew. His dad had told him that if he stood sideways he disappeared. Not that blending in was going to be an issue anymore, what with his getup. His wavy brown hair was beyond the length of needing a trim, his shirt had a ruffle on it, and his pants were held up below his knees with colorful ties. All the crew members around him were dressed similarly, though the ones playing nobles had nicer jackets and felt hats to wear. The costumes made for a cinematic performance.

They weren't putting on a good show for the throng that turned out to see them depart, though, stumbling over the words they'd practiced for months. Nerves, probably. It's not every day that one sets off on a 3,300-mile trek in handmade canoes across two countries, three lakes, and five major rivers all while impersonating 17th-century Frenchmen. Up until the moment they took the stage,

the expedition hadn't seemed real. Seeing Quebec City had been
real, visiting Montmorency Falls and feeling its spray had been real,
the swirling whirlpools of the Lachine Rapids had been real, and
the unexpected culture shock of being an American in French-
speaking Canada was still very real. But the voyage? It had never
been inevitable until this moment on this stage in this waterfront
suburb of Montreal. Now Reid Lewis signed a will as if he were
La Salle, Marc Lieberman towered over him in a tricorn black felt
hat as Henri de Tonty (sans prosthetic metal hand), and George
LeSieutre ambled over to notarize the will the way Jacques de La
Metairie once did. LeSieutre had been the class president before
graduating high school two months earlier. Lieberman had been
a student at Northern Illinois University, Kulick a senior at Elgin
High School. Now they were French canoeists and explorers. They
were voyageurs. Well, pretending to be.

"This guy is nuts," Kulick and his friends had muttered to one
another in the auditorium years earlier. They'd been high school
juniors, and up on stage was French teacher Reid Lewis from their
rival school, Larkin. Lewis had just explained how he planned to
spend two years building six replica birch-bark canoes, then use
them to transport twenty-three men and several tons of gear from
one end of the country to the other—two years of intense planning
and training, followed by eight months of camping, performing
skits, and living three hundred years in the past.

"Now, who would be interested in that?" Lewis asked.

Everyone in Kulick's row of friends raised their hands.

Somehow, only Kulick had followed through after the initial
recruitment. He'd had to give up his job at Jewel, the local grocery
store, and his free time had been gobbled up in chunks by expedition
prep. None of his friends from Elgin had made the cut to be on the
crew, and his relationship with his girlfriend, Kathy, had disintegrated

as well. Though it hadn't been easy at the time, he'd gained plenty of close friends on the crew, including Marc Lieberman and Sam Hess. Signing on to the expedition had meant giving up his old life for the promise of a new one, if impersonating someone who'd been dead for hundreds of years could be considered "new."

Quebec Solicitor General Fernand Lalonde looked out of place in his brown suit as he unveiled the plaque that had been embedded in a small boulder for the occasion. All the young men standing around him wore woolen toques on their heads and leather moccasins on their feet. Colorful finger-woven sashes adorned their waists and leather pouches hung from their shoulders. Their canvas pants belonged to a very limited wardrobe.

The assembled audience had watched in varying stages of attentiveness as a small maple tree was planted. The plaque on the rock next to the tree described the maple's symbolic value in French: ARBRE COMMÉMORANT LE DEPART DE L'EXPÉDITION CAVELIER DE LA SALLE II PROJET DU BICENTENAIRIE AMÉRICAIN 11 AOÛT 1976 (TREE COMMEMORATING THE DEPARTURE OF THE EXPEDITION OF CAVELIER DE LA SALLE II PROJECT OF THE U.S. BICENTENNIAL AUGUST 11, 1976). It was a nice gesture, albeit a strange one. A plaque and a tree to commemorate a voyage that was based off an earlier voyage that had begun 295 years earlier to the day. Layers upon layers of historical interpretation had accumulated, bringing the men to this point—the dedication of a plaque that would remain embedded in this rock for the foreseeable future. But Kulick wasn't thinking much about his participation in an experiment on performed anachronism. He was more concerned with the immediate prospect of saying goodbye, then hopping into a canoe with three other men, and paddling against a strong current for hours.

LaSalle city officials and Quebec government representatives finished their speeches and the last dozen pictures were snapped.

The heartfelt farewells began. Sons hugged their parents, husbands their wives. Kulick had been parting with people for almost a week, first in Illinois and now in Canada. His dad and sister Diane had come to Montreal to see him off, and he had a letter from his ex-girlfriend, Kathy, to carry with him. There would be more letters to come in the future, too, as long as their mail drop points worked out, and he'd see everyone again in several months when they reached Lake Michigan. But that was a thought for another day. Today they were perched with their canoes on the edge of the St. Lawrence, still unsure as to whether they'd actually be capable of paddling the loaded boats down the river. No one they'd talked to seemed to think it was possible for the man-powered vessels to overcome the current.

"*Te Deum laudamus; Te dominum confitemur. Te aeternum Patrem omnis terra veneratur* (Lord, we thank you. Everlasting Father, all the earth worships)," sang twenty-three voices at the end of a benediction from black-robed Father Loran Fuchs, playing the role of Pere Zenobe Membre. "*Sanctus, sanctus*," they concluded. And then they were off, carrying their canoes down the grassy embankment into the reeds on the edge of the river. The water was cool, the sky bright but gray with clouds left over from the recent Hurricane Belle. Kulick hopped into his canoe in front of Reid Lewis and John DiFulvio and behind Rich Gross. Together, the four of them dipped their paddles into the water. Kulick had carved this paddle himself and burned the image of a feather quill pen into the blade, a symbol of his duty as the group's journalist. Now he'd find out how well it worked paddling close to sixty strokes a minute for eight or nine hours each day.

As one of the middlemen (or *milieu*, as they're called in French), Kulick didn't have to worry about anything but pulling his paddle through the water. Gross, the curly-haired teen who'd grown up boating on the Fox River, sat at the front of the boat as the *avant* and was in charge of looking out for debris and hopping out of the boat upon landing. In the back sat John DiFulvio, a burly young man who'd played football throughout high school and had been attracted to the voyage for the physical challenge it presented. DiFulvio was in charge of steering the canoe and keeping it from weaving from side to side in the water, which wastes lots of energy. Compared to the other two, Kulick and Lewis had easy jobs: as *milieux*, their sole focus was providing power to keep the canoe moving forward. But this proved to be something of a challenge within the first half-mile of paddling.

The current on the St. Lawrence varies in strength depending on location along the river and the tide, but even for strong paddlers it can pose a problem. When the fleet of six canoes came around a bend in the river after only a quarter-mile of paddling, the rapids they faced were too daunting to cross, which meant the first portage of the expedition. Portages are the bane of every canoeist's journey, as was quickly proved by this short trek. Land, unload, carry the 175-pound canoes and thousands of pounds of gear down gravel and concrete roads for a quarter-mile, make several more trips back for more gear, sweat, grunt, groan as the edges of the upturned canoes dug into the flesh of shoulders, and double-check that no gear had been forgotten. One of the men had misplaced his musket, but another grabbed it for him. Next time they'd assign gear to each canoe crew. For now, it was time to return to the water.

At first it was a relief to be back on the water after the portage. But after a few hours, paddling was no relief from walking. Kulick's back ached and his arms burned from the strain of moving forward in a river that kept pushing them back. The grip and shaft of his paddle bit into his hands, scraping away skin unaccustomed to manipulating a wooden blade through the water for such an extended period of time. It was tiring, monotonous drudgery. Before the trip everyone had been required to run regularly (with the exception of Father Loran, whose arthritis made it too difficult; he biked) and do some strength training, but they'd done relatively little canoeing in preparation for the expedition, in part because their canoes hadn't been finished. They'd never practiced the kind of distances they'd be covering in the coming months.

The canoes slid past houses and farms on the river, moving so slowly they might've been outstripped by a dog on a leash out for a walk. By the end of the day they'd gone nine miles and were two hours late for their landing in Chateauguay. Most of the townspeople who'd turned out earlier to greet them had already dispersed.

Despite their exhaustion and lack of audience, the crew was in a festive mood. They'd passed their first test. They were capable of paddling the canoes against the current on the St. Lawrence, no matter what people might have said about the probability of failure. Even if it meant blisters and aching muscles and growling stomachs. Fortunately, the hunger would be taken care of in town. Unfortunately, Chateauguay City Hall had planned a fancy meal of finger sandwiches and wine. It was universally agreed upon in private after the dinner: never feed finger sandwiches to hungry voyageurs after a hard day's paddle. Even five sandwiches per man weren't enough to make him feel entirely full.

After giving a performance to a small audience under the lights of a soccer field where mosquitoes feasted on anything that breathed, the crew returned to their camp along the St. Lawrence. One by one they crawled into their makeshift tents, comprised of a canoe turned on its side and covered with a nineteen-by-twenty-three-foot canvas tarp held up by three paddles and some stakes. It was eight men to a canoe-tent, each with his own modern sleeping bag, a concession made for the sake of safety. With all eight men in the tent, there was just enough room for everyone to lay flat on his back without his shoulders touching someone else's.

Kulick stayed up to record the day's events in his journal. In addition to their duties around camp, everyone had work to do on their educational projects. As the crew's journalist, Kulick was charged with recording the official account of the expedition. That meant taking time away from sleep, but he took the job seriously. If everything went according to plan, his notes from the trip would eventually get turned into a book, and who knew, maybe even a movie.

"I am no longer Bob Kulick, I am now Colin Crevel, a voyageur," he scratched into his notebook with a fountain pen. A bottle of ink was open next to him and he wrote by the light of the fire. "We have to forget our old ways, forget about jumping in a car to go somewhere, buying new shoes or new clothes when they wear out. Don't think about what is to come, the cold of winter, the strain of portages, endless hours of work. Think rather of what you are doing now, live the life of a voyageur, live your life paddle stroke by paddle stroke."

He closed his notebook after recording a few more details about the day. His head and torso were sheltered beneath the ribs of the canoe, his legs by the tarp. Some people snored along the row of men, others slept in silence. Peering up into the darkness, Kulick glimpsed a sliver of moon through a gap between the canoe and the tarp. The pale orb was waning gibbous; it had been full two nights earlier and now was slightly diminished. It was like a beacon from the past. The same moon shone on the French voyageurs in 1681, although their moon didn't have human footprints etched into its dusty surface. But from this distance you couldn't see the footprints anyway.

Cornwall, Ontario
August 16, 1976

"Allons les gars!"

Nearly a week into the expedition Lewis's chipper wake-up call was becoming as grating as any alarm clock. His voice rang through the cool air as he went from one shelter to another. It was 6:00, the sun just rising and smearing light across the cold sky. Some men grunted and slowly extricated themselves from their sleeping bags, while others jumped up full of verve, ready for the day. Mark Fredenburg and Sam Hess belonged to the latter group. Fredenburg greeted each day with a loud, "Good morning, world!" while Hess, who slept in the same shelter, tossed away his sleeping bag and pulled out the leather pouch containing his flint and steel. As the fire starter for his module of eight men, the longer Hess took to get moving, the longer it would be before Fredenburg, the cook, could heat up a breakfast. No fire, no food.

Starting a fire with nothing but a jagged piece of flint and a small slab of steel is an art, one that was practiced for thousands of years before matches made their debut. It starts with a piece of steel or iron and a glassy stone such as quartz, jasper, or flint. The stones alone can't conjure up fire; it's their ability to release particles of iron from the steel striker and instantaneously expose the particles to oxygen that coaxes a spark seemingly out of thin air. It was a flashy trick in an age of lighters and matches, but for the crew of the La Salle expedition it was also a matter of survival.

Anyone could learn to make a fire, but Hess was gaining a reputation as the fastest and most reliable fire starter on the crew. He always carried tinder with him, doing his best to keep it dry even on the water. Frayed bark from a cedar tree was the best. He rolled it up into a little mouse nest and laid it at the bottom of the fire pit, then worked on drawing a spark out of his flint and steel.

With one hand holding the angular flint with a small piece of cotton on the edge, Hess used the steel to strike down on the flint at an angle. The flint shaved a sliver of iron off, which reached a molten temperature and created a spark on the cotton cloth. The process took only seconds. Hess transferred the spark to the center of his tinder ball and brought his face up close to the enveloped spark. He blew gently until ribbons of smoke curled out. Once the fibrous ball began smoking, fire was sure to follow. All hail Prometheus.

A tiny fire still needed assistance to grow. Hess fed twigs onto the tinder ball, then sticks, and finally larger pieces of wood. Eventually the crackling fire was hot enough to withstand a breeze and survive an invasion by a black Dutch oven containing the morning's breakfast—unsweetened oatmeal or cornmeal made with water. Sometimes they had maple syrup to pour on top. Just a few days ago the ladies on the liaison team had gone to a store to buy them cinnamon. But there'd been some confusion between the French-speaking shopkeeper and the English-speaking shoppers, and only after the men poured the spice all over the pot of oatmeal did they realize the cinnamon was actually cloves. The taste was terrible, spicy and bitter, but most of the crew were hungry enough to stomach anything. Their food often had a sprinkling of grit mixed in as well. Sometimes the sand was leftover from cleaning the pot the night before, or it was blown in from the surrounding terrain. Hess had learned to chew quickly and ignore the disconcerting crunch.

With the morning's fire blazing away, Hess returned to the tent to pack up his belongings. By that point everyone in camp was bustling around in preparation for the day: packing or eating breakfast by one of the three fires or stretching or having their raw, blistered hands bandaged by Dick Stillwagon. Their muscles were getting stronger day by day, but the toughness of their skin was lagging behind. Hess had layers of blisters across his hands and each day of paddling meant tearing them open again. Today they were traveling from Cornwall, Ontario, to Massena, New York, on the opposite side of the river, thirteen miles against the current.

Despite the thousand little hardships of daily life on the expedition—getting wet, sore, tired, cold, and hungry enough to devour a horse, hooves and all—Hess couldn't be happier. He nearly hadn't been part of the expedition. The teachers had cut him from the original group during the interview process. But Hess hadn't wanted to pass up the opportunity to help create tools for the trip, even if he couldn't participate on the trip itself. His parents had always said he was an old soul. He did things like set trap lines for mink and muskrats in the suburbs, and his summers were filled with camping trips. Learning to craft 17th-century objects would be instructive in and of itself, even without getting the chance to regularly use them. In John Fialko's shop, Hess helped carve knives and tomahawks and pound out steel for the hinges that would be used on wooden chests. Taking note of his diligence, the teachers decided on Hess as an alternate. When someone dropped out a few months into the training, Hess was asked to join the expedition as a regular crew member. He didn't know why the other student had dropped out, and he didn't care. Their loss; his gain. He signed away his social life and took the name Gabriel Barbier without a second thought.

The morning came to a close as everyone swallowed their breakfast and cleaned their wooden bowls and spoons. It was time to be off. They had a full day coming up, including a trip through two locks, the Snell and the Eisenhower.

The St. Lawrence Seaway, with its myriad locks and channels used by massive shipping freights, had not been built with man-powered canoes in mind. The project was quite the opposite;

officials in Canada and the United States had hoped the bi-national engineering marvel would usher in greater economic and technological prosperity. It had also been a significant source of political consternation, with the debate about the project's feasibility spanning fifty years in the American Congress.[6] But eventually, American lawmakers conceded that the project was worth the cost, and construction began. Between 1954 and 1959, engineers and construction workers carved out buried earth, built locks and dams, and created a navigable waterway between Montreal and Lake Ontario that raised ships 225 feet and helped them avoid rapids and shoals. The cost of construction was $470 million Canadian, with the Canadian government paying more than 70 percent of the total bill.

Robert Moses, renowned for his work in New York City urban planning, headed the American side of the project. Once completed, the seaway was heavily promoted by the Eisenhower administration. Some called it the eighth wonder of the world for its incomprehensible scope and the speed at which it was completed. If La Salle had somehow managed to travel forward in time and retraced his trajectory on the St. Lawrence, the river would have been unrecognizable. It might also have been impossible to navigate. Locks and dams are not necessarily helpful to canoes.

The paddlers in the six canoes of La Salle: Expedition II were quickly discovering the challenges posed by modern engineering when traveling in vessels from an earlier era. After paddling only several hundred yards out of camp, they came across dangerous rapids around a bridge. Foaming water seethed up around the trestles and created miniature whirlpools that tugged on the boats as they went by, destabilizing their trajectory through the water. Ron Hobart's boat fought through the rapids just as John DiFulvio's boat, carrying Kulick and Reid Lewis, shot forward. They barely avoided a collision. DiFulvio's boat wound up under a tree on shore and rolled dangerously, taking on a foot of water.

In his boat, Hess focused on digging deep with each paddle stroke. Running through rapids was terrifying and exhilarating. He paddled as hard as he could, fighting forward, the canoe barely moving, and when it seemed like he was getting sucked backward or about to spin out of control, adrenaline spiked through his system and he pushed harder than he thought possible to break free of the current's grip. But he never knew whether he'd be strong enough before he made the attempt. Battling currents on the St. Lawrence sometimes felt like a Herculean task. The river made no concessions for novices. If anyone capsized in the rapids, he'd be swept away and potentially drowned in minutes, regardless of whether he had a life preserver on or not, and plenty of the men didn't bother with the life preservers. Hess never regretted joining the expedition, but moments like this made him question his sanity.

The rapids made for an exciting, if wet, morning. By the time the group reached Snell Lock on the southern side of the river, they'd missed the morning window and would have to wait for the lock to open again. The sun hid behind a dense layer of clouds, and the light wind was growing stronger. Stillwagon yelled at those who were shivering to put on something dry if they wanted to avoid hypothermia. As they changed into dry shirts, a man who'd been piloting a sailboat upriver and was also waiting for the lock offered them hot coffee he'd prepared belowdecks. A warm drink with the kick of caffeine was a godsend. Paddling was tiring work. Just as soon as everyone had glugged down the black liquid, the locks opened and they were ushered into the giant concrete maw.

The taupe stone walls of the lock loomed over the men as they paddled their canoes forward. Built for mammoth freights, the lock made the 20-foot canoes look like toys in a bathtub. The La Salle:

Expedition II was the first group to ever travel the locks in non-motorized boats, and it hadn't been easy to secure permission for the passage. They were followed in by a work boat that would keep an eye on them. After everyone was in, the lower gate folded shut and water began pouring in through the filling valve deep below the surface. The water burbled up, pushing them higher and higher against the wall. The weather seemed to be cooperating more today than it had three days ago, when they had passed through the Beauharnois Lock. It had poured buckets that day, and after only a few minutes it had become apparent that the canvas ponchos designed to keep them dry only served to soak up moisture. Today was gray, but the clouds hadn't turned into a storm.

When the water in Snell Lock was nearly level with the top of the upper gate, the gate opened and the six canoe crews began paddling again. After a quick jaunt two miles upstream the men found Cathy Palmer, Sharon Baumgartner, Jan Lewis, and Marlena Scavuzzo waiting for them outside the Eisenhower Lock with ham-and-cheese sandwiches, jerky, and crackers. They devoured every last morsel while the lock was filled and emptied for the boats ahead of them. As they waited their turn, a crowd gathered along the observation deck, a feature that didn't exist alongside the other locks. A few dozen soon grew to more than a hundred curious onlookers eager to see a 20th-century system put to use by a crew of 17th-century voyageurs.

The gate to the lock opened and crew members who had dozed off during the wait were woken up and ushered back into the boats. Even after the group passed through a couple of locks, the massive walls of the Eisenhower Lock were formidable. To be lifted almost 40 feet on a river without paddling a single stroke was surreal, like riding an elevator in a wooden boat. Relaxing, even though they had to hold on to one another's canoes to make sure the hulls didn't scratch one another. Off to the side of the lock the onlookers standing on the observation deck and leaning over the railing peered into the belly of the concrete drum. They watched as the canoes inched their way up the wall, buoyed by river water. It was a queer juxtaposition of modern and historic technology.

As the canoes rose higher and higher, coming level with the upper part of the river, a breeze ruffled the hats and shirts of those in the canoes. The water stopped rising, the lock gates opened, and a violent windstorm turned the river into a churning mass of waves.

"Did we get dropped off at the Atlantic Ocean?" someone joked.

The waves tossed the boats around as the men paddled. The wind howled in their ears. Soon everyone was drenched. Water sloshed around their feet in the boats, turning their leather moccasins into soggy socks. Occasionally one of the milieu men would stop to bail water out of the boat if it got too high. The river rose and dropped by a matter of feet as the locks closed and opened behind them. Bit by bit the paddlers fought the current and the wind and the waves. Back and arm muscles burned and strained against the water.

"You want the goddamn pants, take 'em!" Terry Cox shouted into the wind. He was a bowman with a temper, and in the wettest seat of the canoe he would occasionally lose it when his pants got soaked *yet again*.

It was a struggle to get to Massena, New York, but waiting for the sopping voyageurs at the end of the river were a number of 4-H kids with a dinner of spaghetti and cake—real food!—and hot showers. God, did showers feel good when most days the best they could expect was a dousing on the river. With full stomachs and clean hair and dry clothes, the sore muscles and blisters didn't bother them so much. And sleep had never felt more satisfying, even if Hess, the group prankster, had scattered sand or ants in their sleeping bags.

⌐━━○

Ogdensburg, New York
August 19, 1976

Twenty-one men sprawled across the lush grass beneath a warm sun, limp and indolent as they enjoyed an afternoon nap. Bob Kulick and Keith Gorse were alone in resisting the soporific ambience of the manicured park. Each of the two men wrote in his journal, Kulick with his authentic-looking fountain pen and characteristic attention to detail.

"I said we pulled into a place that looked like a park—well, it is a state hospital," Kulick wrote. "I guess it is an appropriate place for this group to spend time."

It was early afternoon and the paddlers had made such good time in the morning that they had only two and a half miles to go and three hours before they were expected in Ogdensburg, giving them more than enough time to eat a long lunch and grab forty winks. It just figured that the place they'd chosen for a rest was the grounds of the St. Lawrence Psychiatric Center, treating the mentally insane since 1890.

Whether or not anyone on the crew met the clinical criteria for some form of mental abnormality was almost a moot point. They'd all willingly signed on for the expedition, despite knowing it would involve a great deal of physical agony and the emotional discomfort of close quarters and constant observation. They were spending every waking and sleeping hour together—a group of two dozen, mostly teenage, mostly alpha-male-type guys—and curious onlookers usually watched them from early morning to late at night. It was like living in a testosterone-filled fish bowl. Eight days in, the strain was starting to show.

For some, homesickness struck hard and unexpectedly. Stillwagon, the stentorian biology teacher who'd initially balked at the fact that these teenagers would be addressing him by his first name instead of "Mr. Stillwagon," missed his family and his home so much he wasn't sure he'd survive. As he paddled along the river, occasionally providing a rudder stroke to keep the canoe on course, he was hit by nostalgia so intense it was almost physical pain. One minute he was watching the water glisten below an Arcadian shoreline, the next he was dreaming of his mother-in-law's fudge and toast. He didn't even like toast that much! It made no sense. He'd been away from home plenty of times before, on canoe trips that lasted several weeks, but somehow this was different. His wife, Rowena, was back home in Indiana with their four kids, and he missed them all. The only thing to do was keep to the routine: wake up each morning, paddle all day, perform for the community they were visiting at night, write a letter to Rowena. At least they weren't being 100 percent accurate to the past. In the 18th century, physicians thought homesickness was a physical malady and treated it with purges, bloodletting, and leeches. One Russian general resorted to burying alive his soldiers suffering from homesickness.[7] He reported that after they'd been buried, left underground for a bit, then dug back up, the homesickness had usually subsided.

The second mental obstacle was more insidious and less likely to dissipate with time. It boiled down to clashing personalities—an inevitable result of putting twenty-three men in a pressure-cooker situation, no matter how many psychological team-building sessions they'd attended in advance. Some days, you just didn't want to deal with someone else's bullshit or the fact that one of your socks got lost in the wash. Shouting matches erupted quick and hot as flash fires and subsided just as rapidly. By morning any lingering antagonism was usually forgotten. But some people had the kind of temperaments that seemed to invite simmering, relentless resentment. One such person on the crew was Clif Wilson.

Wilson played the role of a royal, Jacques Bourdon, Sieur d'Autray. He got to wear a fancy jacket and felt hat for their performances. But he carried some of those aristocratic tendencies with him off the stage. He did his work, but he also yelled at everyone else even if they were doing theirs. He was mouthy, emotional, and bossy. He regularly got into vehement arguments with Cox, who could poke a mean finger in Wilson's chest while shouting. Wilson didn't perceive the world in shades of gray; everything was black and white, including his dislike of Randy Foster, who sat directly behind him in their canoe. There wasn't anything logical in the antipathy Wilson felt for Foster, and yet the sentiment stretched back to the years they'd spent training for the expedition. Somehow, despite the animosity between them, the two had been placed in the same canoe, the only canoe without an adult paddler. And that smoldering dislike had no outlet since they spent hours every day in the same small boat.

One of the few ways for Wilson to cope with his dilemma in the canoe was to vent to his friends when they got off the water. The clique called itself the Radical Five and was comprised of Lieberman, Kulick, DiFulvio, Gorse, and Wilson. Sometimes Hess joined their group as well. They were all good friends and would've spent most of their time together anyway, so forming the quasi-fraternity was a logical step. It meant they could share secrets and discuss the people they disliked with the knowledge that most bad-mouthing was done in the heat of the moment and would be kept among themselves. But lately Wilson's disagreements with

Foster had become more severe, to the point where Wilson was considering leaving the expedition.

"You know what a bummer it is to be talking about quitting on the first week out?" he told Kulick and DiFulvio. Kulick figured that if it really came down to it, the adults probably wouldn't let Wilson quit. It wasn't like they were prisoners in the Gulag who'd never see home again, but they'd made a commitment to the expedition and Kulick thought the adults would hold them to it.

Even though paddling all day gave people plenty of time to dwell on their homesickness or stew in anger and frustration, the evenings were full enough to keep everyone busy until bedtime. Today was no different. After leaving the picturesque grounds of the mental institution and paddling the rest of the way to Ogdensburg, the group was treated to another 4-H meal of corn, beans, potatoes, and spaghetti. 4-H clubs (developed by the National Institute of Food and Agriculture and focusing on the development of head, heart, hands, and health) could always be relied on to provide the crew with good, filling food without any of the frills or pretensions that city councils sometimes included with their meals. Not that anyone would turn up their noses at any kind of food served on any kind of dishware. The generosity of communities along the route was the best antidote to daily aggravations and disagreements among the crew members. It was a continual pleasant surprise to see how receptive strangers were of their expedition.

Ogdensburg was particularly welcoming. The townspeople invited the whole crew for a tour of their Frederic Remington Art Museum after visiting hours. The paintings and sketches were beautifully detailed, almost like pictures taken from an era before photography. Sculptures captured bucking broncos, trapped forever on their hind legs, while paintings and sketches depicted life on the Western frontier: cowboys seated around the fire and Indians riding into battle wearing feathered headdresses. In many ways, cowboys were 19th-century versions of voyageurs. They traveled into dangerous lands, trying to colonize, "civilize," and domesticate the wilderness. They were also invaders, like the voyageurs had been, and they co-opted the modes of transportation natives used—horses and canoes.

Pretending to be a voyageur naturally gave everyone on the crew a more visceral appreciation for the ways of the past and the challenges its inhabitants faced. If they could've jumped into those paintings and sat around the fire with the cowboys, would they have had anything in common? Would they've sung songs with a guitar late into the night, maybe taught the cowboys some John Denver or Gordon Lightfoot tunes? That was the thing about acting like time travelers from the past: history felt so close at hand. But the past was still—and would always be—untouchable.

Alexandria Bay, New York
August 23, 1976

The boat appeared around a bend in the river like a ghost from another era, its white hull glowing against the shadowy green of the pine trees on shore. *La Duchesse*, a 106-foot houseboat owned by Andrew McNally of Rand McNally & Co. (a publisher of maps, atlases, textbooks, and globes), was the crew's first rest point on this sixteen-mile day, and it took them five miles off course of their destination.

"Here we go with this song-and-dance routine," Cox muttered as the six sleek canoes whisked across the open river and landed at the sheltered dock where *La Duchesse* made berth. He felt no qualms about voicing his opinion, and he wasn't looking forward to the schmoozing they were going to do today. Cox was like Wilson in that way: straightforward, emotional, maybe a little mouthy. But call a spade a spade. As he saw it, McNally had only invited them for a visit so that he could show them off to his rich friends, like they were a bunch of monkeys in suits.

Not all of the crew shared Cox's cynical outlook on the visit to *La Duchesse*. They spent all day on the water in boats then slept underneath them at night, so they appreciated a well-crafted vessel. And the teenagers didn't know much about the ongoing fund-raising efforts. Lewis hadn't told them how far below the red they still were. Even now he often stayed up late into the night filling out applications for more grants. His departure in the evenings and lack of participation in certain group events and chores was starting to cause some friction. McNally's generosity could be important in that respect. He was on the American Revolution Bicentennial Administration and had already secured $17,000 for La Salle: Expedition II. That's what Lewis told Kulick, at least, and that's why Lewis said they needed to keep "cultivating" McNally.

Kulick was impressed by the houseboat and its history. Only a year ago it had been submerged in river water up to the top of its first deck. McNally bought it for $1.00 and got the fire department to help him resurrect it. Once it was safely docked near his house, it was restored to all its former turn-of-the-century splendor. The woodwork was unbelievable, and details like the original brass fireplace had been refurbished as well. McNally even stocked the cabinets with coffee mugs from the 1893 Chicago World's Fair; he was now using those mugs to serve coffee and Coca-Cola to the voyageurs. Talk about classy: coffee and donuts on a gorgeous antique houseboat. Even Cox was happy to get some Coke.

The tour of *La Duchesse* was enjoyable but short, as the voyageurs still had fourteen miles to go before they reached Gananoque on the Canadian side of the river. Only a couple of weeks earlier that distance might've seemed impossible. Paddling continued to be hard, exhausting work. And taller members of the crew, like Lieberman, were dealing with terrible backaches from having to bend over so much in the little boat. There was a reason most voyageurs had been short and squat. Their physique was matched more closely by Cox, who'd once been a competitive gymnast. But they were all getting stronger, and the miles melted away faster. Everyone's arms and torso were burnt red or had turned golden tan—Gorse looked like a regular Adonis with his wavy blond hair. They were also pocked with mosquito bites. But it was invigorating and liberating to live outdoors. No roof over your head but the sky, which changed every day, no home to call your own but the canoe you turned into a shelter at night. The scenery was beautiful, especially now that they had entered the Thousand Islands region. They'd passed Corn Island, Ontario; Grenadier Island, New York; and Chimney Island, Ontario, the past few days. Today they were paddling along a narrow channel between Wellesley Island and the southern shore. The land was adorned with thatches of cedar and pine trees. Patches of artichoke-green moss covered the rocks along the riverbank. Traveling by water gave the crew a whole new perspective on the world, and sleeping outdoors made them feel like they were part of the beautiful, wild landscape. It seemed like the way man was supposed to live.

The camp at Gananoque turned out to be a perfect spot along the river. Though the men always knew approximately where they were ending the day, oftentimes the suitability of the campsite would be a mystery until they arrived: it could be a smelly morass of mud and weeds, or rocky, or in the middle of a town. If they were spending the night near or in a town, the liaison team coordinated with city officials to pick a spot for the voyageurs, then flagged the men in with a big white banner. Being in a town meant the crew got to interact more with other people, but it also made their campsite vulnerable to theft. They'd had to set guards a few nights because of the possibility of vandalism. If the men were spending a night away from crowds, they chose their own campsite based on which stretch of shoreline looked most inviting. Camp here was just off the water under the shade of trees, and Gananoque community members further warmed the hearts of the voyageurs by providing them with a huge dinner of hamburgers, corn, and potato salad. Kulick ate five burgers on his own to make up for the paltry cheese sandwiches they'd gotten at lunch.

The town had arranged for several other activities in between the voyageurs' presentation in a gazebo near their campsite, including a trip to the showers at the local hockey rink. To top it off, the girls who had served them dinner brought candy bars for everyone. The chocolate and the girls were the perfect treat to end the night. Gorse and Gross were by far the most popular among fawning teenage girls, but the more tanned and muscular everyone got, the more likely they were to elicit looks of admiration and compliments from members of the fairer sex. The expedition had set rules about not going off alone with a girl, but the men couldn't help looking. It was a rush to be the most popular attraction in town.

Back in the camp that evening, Cox, Lewis, and a few others sat up around the fires talking and relaxing while everyone else crawled into their sleeping bags. The burning logs hissed and popped. Cicadas scratched out a shrill symphony from their perches in surrounding trees. The men had a full day coming up in the morning, their last day on the St. Lawrence River before entering the first of the Great Lakes: Lake Ontario.

Around midnight the sleeping crew members were jarred awake by the sound of shrieking and the beating of drums outside their shelters. Kulick tried to shake off some of his sleepy befuddlement.

From a gap in the shelter canvas he could just make out the sight of legs running through their campsite. *Shit.* It was probably some rowdy townies wrecking the place. He pulled on his pants to go help, inadvertently planting a hand in the middle of DiFulvio's chest and shoving him to the ground just as the latter tried to sit up.

When he got outside there was no wreckage or destruction and the voices had quieted. More confused than ever, Kulick made his way down to the last of the three fires they'd built earlier in the night and found several dozen teenagers in Native American costumes and war paint sitting around the fire and passing around a peace pipe with Lewis. He recognized some of the girls from before, members of the Gananoque summer recreation staff and the girls' softball team. Splashes of white light erupted sporadically around the campfire. Kulick blinked and realized it was the flashbulb of a photographer from the local paper. As he watched the bizarre scene, more voyageurs stumbled out of their shelters, having been awoken by the sound.

The surreal peace-pipe smoking lasted a short while, then the "natives" made to leave. Just as everyone crawled back into their beds, the "raiders" came howling through camp again, beating their drums and screeching. It was a ridiculous racket, but Kulick had never been happier to be part of the expedition. Gananoque was, by far, the greatest town they'd been in yet.

Chapter Four

✳

THE BONDS
OF BROTHERHOOD

**Lake Ontario
September 1681**

What kind of person set off into the wilderness for months or years without knowing if he'd ever be home again? What thoughts crossed the mind of the voyageur when he left behind all that was familiar to enter alien terrain? We know only the broad strokes of La Salle the man, a member of the nobility and the man who led the voyageurs, and what we do know is colored by the accounts of his contemporaries. As one historian wrote of La Salle, "He was hated more than he was liked, reviled more than he was praised, denounced and condemned more than he was commended and defended."[1] Even if this historic interpretation of his personality is incorrect, La Salle did seem to excite the ire of his men. On one of his exploratory trips down the Ohio River (all of which took place years before he was granted permission to explore the Mississippi), one of La Salle's servants went so far as to try to poison him by mixing hemlock into his salad. Though the attempt wasn't fatal, it made La Salle ill for more than a month.[2]

But we don't know what La Salle himself would have said in response to accusations about his character flaws. However despised he may have been, he also earned the loyalty of men like Henri de Tonty and Governor Frontenac.

If so many difficulties exist in trying to understand a landed, literate man like La Salle, about whom much is written, discerning the motivations of the illiterate drudges who served as voyageurs is akin to navigating an unfamiliar coastline in the fog. What can be said of the voyageurs as a group is that their reputation preceded them. At certain points in the history of New France up to 12 percent of the male population was working in the fur trade as voyageurs or *coureurs de bois*, men who set off into the wilderness illegally, without permission from the government. They quickly grew into mythic figures similar to those people who populate American tall tales.[3] A voyageur was a man whose central principle in life was fulfilling expectations of masculinity. He passed much of his life in a liminal zone between "savage" and "civilized" (as it was then understood), giving him the opportunity to create new social norms. An individual could earn higher wages for working harder and doing odd jobs such as hunting or learning indigenous languages. These were the types of things that impressed their bosses, the bourgeois leaders. Among comrades the voyageurs built a reputation by gambling, winning boxing matches, and running rapids. Having a good sense of humor and working without complaint were also highly valued personality traits.

Learning the code of the voyageurs and earning the respect of fellow paddlers was no easy task for a novice. As a way of initiating a greenhorn into the brotherhood of paddlers, experienced voyageurs often staged a mock baptism. The earliest known spot for such religious rites was along the Ottawa River at a place called Pointe-aux-Baptemes, Quebec, the first location past Montreal where the landscape suddenly transformed into craggy bedrock.[4] Not only was the scenery starkly different from what the new men had seen before, but going beyond this point meant it would be hard to return to Montreal alone if they chose to desert. The baptism ritual—which could be a bit of splashing or a total soaking, depending on the mood of the initiators—was a symbolic rebirth, a shedding of one's old identity. Welcome to the New World. There's no turning back now. You better learn to blend in if you want to survive.

La Salle's men would likely not have had to worry about initiation rituals on their departure from Montreal. They didn't even paddle past Pointe-aux-Baptemes, since they were traveling along Lake Ontario, two hundred miles south of the Ottawa River. Their mission was different from that of the typical voyageurs. Instead of shipping furs, they were providing manpower for an explorer, an altogether more dangerous task. And with a leader like La Salle, who had a history of inspiring defections, it seemed likely that the thirty men who started the voyage would not all make it to the end before deciding to turn back.

Kingston, Ontario
August 24, 1976

Ken Lewis lay on his back in the scratchy, sun-browned grass of Lake Ontario Park, feet crossed at the ankles, head pillowed by an angular log that would later be used for firewood. His left arm was draped across his chest, palm and one finger wrapped with white tape that had turned a dirty gray over the course of the day. His right arm was bent at a ninety-degree angle at the elbow, balancing a log on its rough end to cast a shadow over his face and keep the sun from his eyes. Tomorrow marked two weeks on the expedition. Two weeks since he'd said good-bye to his wife, Judy. Two weeks since he'd drunk a drop of alcohol. Two weeks since he'd tasted the ashy smoke of a cigarette. Cigarettes were banned on the expedition, but most everyone else smoked tobacco from their wooden pipes. He'd decided to quit both vices at the same time, because the expedition seemed like the perfect break from his old life. He forced himself to abstain from smoking a pipe and resorted to chasing after puffs of secondary smoke that drifted across the water when other people took a break from paddling and lit their pipes. The little whiffs of smoke he managed to catch did nothing to relieve his cravings or reduce his irritability. But at least he could escape in his mind. Eyes closed, he'd fantasize about the Cornstalk Fence in New Orleans. He'd rent a room there at the end of the trip, buy a box of Cuban cigars and a bottle of bourbon, and fill a bathtub with steaming hot water and enough bubbles to form a snowy mountain over the edge. He'd soak, drink, and smoke himself into blissful oblivion. Only seven-and-a-half months and three thousand miles to go.

Until then, he'd have to suffer in silence.

Not that he was all that silent. Some might even call him cantankerous and prone to picking arguments. Not necessarily the kind of person you wanted to sit down and have a heart-to-heart with. At least he had outlets for his edginess, a couple of ways to drain the bile of a bad mood. On the water he poured his energy into paddling. Situated in the middle of the canoe behind George LeSieutre and Sam Hess and ahead of Mark Fredenburg, all Ken had to focus on was raw power. He worked hard to wear himself out. Today they'd gone twenty-three miles from Gananoque to Kingston, and they'd still managed to arrive two hours early.

"La Salle never had to work his ass off in the morning so he could sit outside a town and wait," Bill Watts had grumbled during their two-hour lunch break. But being a little early was a hell of a lot better than being late. The towns were expecting a grand entrance complete with synchronized paddle salute and the smoke and boom of blanks fired from their replica 17th-century flintlock muskets. Even setting up camp was something of a performance, with kids and adults crowding around to ask about the mallets the voyageurs used to pound stakes into the ground, about the knives they wore around their waists, about sleeping under canoes every night.

But the real show was on a stage instead of in their camp. It was in these almost-daily presentations that Ken could once more lose himself. The scripted stage performance came complete with songs, gags, and a smattering of educational information. Ken wrote it and organized the score with the help of one of his friends, Howard Platt. The two met in an acting class and instantly hit it off, bonding over a shared obsession with Mark Twain and paddling down the Mississippi. Platt was off in Hollywood now, making a weekly appearance as the clownish Officer Hoppy in the NBC show *Sanford and Son*, and Ken had transitioned to writing plays and copy for big firms. Given all his experience, it made sense for Ken to take up his pen once more in service of a historical reenactment. He had a turn for the dramatic and was able to slip into new characters with ease. He even had the appearance of a scruffy voyageur: long brown hair pulled into a ponytail, a wiry brown beard, a beak-like nose, and a rugged leanness that suggested missed meals and long hours paddling. But he didn't want to steal the limelight. Plenty of other people had main roles and lines to memorize for their performances.

"You know, it occurs to me that with all the talking we've been doing up here about the voyageur, there might just be a couple of you out there that don't know what a voyageur was," Cox said later that day to the audience spread out before them in the park. For Kingston being home to La Salle's first fort, Fort Frontenac, the crowd was disappointingly small.

"Is that possible? I don't believe it!" Ken interjected with a heavy French accent.

As Cox explained the duties and personalities of the voyageurs, John DiFulvio, who went by the French name La Violette, lumbered onto the stage in nothing but pink long underwear. He was gruff and brawny with a dense, dark beard and brown hair down to his shoulders. His entrance was always sure to elicit laughter. The "dress the voyageur" sketch was so popular, a Chicago-area newspaper had turned DiFulvio into a cutout paper doll, complete with three outfits and a choice of accessories that included his paddle and musket.

"The voyageur's roomy French peasant britches were reinforced in the knees and seat to withstand months of sitting and kneeling in canoes, and they were constructed of very heavy sail canvas," Hobart said as he passed a pair of pants to DiFulvio.

"Heavy leggings, called *mitasses*, were borrowed from the Indians. Mitasses were sometimes made of leather, or, as you can see here, canvas," continued Fredenburg. "They protected the voyageur's legs from brambles on long portages and kept the bottoms of his wide pants from getting in his way."

One by one, crew members brought forward articles of clothing and described their function until DiFulvio had grown even larger and been bundled in every layer he had. From there, they launched into a paddling song called "C'est L'aviron" with Hobart strumming a guitar as they sang. Not everyone had been blessed with a good voice or the ability to hold a note, but after months of training, Hobart had turned them into a respectable group of singers. They hardly ever sounded flat. Although sometimes that meant telling Hess and Gorse to just mouth along.

At the conclusion of the show, the voyageurs were ushered off to a formal dinner. Kingston had been the site of plenty of extraordinary spectacles over the past few years; La Salle: Expedition II was hardly the first group of sportsmen to attempt an unusual feat on Lake Ontario. American athlete Diana Nyad became the first person to successfully swim thirty-two miles across the lake two years earlier. A month earlier, Kingston had hosted the sailing portion of the 1976 Summer Olympics. That had been a memorable event, as much for the stellar abilities of skippers and crews battling for gold as for the antics of one of the losers. The British two-man boat named *Gift 'Orse*, manned by Alan Warren and David Hunt, stole the show. They'd won the silver medal in the boat four years earlier. After finishing fifteenth overall in Kingston, the pair of Brits decided to put the limping stallion out of its misery. On the last day of the races, they brought several gallons of gasoline on board and set the boat aflame while still on the water, sending up clouds of black smoke and drawing the attention of helicopters and harbor police boats.[5] Although the two claimed the fire was caused by spontaneous combustion, Warren later said, "She went lame on us, so we decided the poor old 'orse should be cremated."

By comparison, twenty-three men dressed in 17th-century garb eating a steak dinner with linen napkins and crystal wineglasses didn't seem quite so odd.

In addition to being a popular venue for water sports and a historic city, Kingston also marked the end of the St. Lawrence River and the beginning of the Great Lakes. Paddling on the lakes would be an entirely different experience than traveling along the river. The current and the occasional rapids had been challenging on the St. Lawrence, and they'd all had to adjust to the voyageur routine, but the Great Lakes held their own dangers. It wouldn't be hard to get caught up in a storm and swept away from shore or to capsize in large waves. The six canoes didn't have any kind of entourage following them, so if they got into trouble, they had only one another to rely on. It didn't matter how many times they practiced capsizing on rivers near Elgin before departing; the experience couldn't compare to an unexpected roll.

Ken wasn't overly concerned. They'd all become strong over the past two weeks and proven their ability to handle the canoes. Besides, it was easy enough to take a day off since their schedule had been built with an extra week to take the weather into account. If a storm came up, they just wouldn't leave land.

Sandbanks Provincial Park, Ontario
August 30, 1976

The end of August on Lake Ontario was filled with unpredictable weather and unanticipated difficulties. First there had been the rumor of potential vandalism when they visited the town of Bath. A group of the men were selected for guard shifts, adding sleep deprivation to their list of physical difficulties. Then there were the bugs. They'd seen mosquitoes on the St. Lawrence, and everyone had mosquito netting if the vampiric beasts grew too numerous. But one night while camped out on marshy ground near the abandoned Prince Edward Point Lighthouse the netting proved useless.

The campsite was a disaster from the start, with sharp reeds jutting up from the ground and the smell of rotting vegetation hanging like a miasma in the air. Each footstep squelched and the sleeping bags inevitably got wet. But far worse were the newly hatched mosquitoes that rose from the ground in the hundreds that night. Everyone awoke choking on tiny insects that swarmed around in their shelters. The air buzzed with the droning of thousands of mosquitoes in flight. When Barton Dean, the expedition's photojournalist who occasionally paddled and camped with the crew, flicked on his flashlight (he was allowed to carry one since he wasn't officially a voyageur), the beam barely penetrated the dense thicket of insects around him. It was a miserable night; there was no way to escape the hungry bugs. Dean counted thirty-five bites on his forehead alone the next morning.

Finally, there was the weather. Nothing but rain, wind, and storms practically every day since they'd left the St. Lawrence. On August 28 the water was too rough for the expedition to leave its campsite, and the next day they were forced to stop three miles short of their destination, Point Petre, because of high winds and big waves.

Although nowhere near as dramatic or devastating as the plagues of Egypt, the incidents sometimes felt like biblical trials. Each one added to the normal levels of stress that built up over the course of a day. For Ken, sometimes the accumulating stress felt like layers of calcareous rock slowly accreting on top of him, adding to his growing sense of mental and emotional fatigue and making him appear ever rougher and more unapproachable to other crew members. The lack of alcohol and nicotine was a constant source of irritation, especially around the rest of the crew who were free to smoke tobacco in pipes and drink whatever their hosts might offer them. Ken had been smoking and drinking since early high school, and quitting the two vices at once, especially smoking, made him miserable. Then there was the growing unease he felt about leaving his wife alone for eight months. The decision to participate in the expedition had been an added strain on top of other smaller problems, and now he worried some of those problems might have grown too large to fix when he got back. Everything contributed to the roiling emotions he felt each day. The only person he was comfortable talking to about his struggles was his brother, but Reid already had enough on his plate. There was nothing to be done but push on. He'd never before given up when faced with adversity, and he wasn't planning on starting now.

The morning of August 30 seemed to augur a change for the better. The sun rose into a cloudless sky as the cooks for each of the three modules reheated bean and pea soup leftover from the night before. The resulting glop was thick enough for a wooden spoon to stand straight up in the middle of it and tasted slightly burned. Ken didn't mind the quality of food they ate when they weren't served community banquets. He was always hungry enough that the importance of flavor receded in favor of filling an empty stomach. Sometimes the peas and beans weren't fully cooked by the time a meal was served and you had to chew your way slowly through every fibrous mouthful. The cooks had taken to filling a pot with peas, beans, and water, setting it in the back of the canoe, and letting the legumes soak for the day while they paddled. It seemed to help, but the soup was still thick.

Ken hopped in the canoe after swallowing down all his breakfast, and they shoved off the beach into two-foot waves and a light breeze. They had fifteen miles to cover and it looked like they might finally make some decent progress after two days of being stymied by strong winds. The attitude in his canoe was one of comfortable camaraderie. They didn't always talk or sing, but when they did it proved amusing. Fredenburg, the *gouvernail*, had a great voice and could sometimes be convinced to sing satirical verses from Second City or *Saturday Night Live*. The most popular request made by the other paddlers was the comedic "Saturday Night in Toledo Ohio," written by Randy Sparks and made famous by John Denver on *The Tonight Show*. Fredenburg sang from the back of the canoe while the others hollered with laughter. Hess was also good for provoking a laugh, going off half-cocked on whatever came to his mind. And LeSieutre was a smart guy, never failing to provide interesting topics of conversation. The boat also managed to stay in the front of the pack most days, an ever-important measure of success. Although the crews of the six canoes had been instructed not to race one another, there were feelings of inferiority among the crew members whose boats lagged behind. The crew of the *Fleur-de-Lys*, Ken's boat, never struggled to keep up.

As the fleet of canoes rounded Wicked Point, they paused for Hobart to consult his charts. The wind was steadily building and coaxing the water into higher and higher waves. They decided to try to cut across the big bay and land at Sandbanks Provincial Park. The trek might require extra bailing due to the white-capped waves that rolled the canoes around, but they'd dealt with a little water sloshing around in the boats before. No reason to doubt their abilities now. That didn't stop a few of the men from pulling on the boxy yellow or blue life jackets.

Shortly after the group set off again it became apparent that the conditions were much worse than anything they'd yet faced. The white-capped waves rose higher and higher until they were seven and even nine feet high. Although the six canoe crews tried to stay close together, it was a challenge to keep track of one another. The wind whistled incessantly, deafening the crew. The boats disappeared into the troughs of waves, becoming momentarily surrounded by walls of green water. When the canoes climbed out of each trough onto the crest of a wave, crews frantically reoriented themselves and attempted to locate the other canoes before descending to the bottom of another wave. At the front of Ken's canoe, LeSieutre felt a jolt of fear at the sight of every new wave. The towering wall of water loomed above him at such an extreme angle that he was sure this would be the one to curl down and break over him. But equally frightening was reaching the top of a wave and preparing to surf back down. With such high waves, the narrow canoes could easily be thrown off balance and suddenly roll, sending the paddlers straight into the water. Capsizing now was an urgent danger. The water wasn't cold enough to cause immediate hypothermia, but if someone got injured during the capsizing—if he hit his head on the gunwales or twisted a wrist or an ankle on the way over—there was no telling how long it might be before help could be summoned, or if the other crews would even notice.

In the back of Ken's canoe, Fredenburg struggled to keep the vessel from tipping. Making the task more difficult was the direction of the waves, which rolled parallel to the shore. Though the voyageurs could barely communicate with one another over the sound of wind and waves, it was obvious that they needed to get off the water as soon as possible. But for hours now they'd been paddling past cliffs that went straight up out of the water. At last the sandy shoreline of Sandbanks Provincial Park appeared in the distance—the destination everyone knew they needed to reach. It wasn't going to be an easy journey. If Fredenburg tried to head straight for the beach, the forces acting on the canoe might flip the vessel the moment it came too close to perpendicular with the waves. If he tried following the shoreline, he'd be battling for control of the boat each time they skated down a wave, and they'd never get any closer to landing. The best solution was to quarter the waves, a strategy that meant climbing up and skating down at a forty-five-degree angle. Once they were close enough to shore, the boats could turn straight in. It was exhausting work, but adrenaline kept him and the other paddlers well supplied with energy. Every so often Fredenburg instructed Ken to stop paddling and start bailing. Having one less man paddling slowed their progress, but he couldn't allow the canoe to sink.

No one wore or carried a watch except Reid, so no one knew how long they'd been paddling. It felt like an eternity. At some point between alternating paddling and bailing, Ken realized it had been a while since he'd seen Reid's canoe. He looked up from his work when they reached the zenith of a wave and scanned for the others. Nothing. That didn't initially worry him. The boat crews could see one another only if they were on a crest at the same time, so it might take a cycle of five or ten waves before seeing them all.

But after a bit longer, it became clear that Reid's canoe had gotten separated from the group. Ken felt the first touch of fear, like a cold stone sinking in his stomach. "Where's my brother?" he asked the other three men in his canoe. "Have you seen my brother?" No one had.

Oh no, Ken thought. *He bit the dust somewhere.*

Ken was well acquainted with the precise sensation of dread. He knew what it was like to feel truly at risk of dying. He'd served in the Naval Air Force in the sixties and flown large planes to detect Soviet antiaircraft subs. There had been some hairy moments. Once, his plane had been targeted by Libyan radar as he flew around the Mediterranean. If the Libyans had decided to push one button, missiles would have shot after the plane and taken it down. Evasive maneuvers were impossible in the type of large, slow plane he flew. It was a terrifying experience, knowing that at any moment he might be blasted out of the sky. It forced him to contemplate his mortality in a way he'd never done before. But even that was nothing compared to thinking his younger brother might be injured or dead.

Ken had always been protective of Reid. As kids, they would occasionally get in fights that ended with both of them rolling on the ground pummeling each other. But the moment another person so much as threatened Reid, Ken was there snarling in his defense. As adults, there was much less reason for Ken to jump to Reid's aid. His younger brother regularly managed to take on spectacularly difficult tasks and see them to completion. But that didn't stop Ken from worrying about him. And if something happened to Reid now, what would their parents say? Before they'd left, their mother had told them, "I have all my eggs in one basket, so be careful." And now, on the first day of truly rough conditions, Reid's canoe was the one that had disappeared.

As he was starting to get seriously concerned and trying to formulate a rescue plan, Ken finally sighted Reid's boat. It was at least a half mile away from everyone else and heading farther out into the lake. *Jesus*, Ken thought. *Reid, change your course. You have to take your chance and risk broadside action, at least quarter into the waves!* But whatever telepathic bond they may have shared at certain points in their life, it didn't seem like Reid could hear his older brother now.

Ken felt physically sick. If he could convince his canoe to go out farther, they could provide support to Reid's canoe in the event that anything happened. The canoes were supposed to stay grouped closely together anyway, because they were the only ones looking out for one another. How had Reid let his canoe get out so far? Of course, Reid wasn't the one steering—DiFulvio sat behind him in the gouvernail position, but Reid could've encouraged him to go closer into the beach.

But no, Ken couldn't ask the three teenagers in his boat to risk their lives by heading farther away from the shore. He'd have to focus on getting to land and then do whatever he could from there. He didn't want to think about what that might be. Instead, he told himself to dig in deeper with each paddle, ignore the cramps in his legs and back, ignore the fear for his brother and the fear of being swamped in their own canoe.

Finally, the five canoes surged shoreward on the backs of wild waves. White foam swirled around them and thrust the canoes ever faster toward the beach. One by one the avants gauged the depth of the water and jumped out of the canoes to help slow the boats' momentum—and one by one they tumbled over like a lopsided row of dominoes, unable to stand after sitting so long in the same position. The canoes swept past them and crashed onto the beach, some men falling out while others jumped out to go help the waterlogged avants. Once the boats had been pulled out of the water and everyone had a few breaths to recover from their three hours of barely contained panic, they all began whooping with joy, as exuberant as if they'd just won the World Series. The rush of surviving ten-foot waves in twenty-foot canoes with no damage done to their vessels was unimaginably powerful. It was more than relief, more than excitement; it was bliss. When they went up against the elements, the odds were always against them. It made winning that much sweeter.

And there, one hundred yards down the shore, came Reid's boat. They'd taken a much sharper angle than the rest of the boats, but they'd survived the experience as well. Ken ran out to them and felt the knot of tension in his stomach uncoil. He breathed a huge sigh of relief and watched as DiFulvio hopped out of the canoe and embraced Kulick, shouting, "We did it!" Back at the other end of the beach, where the five other boats had landed, John Fialko declared, "We are now all seasoned canoemen." Coming from him, the crew member who most epitomized a professional outdoorsman, it was the highest praise. They'd all survived. Ken still had a brother.

Scarborough, Ontario
September 7, 1976

Chalky white cliffs running along the shoreline stretched into the distance and towered three hundred feet above the mock birch-bark canoes, providing an impressive backdrop for their landing point. Sunlight glinted off the water, refracting and breaking in the voyageurs' eyes. In any other circumstances, the men would be wearing sunglasses instead of squinting into the glare. But not on this expedition. It would ruin the illusion.

A crowd of reporters and townspeople on the sandy beach watched as the six dark spots on the water drew closer and took on a definite shape. They were escorted by a modern police boat, making an odd fleet. One canoe carried a flapping white flag in its stern. The gold fleur de lys painted on it flickered in and out of view as the fabric rippled in the wind. The voyageurs pulled their paddles through the water in a hypnotic rhythm. The closer they paddled and the clearer the details of their attire became, the more unreal they seemed. Several wore white headbands to hold back their long hair, and one had a leather vest held shut by small, imperfect buttons carved of antler. Another wore a bright red jacket with gold cuffs and a black felt hat. All were bronzed and muscular. Pulling close to the shore, the men raised their paddles into the air in unison, saluting the crowd. They looked like phantoms next to the Scarborough Bluffs, travelers from an era before the bluffs were given their name by an Englishwoman.

The fricative crashing of surf and the noisy splashing of voyageurs hopping out of their canoes to protect the boats from a hard impact broke the sense of fantasy surrounding the ghostly crew. They were real, solid flesh, smelling of campfires and sweat. They could be approached for pictures and answered questions the gathered audience might ask as they set about the task of building their camp.

Scarborough Mayor Paul Cosgrove greeted the voyageurs on horseback, wearing a royal blue coat as if he were the French Sun King. Ken liked to see towns embracing the narrative and donning costumes of their own to briefly inhabit a different persona. Escaping to another character was one of his great joys; it made history much more vivid and approachable. As soon as he appeared in front of a crowd, Ken threw himself into his alter ego, Antoine Brossard. During his previous reenactment voyage, on the Jolliet-Marquette expedition, Ken had interpreted his historical persona as a scurrilous character. This time around he took the opposite approach: he liked to think of Brossard as a decent guy with a fondness for telling long yarns. It was a good persona for interpreting the lives of the voyageurs for the civilians who came to see them. Being Antoine Brossard meant Ken didn't have to worry about fundraising or publicity or personal problems outside of his immediate crewmates. Being Brossard made his life feel appealingly simple.

Scarborough was the expedition's penultimate stop before exiting Lake Ontario. Ahead lay the Toronto Portage, a thirty-two-mile, twelve-day hike through the heart of the city, carrying thousands of pounds of gear and the six canoes. It promised to be a torturous, backbreaking experience unlike anything the voyageurs had encountered thus far. Not that Lake Ontario had been a holiday. They'd almost been bested by the lake at Wicked Point, and even after they put the worst conditions behind them, there had been other difficulties along the way.

On the last day of August the crew had camped on a sandy beach near Brighton where eight five-hundred-pound bombs from World War II lay dormant and unexploded. Among themselves the crew joked about not pounding in their stakes too hard, though they'd been assured of the safety of their campsite by locals. When a massive squall erupted late that night, a reverberating crack of thunder woke half the camp and convinced a few men that one of the bombs had exploded. Antoine Brossard never had to think about hidden explosives, although the risk of having an enemy's tomahawk buried in his skull was probably equally worrisome.

But the main sources of tension had little to do with natural or artificial obstacles along the route. The issues came from within, linked to the various personalities of the voyageurs and the social rules and strictures imposed on them. It wasn't just hunger and fatigue that gnawed on frayed tempers and made people liable to snap. It was an absence of clear leadership.

Reid could be amiable, charming, and inspiring. But he could also be short-tempered and overly demanding. These qualities are not uncommon to leaders, and everyone on the crew exhibited some of them from time to time. In Reid's case, the problem was that half the time he wasn't around. He couldn't always stay to help unload his canoe and cut wood or pitch the shelter because he had to meet with the press and the town officials, or his wife and the other members of the liaison team. Everyone understood that those duties fell to him as creator and public representative number one of the expedition. But it was still irksome that his share of work fell to others. And then at night, when everyone else sat around the fires singing or talking or reading, Reid was often gone, writing applications for grants to continue financing the expedition. They were surviving on loans so far, but Lewis worried they wouldn't have enough to finish the voyage.

But this wasn't a concern he shared with most of the other crew members. For many of them, respect was earned by pulling your weight, doing your chores, being reliable. And since they were, for the most part, oblivious to the financial state of the expedition, Reid didn't seem to be doing anything but ordering other people around and spending time with the liaison team. His absence and his style of leadership—an unclear blend of democracy and dictatorship where he asked for opinions but ultimately made his own decisions—left a void in the chain of command. Power loves a vacuum, and the younger crew members looked to different adults to take a more prominent leadership role. As the group's navigator, Ron Hobart seemed like the most likely candidate, and he was supported by Cox. Both regularly found themselves at odds with Reid.

Ken did what he could to support Reid's decision-making, even when he didn't agree with his brother. The last thing Reid needed was another voice of dissent. Despite help from his brother and some members of the crew, a few days earlier at Newcastle, Ontario, Reid had finally made the decision to abandon his grant applications and extra fund-raising efforts. He feared for the future of the expedition if he wasn't around more, and given the choice between finishing with more debt and not finishing at all, he chose the former. They'd have to rely on the fund-raising apparatus still in place back in Chicago, where Reid's parents continued with the bookkeeping and sent regular updates to their donors. They had enough money for food, and there were plenty of communities along their route who had offered to provide them with a free meal. The main concern would be getting salaries to all the adults and scholarships for the students by the end of the expedition, not to mention paying off the personal loans Lewis had taken out.

Still, even without the added burden of writing letters and fund-raising, Reid struggled to balance all the different roles he had to fill. One of the most trying issues was the liaison team, headed by his wife. They had repeatedly borne the brunt of the crew's ire. Crew members complained that the liaison team was unorganized, lazy, and irresponsible. They lost articles of clothing in the laundry, failed to generate enough publicity for the expedition, and didn't do the necessary advance work with communities the voyageurs planned to visit. Was it so hard to make a phone call a week in advance to confirm arrangements with each town where the voyageurs planned to camp? Reid tried to defend the liaison team's work—there were only four of them attempting to do the work of a much larger team and none of the women were experienced in event planning or public relations. Ken offered his own explanation for the issue. It was a problem he was familiar with in the theater: the stagehand effect.

"The stage crew is totally supporting the actor. If the actor reaches for a prop and it's not there, he feels his vulnerability and trust has been betrayed. A lot of beginning actors, until they learn better, take it out on the stage hands," Ken said. It didn't help that the liaison team got none of the glory the crew members received. No one cheered for them after they drove all day to prepare a landing site for the expedition, and no one wanted to interview them or hear about the kind of work they did to ensure the expedition's success. It was an exhausting, thankless job, and any mistakes were magnified in the eyes of the crew by the fact that they paddled all day in all sorts of weather.

None of these challenges was visible to the crowds that gathered around the crew members. They saw all the details that had been painstakingly crafted to look as authentic as possible—the moose-hide moccasins and matchless fires—and none of the interpersonal drama. The voyageurs lived under two layers of fiction: first, that they were from the 17th century, and second, that their lives were every bit as idyllic and adventurous as they appeared from the outside. This was certainly the impression they gave as they performed on a mobile stage for the suburb of Scarborough. The audience cheered and clapped after the last song, and the mayor returned to present the crew with maple leaf pins and Scarborough medallions.

By this point in the evening, Ken was desperate to use a rest-room. Making matters more difficult was the design of the park. It had been built to fit in with the natural environment as much as possible, and he had trouble locating the dun-colored facilities. They blended right into the bluffs, with their peaked roofs imitating the jagged shape of the cliffs. When he finally found them, he ran into a stall and sat down. Just then a child's voice asked, "Are you one of those La Salle guys?"

"Yes, I am," he said, bemused.

A little hand appeared beneath the stall door holding a pen.

"Could you give me your autograph?"

"Of course." Looking for something to write on and finding nothing but toilet paper, Ken took the pen and signed his name across it in cramped, uneven handwriting that slanted to the left. It never ceased to be a strange experience to have children ask for an autograph. In some ways, being a reenactor was like being a rock star, at least in the eyes of the children who'd never seen anything like them before. However unreal it felt, Ken never hesitated over which name to use when he signed an autograph. To the world, he was a voyageur who felt neither fear nor fatigue nor cravings for alcohol and nicotine. He was *Antoine Brossard.*

Chapter Five

STUCK BETWEEN
TWO WORLDS

Toronto Portage
September 1681

Canoes were an anomaly to the first Europeans visiting
North America. They were sleek and narrow and utterly
foreign. John McPhee writes of the sailors who had just
crossed the Atlantic in enormous brigs: "Longboats were lowered,
to be rowed by crews of four and upward. The sailors hauled at
their oars. The Indians, two to a canoe, indolently whisked their
narrow paddles and easily drew away. In their wake they left a
stunning impression. Not only were they going faster. They could
see where they were going."[1]

This invaluable native technology was quickly adopted by
European explorers. Canoes were the only method of transportation

across the country if you didn't want to travel entirely by foot. La Salle tried to introduce barques to the Great Lakes, but failed miserably when his forty-foot ship, the *Griffin*, disappeared on its maiden voyage. There wouldn't be another ship built on the Great Lakes until 1734. Even a century after La Salle's disastrous attempt to navigate the lakes, only sixteen ships plied their waters.[2]

Canoes became a key part of the voyageurs' identity. The boats La Salle's men used were twenty feet long and three feet wide and could carry up to twelve hundred pounds. They were made of strips of birch bark sewn together with spruce roots and stretched over a wooden frame, with long poles called *grands-perches* laid along the bottom to help distribute the weight.[3] The canoes had to be sporadically repaired through a process called "gumming," which required smearing melted spruce sap along cracks and holes in the bark.[4] According to Nicholas de la Salle, a member of La Salle's crew and no relation to him, one or two men could carry the weight of one canoe when they had to make portages across land.[5] This detail was especially crucial since the men would be portaging to Lake Huron rather than traveling the easier route through Lake Erie.

La Salle knew the southern shore of Lake Erie was populated by Iroquois and worried that running into them might lead to attacks.[6] But as many canoeists will attest, paddling an extra fifty miles is always preferable to a ten-mile portage. The difficult Toronto Portage, established by earlier voyageurs, stretched over thirty miles between Lake Ontario and Lake Simcoe and required the men to carry all the canoes and gear. The portage was named not for the city that would eventually come to sit at the beginning of the trail but for a specific location called Tkaronto by Mohawk speakers to describe "where there are trees standing in the water."[7] The trail started at the Humber River and passed over the Oak Ridges

Moraine. The voyageurs made the backbreaking trek up and down steep hills and through dense forests. Each man was expected to help carry a canoe or several ninety-pound bags, balanced with a tumpline across his forehead. It's little wonder that voyageurs often suffered from hernias.[8]

La Salle and his men got back in their boats on Lake Huron in October. But they would have to hurry through the Great Lakes if they hoped to make it to the Mississippi before the upcoming winter froze all the rivers solid.

⸺

Toronto, Ontario
September 8, 1976

Sid Bardwell scanned the shoreline as his canoe glided past the white geodesic dome and tall stadium lights of the Ontario Center. Only ten or so people were there to greet them. Why was it that big cities seemed to have fewer people interested in the expedition? Maybe because in small towns the voyageurs were the only source of entertainment, like a band of traveling troubadours. In Toronto, the 2 million city dwellers had dozens of other things vying for their attention: the Toronto Argonauts football team played at Exhibition Stadium, concerts drew famous musicians such as Patti Smith and The Who, streets were filled with a plethora of bars and restaurants, and the Toronto International Film Festival was happening in the coming weeks. The sheer size of the city prevented the expedition from having much of an impact. The day was clear and calm and they'd seen the smoggy skyline and needle-like CN Tower from a distance in the morning, but it didn't seem that anyone on shore had been watching their arrival, except maybe the liaison team. Then again, even the ladies might've had too much going on to find a spot on shore and watch their approach.

They were always busy and disorganized, which meant it took twice as long to finish anything. They didn't have a lot of free time to sit on the shore and stare out onto the lake in anticipation of the voyageurs' arrival.

If anyone understood the dynamics of the liaison team, it was Bardwell. Until a week earlier, he'd been traveling with them. Technically, he was still part of that team and was just subbing into the crew since Father Loran had hurt his back. Bardwell, a tall, lanky teen who was rarely without his green-and-yellow-striped hat, had been recruited for the expedition at the very last minute. He hadn't been a student at either of the Elgin schools and was younger than most of the others, having finished high school in three years. Reid Lewis heard about Bardwell from the teen's father, who was the superintendent in Elk Grove, not far from Elgin. Lewis was intrigued when he heard about Bardwell's trip down the Mississippi River a year earlier in a makeshift pontoon boat. He was still searching for an alternate by April 1976, just three months before the expedition's start date. When he offered Bardwell the spot, the teenager got to work sewing clothes and building his endurance. It was a little awkward at first, being the outsider in a group of young men who had spent the better part of two years training together. But the crew was friendly and he was soon accepted into their ranks.

From the outset, the expedition had been the perfect alternative to a fourth year of high school. Bardwell had planned in advance to finish high school in three years instead of four. It required a combination of summer classes and a higher course load, but he wanted that last year to be dedicated to traveling or some kind of adventure before heading off to college. Bardwell loved camping and boating and was fascinated by the physical challenges past explorers had faced. His own great-grandmother had been a homesteader in Iowa in 1874. She remembered Thanksgiving dinners in a barn, when her family welcomed impoverished Native Americans who lived in the area to eat with them. "You can't imagine how much the telephone changed the world," she told her great-grandchildren decades later.

Bardwell could imagine it now; he had the unique perspective of witnessing communication between the crew and the liaison team from both sides. Neither group seemed particularly adept at communicating with the other, but it was especially frustrating when he was on the water with the crew and they had no idea where to land. Sometimes Cathy Palmer appeared at the edge of the water waving a big white flag to signal the canoes' landing spot. Other times the canoes landed without being able to find the liaison team, uncertain if they would have the proper facilities or even permission to spend the night where they'd stopped. These incidents and others had led to some hard feelings on both sides.

Something that particularly irked the crew was the apparent lack of advance publicity. Here they were about to land in Toronto, the biggest city in Canada, and all they had was a minuscule welcome committee waiting for them on shore. But the lackluster welcome the men received was quickly forgotten once the men learned about their itinerary for the rest of the afternoon. Toronto city officials may not have spread word very far that their city was being invaded by a group of scruffy voyageurs, but they had planned a number of promising activities for the men. First they were taken for a tour of the warship HMCS *Haida*, the last Tribal-class destroyer in the world. It had the reputation as being "the fightingest ship in the Royal Canadian Navy." Onboard the ship, the crew got the chance to take showers and learn about the destroyer's history. A few crew members made the observation that everywhere they went, in Canada or the United States, people seemed particularly proud of their military history. No wonder the French were so often forgotten. Their military involvement in both countries was either short-lived or unsuccessful. The men tried to remedy this bit of historical amnesia by performing a musket salute for their hosts, guns aimed toward shore.

Bardwell didn't have a musket of his own; only seven of the crew members had built them, and he'd gotten involved too late to be part of any of the construction projects. The musket men were proud of their guns, but they required a lot of care and upkeep. If they got wet, they would rust and jam up when you loaded the powder and pulled the trigger. Every time the men did a salute, there was always the risk that none of the muskets would work. Most of the time at least a couple went off, and those whose guns didn't were saved from embarrassment by the bang and smoke of the neighboring guns.

With showers and an official welcome out of the way, the crew headed down to Fort York. The military fortifications were built in the late 18th and early 19th centuries and had housed British soldiers during the War of 1812. Today the buildings were among the oldest in Toronto, and the crew had been invited to stay in the barracks. The wooden bunks were only six by four-and-a-half feet and had been shared by two men originally. Luckily no one had to share a bunk now, although some of the men's feet hung over the edge. For Bardwell and Lieberman, two of the tallest men on the crew, it meant sleeping with considerably more than just their feet dangling off the end. It would've been more comfortable to sleep outside beneath the canoes as they were accustomed to, but they appreciated the fort's hospitality. In addition to offering them a place to sleep with a roof over their heads, the men at the fort brought the voyageurs twelve loaves of fresh-baked bread and several cases of Molson Golden, which had become everyone's favorite beer. Nobody felt any qualms about drinking while they were on

Canadian soil, since they were all of legal drinking age there, and several towns along the way had offered them bottles of wine as souvenirs.

That evening the crew sat around a fire with the men from the fort, drinking beer and swapping songs, with the Canadians' songs getting progressively raunchier. The Canadians ended the night with a series of ghost stories about Fork York, perhaps hoping to send the young voyageurs to bed with a chill. But ghosts were hardly the kind of thing they needed to be worried about. The task facing them for the next two weeks—their portage through downtown Toronto—was far more intimidating than imaginary apparitions.

Bardwell woke the next morning to the sound of crew members dragging Clif Wilson out of his bunk and singing happy birthday. "Okay, but where am I going?" he asked as they carried him out into the barracks yard in nothing but his red underwear.

"We're putting you in the stocks!" someone answered.

Outside the barracks, they strapped Wilson's feet into the stocks, locked him in, and posed proudly for photos. Luckily there hadn't been any stockades around during Bardwell's eighteenth birthday a month ago. Instead, he was the first of the crew to experience the Quebecois tradition of being thrown into the air once for every year of birth. Being tossed into the air eighteen times sounded like a recipe for injury, but with so many people pitching in to carry his weight, Bardwell had flown up and down as if on a trampoline. The practice had been continued with other birthdays since then, though he wasn't sure how they'd manage Father Loran, who was in his fifties.

When the morning's entertainment concluded, the crew spent the next few hours working on clothes and moccasins in preparation for the wear and tear that would occur during the portage.

It was another beautiful day, clear and warm. The men sat bare-chested in the sun with their backs against the gray stone wall surrounding the fort or in the shadow of the barracks. Bardwell had a shirt in his lap and was sewing on the deer antler buttons. By this point in the expedition, everyone had perfected his skills with a needle and thread and could put together a pair of leather moccasins or repair a torn seam practically with his eyes closed. Some people wore through their moccasins faster than others and had to make new pairs more often, which seemed like it would be the main problem as they hiked along the concrete streets and sidewalks. Grass and sand were gentlest on the leather moccasins, followed by dirt, then gravel, stone, and concrete. Most of the men had developed the habit of going about barefoot during the day and the soles of their feet had grown thick and insensitive with the practice. Some planned to walk most of the portage barefoot to protect their moccasins.

Though the portage was technically only thirty-two miles, the weight of their gear—six unwieldy 175-pound canoes and 5,000 pounds of equipment—meant they'd be walking at least three times that distance for the multiple trips back and forth they'd have to make. The plan was to cover a half a mile with their gear, drop everything off, then go back for another load. If they put two to four men on every canoe and everyone carried the standard hundred pounds or so per load, it would still take them two or three trips back and forth to transport everything. That meant going four or five miles for every mile they moved forward, with cars zipping past and busy streets to cross and traffic signals to obey.

Not that they had much of a choice. Authenticity demanded they make the trek through the Toronto Carrying Place. It didn't matter that La Salle's route hadn't passed through a major city three hundred years ago; the logic of the reenactment regularly overruled the logic of the real world.

The crew had one more day of respite before they had to set out. After a performance before a sizeable crowd in Nathan Phillips Square, the men had lunch and a tour at the Toronto Maritime Museum. Lewis, Cox, and Chuck Campbell left the museum before the rest of the group to do an interview with the popular radio host Warren Davis. When the fifty-minute show aired later that night, people around the city could listen to the unfathomable lives of the modern voyageurs.

"Give us an example, what's a typical day on Lake Ontario?" Davis asked his guests.

"Get up at five o'clock, make breakfast—which they wouldn't have done, they would've gotten up and paddled two or three hours then stopped and eaten their breakfast. But we're just not that kind of life as far as physical health goes," Campbell said. "We get to our camp at night, we set up camp, cook dinner, then we give presentations when they probably would've gone to bed, gotten ready for the next day."

Davis expressed his incredulity at their ability to do so much every day, wondering if they ever got any sleep. But he was even more surprised to hear about their upcoming trek through Toronto.

"It's thirty-two miles to Lake Simcoe, but we can't do it all in one trip. Assuming we make it in two trips we're talking one hundred miles," Cox explained.

"How on earth then are you going to keep up the pace in order to finish the journey on time?" Davis answered.

"We've asked ourselves that many times," Cox said. They'd managed to stay on schedule so far, but they were at a disadvantage compared to La Salle. The French explorer had only been concerned with moving forward and keeping his men alive. He didn't have scheduled performances for more than one hundred towns along the way; no such towns existed.

"Well, now you are traveling at the time of year that really is going to be the roughest weather that you could be traveling in through the northern part of Canada and the United States," Davis pointed out as he reviewed their itinerary. He listened as the men explained their preparations for winter, then asked, "What motivates you? Why are you putting yourself through this self-induced torture?"

Lewis gave his standard answer about the spirit of the voyageurs and courage and determination and the power of youth. Davis, though, seemed as if he was still concerned about the possibility of danger and the practical side of the expedition, eventually coming back to the "self-induced torture" aspect.

"Do you think the trip on Lake Michigan is probably the most dangerous? What about the possibility of a canoe overturning? Someone being drowned?" he asked.

"When we're on the water we travel in groups of three," Cox said. "Normally all six canoes would be close together, but we try to travel in groups of three so those three canoes don't get more than fifty or sixty yards apart." He didn't mention the incident when Lewis's canoe became separated from the others when they'd encountered big waves in Lake Ontario, or how difficult it could be to corral all their canoes, which traveled at different speeds depending on the day and the weather conditions. "If a canoe did tip over, one canoe rescues the crew, and we've practiced it . . . If there's an accident, we just have to get to shore as fast as we can and get a fire started and get them into warm clothes."

"Because there's a very great danger of hypothermia in those kinds of waters at this time of year," Davis said.

"We received some training in winter survival from the Naval Air Reserve, which gave us—made us aware, anyway—of what we're involved with here. And we have gone through two winters with training . . . We have an idea of what we're getting into," Lewis responded.

Choosing to end the interview there, Davis asked the three men to sing a few verses of a voyageur song for him, then bid them farewell and good luck. Outside, the sun was bright and hot, and winter seemed far, far away.

That night, Bardwell was joined by Sharon Baumgartner at the fire in the yard of the barracks. Baumgartner was a sweet, good-looking girl who wore her hair in a blond bob and woke up early enough each morning to do her makeup, something the other three women of the liaison team normally shirked. Like Bardwell, Baumgartner had been recruited in the early spring of 1976 to join the expedition as part of the liaison team. She had already graduated high school at that point and was in her first year of classes at Elgin Community College, but her boyfriend Marc Lieberman was on the expedition and she heard all about it from him. Baumgartner decided she was ready to take some time off school and go on an adventure. She hadn't known exactly what her duties would be until the trip started. Since then, she'd learned how to drive a green van with manual shifting, how to coerce city officials into finding the best campsites for the crew, and to deal with the sometimes conflicting personalities of the liaison team and the expedition members. She knew all about how hard the crew worked and why they expected some sense of order when it came to the liaison team's side of the equation. Yet she also saw how much work Jan Lewis and Marlena Scavuzzo, the adults of the liaison team, did every day and night. Somehow, it always ended up being *their* fault when things didn't turn out. This seemed to be the case yet again with the Toronto camping debacle.

Marlena and Jan were *sure* Cox and Hobart, who had planned the expedition's route through Toronto, had secured campsites ahead of time, so they hadn't bothered with it. Cox and Hobart were equally certain they'd been told the liaison team would be coordinating their campsites. Somehow neither group had caught the other's mistake until everyone arrived in Toronto. Now, the night before the crew's first day on the portage, they still had nowhere to camp in the coming nights. Jan and Marlena were both peeved at Cox and Hobart and tired of being blamed for everything that went wrong, and it didn't seem like the women had a plan for finding all the necessary campsites. Palmer and Baumgartner were going to have to tackle the issue of where the men would camp at night on their own, in addition to finding places where the men could deposit their loads in between trips. Baumgartner related all this to Bardwell, adding that both of the team's vans were acting up. The red van, which Bardwell drove when he wasn't paddling with the crew, had been in an accident a week earlier and needed repairs, and the green van's brakes were locking. All in all, it seemed like the next twelve days were gearing up to be a test of strength and willpower for both the voyageurs and their support team.

⊶

Weston Road, Toronto, Ontario
September 12, 1976

The man in the yellow Alfa Romeo Spider Veloce stared at the unusual characters who had just walked by his parked car. Two men's heads were hidden beneath the canoe they carried on their shoulders down the sidewalk of Weston Road. Their torsos were bare and on their legs they wore dirty canvas pants rolled up to the knee. The driver watched as the canoe and its headless carriers trotted past the storefront of Meats and Groceries Delicatessen. In the shop's open doorway a young blond boy stared just as incredulously at the voyageurs. Following the first canoe came another, and another, and more oddly dressed men with ludicrously large loads balanced on their backs. They trudged past shopping carts and bicycles parked on the side of the street, struggling under the weight of their packs. At bus stops more people stood watching, wondering who these strange men were.

Despite not initially knowing where they were going to stay in the evening, the crew had managed to survive the first few days of the portage through Toronto. They survived, but they didn't enjoy it. Whatever hardships anyone had envisioned in advance of the twelve-day carry paled in comparison to the reality. The walk was a more grueling ordeal than they could've imagined. Paddling a canoe for ten hours straight had in no way prepared them for the physical drudgery of moving all their gear through a crowded city, and the earlier portages they'd done had been much, much shorter. On the first day, no one could get their tumplines to work properly. The ropes hadn't been a problem when they were going short distances, but now they were proving troublesome. The system, which had been used by the original voyageurs, was meant to spread the weight of their packs across the neck and back. A leather strap rested on the forehead and was attached to ropes on either side, which wrapped around the unwieldy wooden crates and other gear. A great idea in theory, but in practice it was proving to be exceedingly difficult. On the first day the ropes hadn't stretched to the end of their elasticity, meaning the load shifted progressively lower down their backs. No one had yet figured out a comfortable rhythm for picking things up and setting them back down, since their previous portages had been significantly shorter and required less advance organizing. The canoes were hardest of all, and different teams tested out carrying them between two men, three men, and four men. The fewer the men, the harder the carry, but it meant more people were freed up to take loads of gear to the half-mile rest stop, so everyone made fewer trips overall.

The oppressive fug of damp heat and car exhaust didn't help anyone's mood. By the end of each day, the crew felt so battered and exhausted it was all they could do to numbly eat their dinner and crawl into bed at their new campsites, most of which ended up being city parks that the liaison team found for them at the last minute. An incomplete list of injuries that occurred thus far during the portage included: a strained tendon (Sid Bardwell); the flu and a mysterious allergic reaction (John DiFulvio); pain in legs related to prior surgery (Bill Watts); and an ever-growing number of bruises, blisters, and falling arches of the feet (everyone). They'd also learned that not everyone enjoyed the 17th-century invasion occurring in the city. The police received numerous reports from residents complaining about a band of gypsies, and the men caused several small traffic accidents when drivers were distracted by their presence on the streets and sidewalks. But at least one citizen of Toronto was thrilled with the portage, telling a reporter that the men "should all be knighted by the Queen [of England]."

For the crew members, each day was a repetition of the last, and the work wasn't getting any easier. They began the morning with a stop at Stillwagon's makeshift infirmary, where he taped feet and ankles and worried over their collapsing arches. He'd checked with a podiatrist, who said as long as the men could handle the pain, their arches would eventually rebound. After their visit to the infirmary, it was off on an agonizing march with a hundred pounds of weight pressing uncomfortably into their backs and shoulders, a walk back to get more gear during which they felt light as air, and then another painful march back to the drop spot with another load slowly crushing them. Cathy Palmer always made the first walk with the men to direct them where to stop, then stayed there until all the gear had been deposited and was ready to be hauled to the next rest stop. Oftentimes the hosts on whose lawns the men dropped their gear would offer the use of their bathrooms as well, and some provided snacks or drinks. The kindness and generosity was a spiritual balm in its own way, but it did little to alleviate the physical pain of such heavy burdens. Whenever the men were out of earshot of civilians, they let loose profanity-laden diatribes from beneath their heavy cargo. At one point, Hess and Kulick were carrying a canoe together and approaching a school. Rather than asking him to stop cursing, Kulick told Hess they'd need to switch their swearing to French. Despite the warning, Hess couldn't stop himself from saying, "This is fucking merde!" as they continued past the school grounds.

Palmer and Baumgartner had been working double-time to find rest stops and campsites for the crew as they crawled through the city like mules. Based on how far the men planned to go each day— anywhere from two and a half miles to four and a half miles—the girls would hop in the van and use its odometer to find the closest campground to the endpoint. From there, they had to backtrack along the crew's proposed route for the day and find rest stops every half mile. This meant walking up to a stranger's house, knocking on the door, introducing themselves, and asking if a group of sweaty, curiously dressed guys carrying thousands of pounds of gear could stop on the front lawn and maybe use the bathroom. At first, Palmer hated the process. Having grown up with six brothers, she was more than happy to deal with the crew and get them whatever they needed, but none of her earlier life experiences had prepared her for talking to strangers and asking them for things. Baumgartner had handled most of the publicity work from the start. She was always so put-together and never seemed nervous. She charmed everyone she met, with her huge smile and bright lipstick. For Palmer, going up to someone and saying, "Hi, I'm with the La Salle: Expedition II and we're looking for a rest stop," was a challenge, but what else could they do? Baumgartner was busy coordinating other tasks, securing permission for the men to camp in various parks and relaying all these plans to Jan and Marlena, who were staying in a hotel and were too fed up to deal with the crew.

The Torontonians made the task much easier with their generosity and hospitality. The first night, when the crew was setting up shelters in Etienne Brule Park, Palmer and Baumgartner set to erecting their own orange tent. As often as possible, they camped out to help save money. There had been discussions earlier in the trip about getting rid of the liaison team altogether because of the cost of paying for hotel rooms and gas and the inordinate amount of pizza they seemed to consume (the last of which particularly grated on the crew members, seeing as they were stuck eating sludge-like peas and beans). That suggestion had been dismissed. Whatever tension the liaison team caused, their work was necessary. To minimize their expenses, the women sometimes slept outside in tents and asked for pocket money from home to buy shampoo and other toiletries. But that first night in Toronto, a married couple saw Palmer and Baumgartner getting ready to spend the night outdoors with twenty-three men and offered the two of them beds in their home. Every night afterward for the duration of the portage they were hosted by a new family. The families of Toronto adopted the women of the liaison team in much the same way they adopted the crew members.

The random acts of kindness were as small as a Sicilian man offering Lieberman and Kulick a ripe tomato from behind a fence, and as large as a family allowing the liaison team to store all the extra gear that they usually kept in the van in their entryway while the van was being repaired. This latter bit of generosity was offered by Fred and Meryl Leslie, a couple who had taken a particular interest in the expedition. Not many Americans seemed interested in the history of their country before the Revolution. The Leslies appreciated these nice young men who were doing such a good job presenting living history. The two brought their children out to see the voyageurs tromp through town and planned a spaghetti dinner to celebrate the end of the portage. The expedition members were so grateful for the unanticipated support that they brought the Leslies into their fold, inviting them to come celebrate the end of the expedition in New Orleans in April. Everyone promised to keep in touch with the family via voyageur post (the liaison team made regular mail stops for the men as they went along their route).

Countless others demonstrated Canadian hospitality, buying the men meals from McDonald's or bringing them coffee in the morning, following them as they walked, listening to their stories about the trip. If not for such people, everyone on both sides of the expedition—crew members and liaison team—would've struggled even more to overcome the physical and psychological challenges of the portage.

<hr />

Sparrow Lake, Ontario
September 25, 1976

Dear Mom, Dad, San, and Rod,

I'm sorry I haven't written again, but time slips away so quickly up here. I just received a letter from Gram—boy was I happy! That was my 1st letter in 3 mail pickups. So far I haven't heard from any friends except Jill and Dave.

The whole of the portage went well although the first couple of days were madness. As the guys got it down to a system and we got arrangements made, things went pretty smoothly. Of course, Jan thought Ron made advance plans for those 12 days and vice versa, and that made for hard feelings between the crew and the liaison team (they thought we weren't doing our job). In fact, it grew to the point where crew members made snide and sarcastic remarks about Jan and Marlena both to their faces and behind their backs . . .

In a letter to her family, Sharon reflected on the two weeks she'd spent traveling through the city making last-minute arrangements with city parks and private homes where the men camped out for the night. It hadn't been easy for anyone.

I finally got infuriated with Clif and John D. and had a nice long "discussion" on what the liaison team function was. Not long afterwards John got sick and had to be with us. In 3 days time, he changed his tune and promises never to badmouth us again.

The dissension and dissatisfaction with the liaison team's work had spread to other members of the team, namely Palmer and Bart Dean. Dean had always been a man unto himself, stuck somewhere between crew and liaison team like Bardwell. As the group's photojournalist, he had to be present to witness the crew's daily life, which meant participating to a certain extent but maintaining enough distance to get photos. He was assisted by two crew members, who took photos from their canoes when Dean wasn't around. Sometimes Dean hopped in and paddled with the crew so that he could get action shots. In Toronto, however, he hadn't been carrying any of the gear. The city was a big media market, and he wanted to get as many stories and pictures published as possible. Dean's discontent about the liaison team and the general leadership of the expedition stemmed from financial issues. He'd graduated from Northwestern's Medill School of Journalism in the spring of 1976 and was enthralled by the opportunity to shoot an expedition and go on an adventure. The pay was only $800 a month, a lousy salary for a full-time journalist, but he didn't care. It was going to be the journey of a lifetime. Unfortunately, it was looking less and less like he would actually get paid during the trip, because the expedition was so low on money. Not knowing if or when he'd be paid had corroded some of the joys of traveling with the canoe crew.

Then there was Palmer, who had spent most of her time on the portage walking with the crew members to show them their rest stops. She also helped them get the supplies they needed, be it tubs of peanut butter for their lunches or clean clothes at the end of the day. With her proximity to the rest of the crew, she heard plenty of the crew's complaints about Jan and Marlena's dysfunctions. Whatever she may have heard or said, Palmer's more intimate relationship with the crew didn't endear her to the adults she reported to. At the end of the Toronto portage, Jan gave her a stern talking-to about not undermining the liaison team that left Palmer in tears and did nothing to improve her relationship with Jan and Marlena. At least she had Baumgartner to keep her company. Having grown up surrounded by brothers, Palmer was grateful for Baumgartner's sweetness and femininity. It was like having a sister, only they didn't argue. The two young women's differences had always seemed superficial—Palmer didn't like wearing makeup or worrying about her hair, and she was more interested in camping out and roughing it than Baumgartner—because both were caregivers at heart. They wanted to make the expedition a success and do whatever they could for the crew, though they went about it in different ways.

Baumgartner didn't have as much difficulty getting along with the women on the liaison team, perhaps because she was a year older than Palmer and closer in age to the adults—Jan was only twenty-five and Marlena was twenty-four. Of course, her closeness with them could also have been the result of working with them and not with the crew.

> *I've finally gotten to know Jan and Marlena and love them both dearly, I saw all the paperwork they had to contend with and helped them by doing what I could . . . Mom, you thought MY makeup habits would change—HA! Now I have Jan buying makeup galore and doing her nails every night, which she's NEVER done before!*

For their part, Jan and Marlena appreciated Baumgartner's cheerful, capable presence on the team. At times they felt like everything was falling apart around them. Neither had any previous experience with logistics or organizing an extended wilderness outing, nor had they anticipated how much work leading the liaison team would turn out to be. The days were often filled with thankless toil. When the women visited a community in advance to check if a campsite would be suitable, they would sometimes request extra firewood or access to bathrooms for the soon-to-arrive voyageurs, and city officials would tell them it was impossible. Then, as soon as the crew members arrived, all those requests were suddenly fulfilled without a second thought. The costumes the men wore imbued them with a kind of magic. Their arrival would sometimes bring tears to people's eyes, and it inspired communities to cook banquets and hold ceremonies in their honor. None of the women had period outfits or props or any other physical signs that marked them as part of the historic reenactment, except for a slip of paper behind the windshield of the van that proclaimed they were with La Salle: Expedition II. No one paid much attention when the liaison team drove into a new town, regardless of that sign.

It had also been a challenge to go from being a teacher, an unquestionable authority figure, to taking orders from someone else and trying to cater to the demands of twenty-three men. Jan and Marlena were accustomed to being decision-makers and disciplinarians. On the expedition, Reid was the final decision-maker, but no one was really playing the role of disciplinarian because everyone was expected to act like an adult, despite the relative youth of the crew members. Jan and Marlena weren't much older than the teenagers and didn't have the experience or confidence to address concerns in a productive way. Criticism from the crew felt like personal attacks, and hearing complaints over and over again left them drained and stressed. If they'd had ten more years under their belts, maybe things would've been different. But as it was, it never felt like what they were doing was good enough.

Baumgartner found her own ways of calming down on hard days. She'd asked her parents to send books on philosophy and piano music to keep her mind busy when they had spare time. In Toronto she'd stayed with three different families who owned pianos and practiced playing Carole King songs. She also got to spend some time with her boyfriend, Lieberman, although they often had to settle for a smile and a wink as they passed each other going about their respective duties. Lieberman was hoping to visit his father in Florida at the end of the expedition and had invited Baumgartner to come down with him, if all their plans worked out. She was very much looking forward to that kind of trip. Sun, sand, and relaxation. For now, she just tried to enjoy living in another country. It was less noticeable in Ontario than it had been in Quebec, since most people spoke English instead of French, but there were little reminders all over the place: the Esso gas stations and Bonimarto shopping stores, the butter tarts and burned pepperoni pizzas, the restaurants that never served water with meals, the beautiful rocky terrain along highways between fields of cattails. Even though they were traveling all the time and never stopped in one place for long, Canada had come to feel comfortable and welcoming, even when their accommodations left something to be desired, due to the fact that they had little money to spend on hotels. Still, she couldn't help but feel the occasional pang of homesickness, as she wrote in letters home.

How is my room? I miss Elgin. Mr. Kerr, that econ prof, reminded me of Mrs. Pool and ECC [Elgin Community College] and all the students and classes and home and everything. I'm glad I'm busy and don't have much time to dwell on it . . . The past 3 nights the liaison team has spent in an old "farmhouse." There are 3 broken windows, no heat, 1 light bulb, bird's nests—(we're staying in the upstairs), the downstairs has broken furniture, a burnt out gas stove, a hole that goes to the basement—all in all, it's a terribly interesting place to stay. We sleep in our bags on the floor or sofa.

Fortunately, they didn't have to spend long in the crumbling farmhouse. Having finished the portage through Toronto and paddled up Lake Simcoe and the Severn River, the crew would soon be entering Georgian Bay, and the liaison team planned to rent a nice cottage along Lake Huron. This Canadian region was going to be the most remote stretch of their trip yet, and the men would be out of touch with the liaison team for much of the three weeks they were spending in Georgian Bay. Everyone was preparing physically and mentally, working on warmer clothes for the approaching winter, making extra moccasins, enjoying the company of other people while they were still in civilization. They anticipated making a small adjustment to the crew as well, since

Father Loran was still having back problems. He'd sat out during the portage, sleeping on the HMS *Haida* and trying to recuperate. Paddling continued to be hard on his back. He was going to rejoin the crew in Georgian Bay, but if nothing improved, he would permanently give up his spot and Bardwell would take over.

After hiking with the crew through Toronto, Bardwell felt strange going back to the liaison team. He wasn't used to wearing real shoes or being able to watch a movie on TV. Even eating dinner at Kentucky Fried Chicken was a disappointment. The food tasted terrible. He missed the crew's dinner of dried peas and being able to wear the voyageur clothing. Being stuck between two worlds continued to be a struggle. It was the constant uncertainty of each day, not knowing if he'd be paddling or helping the women. It was hard to watch the rest of the guys jump into the canoes and leave without him, especially now that there was such animosity between the liaison team and the crew. Where did Bardwell belong? If he had his choice, he'd move to the canoes full-time. But that would leave the ladies of the liaison team to fend for themselves.

Chapter Six

NO TRAILS BUT THE
WATERWAYS THEMSELVES

Georgian Bay, New France
October 1681

La Salle's voyage is often described as a "discovery" that benefited France and the Sun King, and it was an impressive feat, especially by 17th-century standards. The privations he and his men endured are hard to imagine in a world of twenty-four-hour fast food restaurants and walk-in health clinics. The voyageurs regularly faced starvation and lived on rationed diets, despite expending thousands of calories paddling from dawn to dusk. At one point in his travels, La Salle's trusted lieutenant Tonty ran out of food and was forced to live on acorns for three days.[1] The nuts provide a good dose of nutrition in large quantities, but when eaten raw they're incredibly bitter and can cause digestive problems.[2] And raw acorns were hardly the worst option when it came to survival food. Rock moss, boiled in water to make a meager soup called tripe-de-roche, often saved voyageurs from dying of hunger.[3] Considering what La Salle and his men had to go through to reach the end of the Mississippi River, the voyage could certainly be considered an ordeal, but it was one they overcame to make a great discovery. That said, the "discovery" only counted from the European point of view.

Native Americans knew their continent at least as well as Europeans knew the entire continent of Europe. They traveled regularly—sometimes by choice, sometimes by necessity. When Europeans arrived, Native Americans frequently aided their navigation. They would draw maps on deerskins or buffalo hides, in the sand, and on ribbons of bark.[4] La Salle himself was the recipient of numerous natives' advice when it came to traveling the Mississippi. While Europeans may have believed they were taking advantage of the knowledge of the unsuspecting indigenous people, it's just as likely that the native guides were steering early Europeans away from sacred sites that they didn't want visited. But the Europeans had their own religious agenda in the New World. Jesuit priests regularly made treks into Native territory and built missions, even in places where they weren't welcomed.

As La Salle paddled through Georgian Bay on the northeastern side of Lake Huron, he and his men passed two such failed experiments in religious cohabitation. The first of the two abandoned missions was Sainte-Marie Among the Hurons, located on the land of the Wendat (also known as Wyandot) at the southern end of Georgian Bay. The Jesuit establishment was founded in 1639 and destroyed a mere ten years later after eight of the missionaries were killed in the Huron-Iroquois wars. The second site was on Manitoulin Island, the largest island in a freshwater lake in the world. In 1648 Father Joseph Poncet set up a mission near the village of Wikwemikong on Manitoulin Island that fared no better than Sainte-Marie Among the Hurons. Just two years after its founding, an Iroquois raid sent Father Poncet and the Hurons living on the island running for the barricaded village of Quebec City hundreds of miles away on the mainland. Within the year, two hundred people left the island in forty canoes, and a final Iroquois attack in 1652 drove the remaining native residents, the Odawa (or Ottawa), away from the island.[5]

Even with an entourage of thirty men armed with rifles, La Salle knew what the consequences would be if he encountered an Iroquois war party. Such a meeting could forever put an end to his quest. However highly the Frenchmen thought of themselves, with their "civilized" behavior and superior religion, the fact of the matter was that they were still visitors in a land very unlike their home.

⊶

Midland, Ontario
September 30, 1976

John Fialko hobbled into the fenced yard of the mission, taking care not to place too much weight on his right foot. The swollen instep ached with any movement, but at least he wasn't carrying a canoe over his head anymore. The doctor he'd just seen assured him the foot wasn't broken, despite the bruising and swelling. Lucky, considering the weight of the object he'd dropped (a 175-pound canoe) and the way it had landed (with the sharp, angular gunwales of the bow pointed right at his foot). It was also a bit of good timing. The portage was over. There'd be much less walking for the next few weeks as they paddled across Georgian Bay. Life would be lived in the belly of the canoe.

Fialko, who went by the name Pierre Prudhomme when in camp and on stage, was the epitome of a wilderness man. The original Prudhomme had disappeared for ten days in the wilds around the Mississippi River when he got lost on a hunting expedition. Against all odds, he found his way back to La Salle's men, starving but alive. Like his namesake, Fialko seemed to have a limitless knowledge of survival, though he'd been fortunate enough not to need it yet. He quickly learned new skills, from building a spear to throwing a tomahawk. Though he could be reticent and preferred a subdued method of leadership, his commands were obeyed immediately and without question. If the crew had any word that most embodied Fialko's attitude and abilities, it was "capable." He relished the moniker. After all, being an expert outdoorsman was all about having the flexibility and ingenuity to adapt to whatever situations arose.

He looked the part of a frontiersman as well: dark brown hair that came past his jaw, a tangled black beard that obscured half his face, and muscle all over his body. A smile that stretched up to his crinkled eyes saved him from fully incarnating a gruff mountain man. His tendency to provide a helping hand whenever it was needed without complaint further endeared him to the rest of the crew. As the group's "armorer," Fialko had helped the teens build their rifles and overseen the canoe construction. Now he was tasked with making necessary repairs to keep the boats floating. Without his diligence, the crew would have quite literally sunk by this point in the trip.

The group would need capable leaders now more than ever if they planned to succeed in the next stage of their journey. Georgian Bay was the most isolated body of water they would have to paddle across. They would make only three stops in towns over the course of three weeks. They'd have minimal contact with the liaison team, and the only food they'd have to eat was what they carried and what they caught. If anything happened, no one would be there to help. They prepared for the month-long wilderness trek by getting weighed and measured for body fat before their departure. Belts might have to be tightened at some point. This bit of the trip was the closest they could possibly come to experiencing life as the original voyageurs had lived it, rationed diets and all.

Getting lost was the real danger. Georgian Bay is 120 miles long and nearly 80 percent as large as Lake Ontario, the last lake the group had crossed. Sometimes called the "sixth Great Lake" for its size, the bay is filled with tens of thousands of islands. When navigator Ron Hobart had looked at the bay's charts for the first time, he realized there were a disconcerting number of blank spots. The expedition would be navigating uncharted territory without the benefit of GPS assistance, just as La Salle once had. What's more, large parts of the eastern shore of Georgian Bay still belonged to First Nation indigenous people of Canada, including the Anishinaabeg, who belonged to the Algonquian group (a designation made on linguistic similarity that includes groups such as the Ojibwe, Cheyenne, and Loup). Chief Max Gros-Louis of the Huron had given the group permission to travel through his people's land when the men departed from Montreal, but they were a long way from Quebec and were portraying an era of history that had resulted in the devastation of native people and their culture. Only a few years earlier, when Lewis was leading the Jolliet-Marquette Expedition down the Mississippi, he'd been given an FBI entourage for fear that members of the American Indian Movement would attack the crew. The group was known for its large protests and the occupation of historic sites, including a seventy-one-day occupation and battle with U.S. armed forces at Wounded Knee, South Dakota, in 1973. And in the case of historical clashes between peoples of different societies, one culture's hero can be another's augury of destruction.

There had been no threats made against them on this voyage. They'd have to hope Gitche Manitou, the Algonquian incarnation of the Great Spirit, allowed them safe passage despite the misdeeds of their predecessors. And anyway, history was more convoluted than labeling the French as evil and the indigenous people as victimized. Some voyageurs married native women and never returned to the French colonial towns, and native people worked with the French as guides, interpreters, or soldiers. The Europeans who worked closely with them sometimes adopted native clothing and learned native languages. Their 17th-century world wasn't one of a simplistic division between conquerors and conquered.

But the crew usually had an hour to give their show, and it had been written with a focus on the French voyageurs, not the Native Americans and First Nations they came in contact with. Capturing that level of nuance in a historic reenactment was difficult, and even if the men had wanted to stage a meeting between Frenchmen and natives, most of the country they traveled through was populated by the descendants of European immigrants. They'd be passing close to reservations on Georgian Bay but hadn't planned any stops in those communities.

While some crew members contemplated the absence or presence of native spirits in the territory they were about to enter, Father Loran turned to Christianity for divine assistance. He felt an especially close connection with Saint John Brebeuf, with whom he'd recently become acquainted. For the past three nights the crew had been guests at the reconstructed Jesuit mission at Sainte-Marie Among the Hurons. Brebeuf was a resident at the mission when it was destroyed in a battle between the Huron and the Iroquois in 1649. He and another missionary were taken captive by the Iroquois, who tortured then killed the French priests. For his work as a missionary, Brebeuf was canonized. A church called Shrine of the Seven Martyrs was erected in the early 1900s near the reconstructed Sainte-Marie Among the Hurons mission in Midland, Ontario, to honor Brebeuf's work and that of the other Jesuit missionaries who had come from France to spread Christianity in North America. Inside the reconstructed mission there was also a tombstone for Brebeuf. It lay below a window, allowing rays of sunlight to illuminate the stony gray sculpture of the martyr.

It could've been eerie sleeping on ground that was the site of a bloody battle several centuries earlier. Instead, the mission felt homey. It also matched the historic aesthetic of La Salle: Expedition II. The buildings were precise replicas of the originals, filled with tools of the era, handcrafted furniture, and bunches of dried tobacco leaves hanging from the rafters. None of the historic buildings were equipped with electricity, so at night the men wrote or read by candle- or firelight. The crew slept in the Upright House and stored their canoes and gear in the "non-Christian" area where unbaptized indigenous people would've once come. After the noise and commotion of Toronto and the accumulated fatigue of the portage, the mission was a much-needed rest stop—even if it was built on top of a battleground.

The crew spent three days giving presentations and lolling in the tall grass around the mission, sewing clothes and moccasins beneath a warm sun. School groups and tourists who had come to the mission for a guided visit were treated to a surprise when their guides introduced them to the 17th-century voyageurs passing through before they continued on their way to the Mississippi River. One guide even said she was skipping the museum so that her group of elementary school kids could talk to the voyageurs. Doug Cole, the director of the re-created historical site, was so impressed with the crew's commitment to authenticity that he offered the teenagers summer jobs for the year they finished the expedition, even though the positions were normally open only to Canadians. He also bought them dinner for their last night at the mission.

In many ways, the men felt they had become true voyageurs: comfortable with the heft of a wooden paddle in their hands, inured to hardship, familiar with the rhythms of wind and waves. The days of painful blisters on their fingers and unease in woolen shirts were far behind them. This life of constant travel, rigorous physical activity, and campsites on beaches and in forests had become satisfyingly routine. And now that they'd be free of scrutiny from the public for almost a month, they were even freer to embrace their newfound identities.

Shortly before noon on September 30, the voyageurs' last day at the mission, the canoes were floating in the Wye River and loaded with gear. To the equipment they'd arrived with, they added bundles of dried tobacco and some modern foul-weather gear, including insulated diving gloves, yellow waterproof pants, and thigh-high waders. The boots were solely for the avants to wear when the weather grew colder, since they'd be required to jump out of the canoes into icy water. The justification for these concessions to modernity was that the crew would be traveling in weather that La Salle might have avoided, since they had communities to visit on specific days. The crew's commitment to authenticity didn't extend to putting themselves in as much danger as the earlier voyageurs would've faced, and the risks would only grow as the weather became colder. Trees around the mission were beginning to change color. The tall sunflowers in the mission's garden were still standing, but their leaves had turned black and the buttery petals were limp. Canadian waterfowl and songbirds were preparing for their long migratory flights south. Though it felt warm now, all of nature seemed to be united in a single message: *winter is on its way.*

The crew departed, however, under a sunny sky with the well wishes of the staff at Sainte-Marie Among the Hurons at their backs. The men faced their impending isolation from society with a variety of emotions: excitement, trepidation, determination. No doubt it would be different from the experience of having an entourage of enthralled people anticipating their arrival and departure every day. No one would be there to encourage them and stroke their egos. They would be alone with one another in the expansive northern wilds. Who knew what kind of men they'd be when they reached the other side?

Philip Edward Island, Georgian Bay
October 6, 1976

"There is magic in the feel of a paddle and the movement of a canoe, a magic compounded of distance, adventure, solitude, and peace. The way of a canoe is the way of the wilderness and of a freedom almost forgotten. It is an antidote to insecurity, the open door to waterways of ages past and a way of life with profound and abiding satisfactions."[6]

Ron Hobart had discovered the writings of environmentalist Sigurd Olson while studying biology at Gustavus Adolphus College in St. Peter, Minnesota. Reading those words for the first time had been a moment of profound recognition, like making eye contact with one's soul mate from opposite sides of a crowded room. Never before had Hobart connected so intimately with the written words of another human. Olson's experiences and views on nature, the past, and canoeing all resonated with Hobart and mirrored his own beliefs. The connection to Olson and the singing wilderness felt stronger than ever in Georgian Bay. Like one of the well-tuned strings on the guitar he played every night, Hobart felt in harmony with all that surrounded him. The granite mounds of the Canadian Shield, the splendid eruption of crimson and orange leaves on deciduous trees, and the soft whisper of wind blowing through the uplifted branches of the eastern white pines. Sometimes at dusk they sat around the crackling campfires and listened to the tremulous call of a loon crying for its mate. It was an eerie, beautiful symphony directed by a silent conductor, playing for whomever happened to be listening as stars appeared in the darkening sky overhead. In Georgian Bay, time no longer felt linear. Instead it seemed entirely possible that they might round the point of a small island and come face-to-face with La Salle and Tonty dressed in the finery of King Louis's court.

Each new day brought the men a deeper appreciation of the spectacular wilderness. No other part of their journey had felt so genuinely authentic. They rose before sunrise and broke camp, then paddled for several hours before stopping for breakfast. Fialko was charged with signaling when they would take a break from paddling. He had to rely on his own judgment without the benefit of a watch to call out the hour mark that meant they could rest for ten minutes. Occasionally Father Loran would turn around in their canoe to ask, "About time, isn't it?" Fialko usually had to tell him to keep going. When he deemed it time for a break, both he and the Franciscan priest broke out their pipes and smoked while the canoes drifted across the water. In other boats the men chatted, closed their eyes for a few minutes, or pulled out their own pipes. When all the tobacco had burned down, it was time to move on again. The same practice had been used by the voyageurs, giving rise to the use of the word "pipe" to mean break.

The day on the water ended when the sun sank below the horizon and the men found a place to land. They ate a meal of cooked peas or beans and drank water straight from the bay. They camped on the granite boulders so common to the area, sometimes erecting the three shelters on separate small islands. The shelter builders used rocks to hold up the tarps instead of the stakes they normally drove into the ground. Sleeping on stone could be surprisingly comfortable, especially after a full day of paddling thirty miles and unwinding around the firelight. Some of the cooks spent their free time frying up bannock, made from a mixture of flour, sugar, and water. Others wrote in their journals or read books. Hobart often pulled out his guitar to serenade the crew with songs by John Denver. His favorite was "Rocky Mountain High." *I've seen it raining fire in the sky / The shadows from the starlight / Are softer than a lullaby.* The lyrics seemed to describe the vast ceiling of stars above them.

On the morning of October 6, Hobart followed his typical routine of consulting the charts in preparation for leading the fleet of canoes through the countless islands and islets. Since no one else was allowed to view the maps, it was left to Hobart's judgment to pick their route. Making the task more difficult was the lack of detail on the charts. Often an area would be marked with "numerous small islands and shoals" without showing where exactly those islands appeared. Today was one of those days when it was impossible to tell what the terrain they'd pass through would look like. All Hobart knew was that they needed to make their way to Voyageur Channel, a protected passage between some islands and the shore that would shield them from wind and waves on the exposed bay. It had been used by paddlers crossing Georgian Bay for centuries. To get there, however, they first had to make their way around the Chickens.

The Chickens are a series of huge boulders that were dragged into the bay at the end of the last ice age. Left in the wake of the retreating glaciers, they became submerged when the lake formed. The exposed granite rocks protrude from the water like the backs of enormous white whales surfacing for a breath of air. Some of the boulders are low enough to see over, while others are tall and covered in pine trees. They stretch across almost two miles near the shoreline and extend out into the bay for a mile. In some areas the boulders lie close to one another, presenting an impenetrable labyrinth, while other boulders are far enough apart to allow passage for slim canoes.

Hobart couldn't tell from his charts whether it would be possible to safely travel through the Chickens. He didn't want any of the canoes to become damaged by paddling over rough rocks that were closer to the surface than they appeared. Before setting out he instructed the crew to paddle out and around the boulder field. The route would mean traveling farther and putting their boats at risk in the larger bay. A cold drizzle was coming down, but the water was calm and there was little wind. Conditions could always get worse, but they wouldn't be in the bay for long. It seemed safe enough.

Hobart's canoe was last in line to make the turn around the Chickens and out into the lake. As he steered the canoe from his gouvernail position, he noticed a small opening between the Chickens and the coast.

"Hold on a minute," he said to his crew. He whistled for the rest of the canoes and, one by one, they came back. Hobart pointed at the passage between the boulders and suggested they attempt to find their way through. Since he was navigator and had successfully seen them through everything else to this point, no one disagreed. With Hobart leading the way, the six canoes nosed their way through the dense array of boulders. The cold rain turned the granite splotchy gray and seeped into patches of moss that grew in rocky crevices. The droplets splashed gently into the water, creating a rhythm with the sound of paddles pulling the canoes forward. After half an hour of following a combination of instinct and chance the expedition reached the end of the Chickens. Before them was the entrance to Voyageur Channel. The shiver Hobart felt had nothing to do with the chilly weather. It was spooky. Almost like they'd been guided by the old voyageurs. He'd never been to this region before, could've gotten everyone hopelessly lost in the boulders and been forced to turn back, adding time and miles to the day and putting the crew at risk of hypothermia. Instead, he found a shortcut.

Once more the words of Sigurd Olson seemed appropriate: "I have seen what happens when food and equipment are lost far from civilization and I know what it takes to traverse a wilderness where there are no trails but the waterways themselves. The elements of chance and danger are wonderful and frightening to experience and, though I bemoan the recklessness of youth, I wonder what the world would be like without it. I know it is wrong, but I am for the spirit that makes young men do the things they do. I am for the glory that they know."[7]

Although Voyageur Channel was protected from wind and waves, the men found themselves wedged between towering granite bluffs, Philip Edward Island on one side and mainland Canada on the other. It was the end of the day, and they had no idea where they could land. Cliffs as high as fifty feet forced them to stay on the water. That was always the risk in Georgian Bay—since no one had planned out the specifics of where the crew would be camping, campsites could be less than ideal. At last they happened upon a grassy hill with a hunting and fishing lodge at its peak. The sight of such a lodge wasn't uncommon in the region. Most were empty at this time of year—the summer tourism season was long over. Still, best not to trespass without permission. Several of the crew jogged up to the lodge to check if anyone was home. The owners answered and welcomed them to Mahzenazing River Lodge, site of a former logging operation. Despite the scruffy appearance and pungent smell of the young men (the water was too cold for bathing, so everyone had done without for the past week), the owners happily consented to the voyageurs camping on their lawn. Perhaps the act of hospitality was inspired by admiration for the group's odyssey through remote Georgian Bay, or maybe the couple were simply happy to see any visitors at all, no matter their odor, since the hunting lodge could be reached by only water or air. Whatever the reason for the friendly welcome, the men were happy to have soft terrain to sleep on, and even more grateful for the fresh bread and jam offered by their hosts.

It had been a relatively short day on the water in spite of the prolonged search for a campsite. Only nine and a half miles covered, thanks to the shortcut through the Chickens. Unfortunately they were still eighteen miles from Killarney. The small town was the crew's first stop since entering the territory, and a brief return to civilization was appealing for several reasons. First, Sam Hess needed a doctor. The fire starter had been chopping wood when a stray shard flew into his face and struck his eye. He could still see a little out of the injured eye, but it was swollen and bloody. Still-wagon didn't trust his limited skills as a medic to treat the injury and prevent infection. He wanted a real doctor to take a look. Next, the crew was running worryingly low on food. They'd planned on reaching Killarney and the liaison team three days earlier to resupply, but several days of high wind and waves had delayed their progress. Who knew what the liaison team was thinking at this point. There was no way for a message to be sent to them.

Second, the crew was surviving on rationed portions of beans and oatmeal, and could probably manage for a few more days at least. No one was about to starve. But hunger had become an incessant, bothersome companion. The men joked about boiling up pots of moss for a nourishing stew the way voyageurs of old had done, or foraging in the woods for pinecones and rose hips. The possibility of hunting or fishing was discussed more seriously. Georgian Bay supported a profusion of wildlife: raccoons, bears, beavers, deer, fish, and fowl of all kinds. More than enough to feed a ravenous crew of twenty-three men, if they could only figure out how to catch them. Though they carried two ten-pound bags of lead shot for the muskets, hunting was deemed too lengthy and impractical a process unless it became absolutely necessary to prevent starvation. The blast of firing was likely to scare away anything with legs, and few of the musket men had practice aiming with the loaded guns. They only ever shot blanks straight into the air. Fishing was the more feasible option. Fialko and Mark Fredenberg managed to catch several pike and perch with makeshift spears, but the fish were hardly enough to be a feast. And they hadn't been the most toothsome addition to their meal, though that was a failure of the preparation rather than the fish themselves. They'd removed the heads and scales then put the whole fish on spits, but some of the sticks they used turned out to be full of pine sap that leaked into the flesh. The resinous flavor wasn't appetizing.

If they could've caught and eaten the massasauga rattlers that abounded in the area, they might never be hungry. The splotchy brown snakes slithered through the foliage and basked indolently on sun-warmed rocks, making themselves easy targets. But they were also venomous. The few close brushes crew members had with them made everyone overly cautious around the snakes. Ken had woken in a panic one morning when he felt sweat trickling down the side of his face and was convinced it was a small snake. Once a snake had slithered between Cox's legs when he and Hobart were walking through the woods, sending him straight in the air. Cox landed with both hands held out like guns, making *pewpewpew* noises at the departing serpent.

The only real option for assuaging their hunger was to snack on dwindling boxes of golden raisins and the last of the bannock—and pray to whichever gods might be listening that they wouldn't be delayed from reuniting with the liaison team much longer.

Even with Hess's injured eye and everyone's empty stomachs, the men reveled in the beauty of their surroundings and the simple joys of living outdoors. Distraction from discomfort wasn't hard to come by. One afternoon photographer Bart Dean, who'd decided to travel with the crew part of the way through Georgian Bay, found a dead fish and tied a string around it to use as a limp sword. He called for Chuck Campbell, the once-shy teenager who had since grown comfortable with voicing his opinions among the crew. Back at the beginning of the expedition Cox had jokingly given Campbell a moniker celebrating his habit of wearing every sack and sash he could find for performances, resulting in a strange, jumbled collection of apparel. Adding to the name's suitability was the fact that Campbell loved wildlife, whether it was living and breathing or in the final stages of rigor mortis. Dean decided to celebrate Campbell's affinity by knighting him. He swung the dead fish over Campbell's shoulder and officially dubbed him with the name Cox had earlier bestowed: "Roadkill." The newly christened Roadkill wore the fish on his shirt for the rest of the day.

Whether on land or water, the key to keeping morale high was refusing to let boredom get the best of them. They were traveling without access to news, media entertainment, or the companionship of other people. Even with the most verdant surroundings and a religious respect for nature, paddling every day could become tedious, and too much tedium invited a host of other emotions: frustration, annoyance, anger. So the crew came up with a number of ways to amuse themselves. Hobart and Cox, paddling at opposite ends of the same canoe, worked with their canoe to perfect the Ojibwa stealth stroke (lying all the way down in the boats so only their arms protruded) and snuck up on flocks of floating birds. They invented other new strokes, like the Rodney, where Cox held his paddle with one hand and Keith Gorse, sitting behind him, reached over his head to push it down into the water. Sometimes they sang popular songs or told stories. The two canoes of the gold module—one driven by Hobart and the other by Stillwagon—had to work harder to keep up, since they had seven men between them instead of eight. Campbell was in the swing position, alternating between the two boats. But even one man short they managed to make more noise and merriment than everyone else. They'd dubbed themselves the Paddlin' Madeleines.

In the evening chores were divided up among members of the same module, so the men who had spent the day paddling together often spent all evening together as well. There were no formal rules dictating who everyone had to spend their time with; some men formed tight cliques while others bounced between groups of friends. But the module structure tended to limit movement, since each module had its own chef, its own fire, its own shelter. It produced a strong sense of camaraderie between members of a module. They talked about anything and everything. Many came to know one another like family members. The adults particularly enjoyed seeing the way the teenagers had changed and matured since the start of the trip. They may have been typical high school students at the outset, but the past two months had made them into men.

Cox and Hobart, who were friends before joining the expedition, had grown even closer as the trip went on. Like all the best duos, the two had temperaments and personalities that complemented each other. Hobart was tall, with curly, fawn-brown hair and big glasses that magnified his blue eyes. He wore a patch embossed with a musical note around his neck since he was in charge of the musical portion of the crew's performance. He also led some of the science projects, including creating a map using 17th-century tools and collecting water samples wherever they traveled. Hobart was friendly and generous with advice without being overbearing, which made him a popular confidante. Before the trip he hadn't had much self-confidence, and it was a defect he'd always felt. As the expedition progressed, Hobart seemed to be gaining an ever-stronger belief in his abilities. He liked the trust the young men placed in him and was flattered to be thought of as a leader. Cox, on the other hand, was short, stout, loud, and opinionated. He was impatient and had a temper, but also the best sense of humor of anyone on the trip. Even when he was at his most frustrated, he was often cracking jokes.

Almost every evening, usually after all the others had gone to bed, the two men stayed up, entranced by the stars and the sound of the water and the firelight. Sometimes Cox read. He was a voracious reader and had adamantly refused when someone suggested they ban books while they were in Georgian Bay so as to be more wholly authentic. Sometimes they both wrote in their journals. Sometimes they talked. They also rehashed the day or discussed friends back home or what their futures held at the end of the expedition next April.

Like everyone else, the two thought often of loved ones they'd left behind. In January 1976, Hobart had divorced his wife, Helen, for a variety of reasons. Though he didn't regret agreeing to come on the expedition, the strain of the upcoming eight-month-long voyage was one of the factors in their separation. Hobart wished things between them could've happened differently; he also left behind a three-year-old son, Seth, who wouldn't recognize his father when they saw each other in December.

Cox had been married for six years to a woman named Pam, another teacher, and he constantly thought of her. However much he changed, she was sure to be changing even more. She'd been left on her own to pay the bills, earn a living, and keep herself occupied. Cox only hoped that both of them would be changed for the better.

Stillwagon, also married and with four children, felt guilty at times that he couldn't share the experience with his family. "Last nite [sic] I got up during the nite [sic] and could not believe how the stars looked. I've never seen a clearer sky . . . It hardly seems fair that I have all these great experiences w/out you!" Stillwagon wrote to his wife, Rowena. Fialko wrote letters of his own to his fiancée, Linda, and thought of her frequently. They were going to be married in June, two months after the conclusion of the expedition. He felt bad for leaving her behind while he had the experience of a lifetime. But they'd known at the start of their relationship that this expedition would happen. The expedition was actually part of the reason they'd started dating—he met her when he went looking for a teacher who could translate some documents from French to English when the expedition was in its earliest stages.

Among the younger crew members there were fewer romantic attachments. Most enjoyed the adulatory attention of young women in the towns they visited. Those who remained in relationships with girls back home had their own methods for dealing with homesickness and heartache. George LeSieutre, whose girlfriend, Annie, had started college classes at the University of Illinois, wrote dozens of letters and made phone calls to her dorm whenever he could. Sometimes he played his harmonica to keep from getting blue, and he always wore the silver Saint Christopher medal she'd given him before leaving. It was getting tarnished, but he was reluctant to take it off for a polish.

The next day, as long as the weather was fair, two of the other romantically attached young men would get to see their girlfriends. Lieberman, who was dating Baumgartner, and Fredenburg, who had started a relationship with Palmer, were excited for more than just the food that awaited them. And Reid Lewis would get to see his wife, who would probably be relieved that the men had made it out of the wilderness unscathed. But however necessary her presence was as head of the liaison team, the fact that Lewis had so much contact with his wife when no one else could seemed to be just another way that he was different from the other adult crew members.

The following morning the men were finally greeted by good weather. They paddled for Killarney, the town where they'd planned to meet the liaison team several days earlier. The women were jubilant to see the men after worrying about their location. Jan and Marlena admitted they'd considered sending out a search party if the men's arrival was delayed much longer. It had been a nerve-wracking forty-eight hours, but the women never really thought the men were in serious trouble. After all, they weren't entirely like the original voyageurs, whose risk of injury or death was much higher and the distances separating them from people who could help much farther. With the modern voyageurs, everyone suspected injuries would occur. But death seemed beyond remote.

Near Blind River, Ontario
October 11, 1976

Wind, rain, and waves battered the fleet of canoes. All morning the paddlers had muddled through the dismal mess of water. Whatever luck had been with them during the first few days of beautiful weather in Georgian Bay had long since disappeared. Maybe Gitche Manitou was testing them—or maybe it was simply a bad time of year to attempt traveling through northern lakes. On its own, getting wet was a common enough occurrence and could be ignored for the length of a day's paddle. But getting wet and being exposed to a cold wind was more than miserable. It was dangerous. Already some of the skinnier men like Clif Wilson and Jorge Garcia, who paddled in the same canoe as Wilson, were shivering and pale. If they spent much longer on the water, they'd risk hypothermia.

Hobart consulted his maps in the back of the canoe. The group had stopped at the tip of a spit of land to decide what to do next. The boats lurched over four-foot swells. The occasional breaker splashing in over the sides sent men reaching for bailers to dump the water back out. With a howling wind coming from the southwest, there was no way to avoid being exposed to waves. Behind them there were several islands they could paddle around for shelter. The rocky shoreline would make landing hard, but not impossible, especially since the wind and waves wouldn't be pushing them forward. Around the point ahead of them was a bay that stretched back for slightly more than a mile. They could paddle two miles to get to the opposite side of the bay, but that might be risky due to the direction of the waves. If they went straight into the bay, they'd have to hope for a soft landing site because the waves would be coming from directly behind them, forcing them ahead at uncontrollable speeds. Landing on rocks at high speeds could easily damage the canoes, and counting on a landing spot that wasn't rocky was a gamble in Georgian Bay, where the shoreline was often granite boulders.

"Given what I can see of the terrain, I don't think we should head into the bay," Hobart said. Instead, he thought the crew should backtrack and find a sheltered landing spot to get the canoes out of the water. Not a wonderful prospect for the night, but probably safer than paddling into unknown waters. Many of the crew members agreed with his assessment, even if it meant turning back and camping on the cold, wet rocks for a night. Just when Hobart thought they'd come to a decision, Lewis said something to the men in his canoe, and they started paddling. In a moment, they'd disappeared around the point.

Hobart and the others exchanged incredulous looks. What the hell had just happened? What were they supposed to do now?

"If he's gonna go, we have to go," Hobart said. "We can't be separated."

As soon as they made the turn into the bay, the boats were caught up in the grasp of rolling waves and rocketed forward. All around them were walls of rock. Hobart, already angry with Lewis for making a decision without consulting the rest of the group, was growing more and more concerned that they'd find nowhere to land. They drew closer to the shoreline, shooting forward in the surf. Waves crashed around the canoes and poured in over the gunwales. It felt like the rough ride they'd had on Lake Ontario all over again, only today it wasn't sunny and the beach ahead wasn't sandy, and Hobart hadn't wanted to come this way. Just as it was looking as if the canoes were about to become splinters in the rocky teeth of the bay's shoreline, a tiny sand beach came into view. The canoes flew onto it one after the other, tipping over on their sides and sending the crew sprawling, then scrambling to their feet to get out of the way of the incoming vessels. In minutes they had all safely landed.

Despite the fortuitous conclusion of the day's misadventure, Hobart had never been so infuriated in his life. He volunteered to get firewood to start warming people up and stomped off to the woods with an ax. It felt good to turn the logs and driftwood into kindling. Cox, equally riled by what had happened, joined Hobart in turning branches into toothpicks. What had been the point of that maneuver? To put them a half mile closer to their destination, Blind River? Because Lewis had planned a rendezvous no one else knew about? Because he thought it was safe enough? Where exactly did he draw the line when it came to safety? Sure, everyone had known the inherent risks when they signed up for the expedition, but that didn't mean they needed to purposely court danger. Hobart felt some sense of responsibility for the crew and would do whatever he could to prevent any accidents. And if that meant stopping earlier than they'd planned, so be it. Was their schedule more important than their lives?

When Hobart and Cox came back to the campsite with armfuls of splintered wood, Lewis was gone. It seemed he'd wanted to meet with the liaison team and that was part of why he'd been so determined to reach a landing spot that put them closer to Blind River rather than turn back to one of the sheltered areas they'd already passed. It would've been helpful if he'd filled everyone else in. Still, the thought made Hobart slightly calmer as he continued to help set up camp. A bit later, DiFulvio approached him. As the gouvernail for Lewis's boat, he'd been part of the initial breakaway and had heard Reid discussing it with Ken after they landed.

"What's this I hear about you being afraid to paddle?" he asked Hobart.

"What the hell does that mean?" Hobart said.

DiFulvio explained that he'd heard Reid and Ken making disparaging comments. Hobart's temper flared right back up again, and he fumed for the rest of the night. *I vow never again to put the crew in jeopardy because Reid wants to do some dumbass thing,* he thought. *This is where it changes.* He wasn't going to sit back and listen when Lewis made a decision for the group. They were supposed to decide things democratically. If he had to shout himself hoarse until they came to a resolution, he would do so. He was the navigator. He had a responsibility to see the men safely to their destination.

⚬

St. Ignace, Michigan
October 21, 1976

The snowflakes fell thick and heavy as an opaque curtain, momentarily blotting out the shoreline. The men were less than two miles from their landing site but so snow blind they had no way of knowing if they'd made any progress. The sky had been clear and sunny when they set out, then rain clouds rolled in, and now snow. Three seasons in one day. By the time they got close to shore, the clouds had rolled back and the sun was peeking through the flurries. To the crowd on shore at St. Ignace, the incoming voyageurs were like ghosts emerging from a storm.

In the ten days since they'd crash-landed on the beach outside of Blind River, the expedition had undergone several major changes. First, winter had roared in with a fury, bringing freezing temperatures, frost, and snow all within twenty-four hours. The crew had awakened the morning of October 15 to a silver layer of frost feathering across everything. Their leather moccasins had hardened into unwearable lumps, and any of the canvas ponchos that had been propped up on sticks to dry overnight were now solid enough to stand on their own. Everyone spent a few minutes in front of the breakfast fire coaxing malleability back into their leather shoes. Every day since then, they'd seen sporadic snow flurries. Thin icicles were growing along the gunwales of the canoes, and the air had a sharp nip. The snow roused everyone's spirit. The crew agitated for a chance to take on a full blizzard, since it wasn't yet cold enough to be unbearable. Lewis wasn't as thrilled with the changing seasons, though not for reasons of personal discomfort. The crew was taking longer than ever to get moving in the morning. It was as if the cold had turned them into half-asleep bears, ready for several months of hibernation. And it was only October! At this rate they'd never get any paddling in by the time December rolled around.

In addition to the arrival of a new season that brought with it harsher, more dangerous weather, the crew was also adjusting to a reshuffling in the ranks. Back in Blind River, Father Loran made a permanent departure, ceding his spot to Sid Bardwell. The priest said he simply couldn't stay warm and maintain the energy to paddle all day long, and his back continued to bother him. Instead of paddling, Father Loran would travel with the liaison team and do advance work while continuing to perform masses for the crew and their audiences. Bardwell would join Fialko's canoe for the remainder of the trip. He'd finally gotten his wish. No more back-and-forth nonsense. He was a milieu, part of the red module, and could say good-bye to hotel beds and fast food.

The first week as a permanent crew member didn't go quite as smoothly as Bardwell had hoped. It was actually something of a living hell. Freezing cold every night, no sun to speak of, bland food for dinner, cornmeal in the morning—not his favorite breakfast to begin with, made that much worse when you had to eat it every day—and tempers always flaring. Hobart, Cox, and

Stillwagon always erred on the side of caution, wanting to avoid bad weather and hypothermia. Reid and Ken took the other side of the argument. They needed to keep moving, keep ahead of schedule, press forward. Bardwell thought Lewis might just send the crew out into a tornado, the way he talked. But for all the annoyances, Bardwell was happy to be experiencing hardships with the crew. Now he could join in their commiseration. He wasn't just watching the men go through terrible weather and frigid nights—he was part of it.

Last of all, the crew had said a final farewell to Canada. For the rest of their journey they'd be paddling American waterways. They exited Canada on October 18 at a minuscule town called DeTour Village. The customs office was in the living room of a private home, and the woman who checked their paperwork and welcomed them back to the United States was also the town's reporter. She took pictures of the canoes down by the water and interviewed a few of the crew members for a story before they set off onto Lake Huron. The Georgian Bay experiment was over.

It had been a successful one in many ways. The prolonged isolation from civilization had given the crew a deeper sense of connection with the original voyageurs. They had new experiences to share with people along their route. They'd also proved that modern men could survive on essentially the same rations the voyageurs would've had. Many of the crew members had lost weight over the three weeks they were in Georgian Bay. Others who had been skinny to start were gaining weight in muscle. Their various interdisciplinary projects were also moving forward. Water samples had been collected, maps drawn, and the official journal had grown by several thousand words.

But the time spent far from society had also revealed some defects in the group. Their language had grown more than a little salty out in the wilderness where no one was around to hear them. They'd have to tone it down now that they'd be traveling through populated regions again. More troubling than curses were the ever-deepening divisions. Fialko had hoped Georgian Bay would forge them into a true team in a way they hadn't yet become. Instead, the mistrust in leadership led to increased discord between the adults. Hobart and Cox were perpetually poised to go on the attack against the Lewis brothers. Fialko felt torn by the conflict. He respected everyone on the crew as individuals and disliked the amount of arguing that went on between them. They all had fair points to make, and he didn't envy Reid's position. There was no winning as leader of the expedition and its main media representative. Those two identities were too incompatible. Lewis was either trying to perform stunts that put the crew in harm's way to get a good photo, or he was being dictatorial with the crew's schedule and daily progress. In some ways, he seemed to be turning into the embodiment of La Salle: aloof, overly demanding, and unable to relate to his men. Fialko only hoped all the adults could come to some sort of truce. That said, Fialko sided with Hobart and Cox on one issue: it always made him nervous to be traveling based on a schedule rather than the elements. This was especially true now that they were paddling through minor snowstorms.

As the crew pulled up to shore at St. Ignace, the snow-bearing clouds were blown away and the sun shone down brightly once more. Fall hadn't quite given into winter yet. Maybe they'd have a few more warm days before they were stuck wearing wool long underwear and multiple layers of shirts.

Now that the flurries had abated, Fialko could see the people on shore. To his complete surprise, his fiancée, Linda, was standing among them, distinct with her long brown hair.

As soon as his canoe touched ground, he hurtled over the three men in front of him like a kid playing leapfrog and ran to her. The homesickness that had come on for the first time in Georgian Bay evaporated. Stress from the disagreements within the expedition vanished. With her, he didn't have to be Pierre Prudhomme, 17th-century armorer and wilderness survival expert. He could just be John.

Chapter Seven

TRAPPED AT DEATH'S DOOR

Michilimackinac, Lake Michigan
Late October 1681

La Salle wasn't the first European to reach the Mississippi, nor was he the first Frenchman to have contact with tribes along the Great Lakes region. There had been a European presence in North America for close to two hundred years by the time La Salle arrived. Yet all the discoveries of his predecessors had done little to fill in blank spaces on the map. There were plenty of unsolved mysteries and misconceptions about North America, caused in part by misfortunes such as the disastrous culmination of Louis Jolliet and Jacques Marquette's voyage. The two Frenchmen traveled together to discover a route from Lake Michigan to the Mississippi River in 1673 and continued on to Arkansas before turning back due to fears of meeting with Spanish colonists farther south. Jolliet, trained in cartography and geography, almost certainly made a map of their route. But when he returned to Quebec after parting ways with Marquette, his canoe capsized in the Sault Saint-Louis rapids just outside of Montreal. Three of the men traveling with him perished, and although Jolliet survived by clinging to some rocks until he was rescued, all of his notes were lost. He was forced to make his report on the journey down the Mississippi solely by memory.

Such gaps in the voyageurs' knowledge of North American geography—and with it, Native culture—were common. Though it was given the name "America" decades before La Salle's birth, the continent was still the "fourth part of the world," an unknown element.[1] In the 16th century, Europeans were at least somewhat familiar with Asia, Europe, and Africa, but the world beyond the Atlantic Ocean was a land populated by monsters and men with no heads. There was little reliable cartographical information for anything beyond the East Coast, and one misstep could mean death. Considering the thundering waters of Niagara Falls, who could predict that early explorers wouldn't encounter such fierce rapids as they paddled farther into the interior? None of them knew what they might encounter.

By the time La Salle arrived in what would later be known as the Midwest, he had to rely mainly on his own previous experiences and the information he was given by Native American guides. The latter could be a gamble, because La Salle and the other Frenchmen were hardly the most powerful players in the game of exploration. Native American tribes could and did exploit the voyageurs to their advantage, whether it meant trading for European weapons in wars against other tribes or directly involving the Europeans in Native disputes. Every bit of advice had to be placed in its proper context: La Salle was a foreigner traveling through occupied territory rife with political alliances and enmities about which he had little knowledge, and there was always the possibility that he was being manipulated.

Fortunately, the next section of La Salle's journey involved navigating a well-known strait in Lake Michigan. Less fortunate was the passage's notorious reputation for leading to the deaths of even the most experienced voyageurs. The passageway linking Lake Michigan with Green Bay was known as La Porte des Morts (Death's Door). All mariners treated it with caution. According to the legends of the local Potawatomi tribe, the name was derived from a battle between their warriors and the warriors of the invading Winnebago tribe. As the Potawatomi paddled along the strait, they were attacked from the cliffs of a nearby island, and many died in the rough waters.

Whether or not the legend held any truth,[2] La Salle was already intimately familiar with the dangers of Death's Door Passageway. During an earlier attempt at reaching the mouth of the Mississippi, La Salle's fleet of canoes was almost dashed against the rocky shore when a storm blew up while they were crossing the strait. And there was the matter of his ship, the *Griffon*, the first sailboat to ever travel across the Great Lakes. The ten-ton, forty-foot vessel was built to easily transport furs and carry supplies for La Salle and his men down the Mississippi River, but the boat had disappeared years prior, after its maiden voyage in 1679. He may well have wondered if the ship was wrecked in the shallows of Death's Door, but there was no way of knowing.

This time around, in October 1681, luck was with La Salle and his men. After a brief stop at the mission at Michilimackinac, the northern tip of modern-day Michigan, the men quickly made the crossing from Lake Michigan to Green Bay. By the beginning of November they were already approaching the Illinois

River, moving faster than the cold weather could freeze up the waterways.

Washington Island, Wisconsin
November 4, 1976

For two days the team had been confined to dry land by the howling wind that stirred the lake into a mass of hard-edged chop. They'd risen before dawn to prepare for the normal paddling routine. They'd organized their gear, broken down the camp, and packed the canoes. But instead of heading onto the lake to do battle with the foaming waves, they'd been told to rebuild the shelters. The water was too rough to paddle across.

The residents of Washington Island had been more than hospitable during the voyageurs' extended stay. The young men were welcomed into homes to watch the news and listen to radio reports of the presidential election. Everyone had submitted their absentee ballot for either Jimmy Carter or Gerald Ford weeks earlier. The team consensus seemed to be that Ford, the incumbent, would be re-elected. To their surprise, he was overthrown. Another new start for the United States.

One Washington Islander in particular had done everything he could to accommodate the crew. Thor Williamson, the community action program director, was a tough old marine who acted as the group's host while they were on the island and was determined to make their stay as enjoyable as possible. He drove down to the expedition's campsite each morning with a breakfast of steak, eggs, and donuts to get them started on the right foot. The hardy breakfasts were some consolation for not keeping to the schedule. At least Thor would be back the next day with more of his excellent food. He also gave them use of his Travelall utility truck to check out water conditions on the eastern shore of the island and he spread the word around the small Washington Island winter community that the northern side of the island was being visited by a crew of voyageurs. Meeting with townspeople was a kind of palliative. It helped prevent a lethal level of boredom while the crew waited to depart.

Originally, Lewis had planned for his team to stop at Washington Island for a night or two, perform their regular routine for the five hundred year-round inhabitants, then depart. The island was the perfect resting spot before making the treacherous journey across Death's Door Passage. The strait, which runs between the tip of Wisconsin and the Potawatomi Islands, had long held a degree of notoriety among locals. But Lewis was confident in everyone's ability to handle rough waters. At this point they'd canoed over nearly one thousand miles of lakes and rivers, surviving passage through locks, unpredictable weather on the Great Lakes, and the thousands of islands of Georgian Bay. Lewis was impatient to be on the way again. As much as flexibility was a necessity in this undertaking, he knew they'd likely encounter more bad weather and delays now that winter was approaching, and he hated to miss any of the performances he'd scheduled months earlier. But there were no scheduling solutions to bad weather.

Despite their relatively diminutive size compared to the oceans, the Great Lakes are among the most treacherous bodies of water on earth. Squalls blow up without warning, dark waters hide reefs, foggy nights send ships unfamiliar with the shoreline straight onto the rocks. Historian and mariner Mark Thompson estimated that as many as twenty-five thousand people have died in shipwrecks on the Great Lakes; between 1878 and 1897 alone, 5,999 shipwrecks were reported.[3] The Death's Door area is a particularly dangerous part of Lake Michigan. In one seven-day period in 1872, the insidious shoals sent eight schooners to the lake bottom. And if history had taught Great Lakes navigators anything, it was that November was the most wily and unpredictable of months.

Following on the heels of Halloween, strong winds nicknamed the Witch of November blow across the Great Lakes each year. The winds are caused primarily by low-pressure systems that sit implacably above the Great Lakes for weeks, pulling in cold Arctic air from the north and warmer air from the Gulf in the south. When the two fronts meet over the lakes, they can create horrific storms capable of producing hurricane-force winds. In 1913, a November squall-blizzard dubbed the "Freshwater Fury" killed more than 250 people, caused around $5 million in damage ($116 million in today's currency), and stranded or destroyed thirty-eight ships. Winds reached ninety miles per hour and produced waves more than thirty-five feet high.[4] The storm's intensity was unusual, but plenty of large storms battered the shores of the Great Lakes every year, especially in November. The Canadian vessel *Bannockbarn* was sunk in November 1902, the *Rouse Simmons* disappeared in 1912, and the *Daniel J. Morrell* was broken by a storm in 1966.

The years that followed the Freshwater Fury were spent developing better weather forecasting tools and more advanced preparedness systems. But that didn't stop another intense storm from killing twenty-nine men in November 1975, just one year before the La Salle reenactment expedition. The 729-foot ore ship *Edmund Fitzgerald* had been on a course for Cleveland when a powerful storm engulfed it on Lake Superior, leaving no trace of ship or crew. Despite an exhaustive investigation of the incident by the U.S. Coast Guard National Transportation Safety Board, no definitive reason was ever provided for the shipwreck. The twenty-nine men aboard the ship joined thousands of other mariners who have died on the Great Lakes. The incident was even marked by pop culture: Canadian folk singer Gordon Lightfoot released a song commemorating the tragedy in June 1976, just two months before the La Salle reenactors set off from the banks of Montreal. In the first verse of "Wreck of the Edmund Fitzgerald," Lightfoot introduced his listeners to the legendary ore ship and the storm that brought her down. "The lake, it is said, never gives up her dead / When the skies of November turn gloomy," went the lyrics.

On the morning of November 4, the third day of camping on Washington Island, Lewis, Hobart, and Fialko drove along the shore to scope out the wind and water conditions. If they left that day and paddled from the northern part of Washington Island down to a new campsite just six miles away on the southern shore of the island they'd be better positioned to cross Death's Door Passage the following day. It would mean another night on Washington Island but would still cut some of the distance off for the following day's paddle. From their perspective on shore, the lake looked as if it might be rough for a mile or so, but after that the water would be calm enough. Certainly nothing worse than what they'd experienced in the past. They decided to go for it. Having been trapped on shore for three days, it felt good to have a plan of action, to be doing something. The crew was cheered by the news as well. They'd been getting antsy to leave.

It was a later start than usual. The sun had been up for an hour when the canoes launched from Jackson Harbor at 7:45. Even with the warm daylight there was ice to chop away along the shoreline before they could get the boats in the water. Ice, at the beginning of November. Less than a week ago they'd celebrated Halloween on Big Summer Island; the name had seemed less than suitable considering the weather. They'd finally made the turn south around the west side of Michigan after spending a third of their journey traveling west, but several months of Midwestern winter lay ahead of them before they would reach the milder climate of the south. Already the water was a frigid thirty-nine degrees and ice formed rapidly on the canoes. Everyone was dressed in wool hats and mittens, but there was little they could do to protect their faces from the stinging spray. Luckily the wind was blowing from the northwest, so the paddlers would be sheltered by Washington Island as they made their way down its east side.

The boats glided onto the lake in splendid unison, as if they'd rehearsed the launch hundreds of times. And of course, they had—every day of paddling for the past three months had been a lesson. They were practically experts at this point. The cold wind nipped at any exposed patches of skin, and the choppy surf slapped the canoes as they slipped along. The day was overcast and the air cool, but nothing out of the ordinary. There was no reason to think the six-mile journey down the coast of Washington Island would take much longer than an hour.

But after less than a mile of paddling around the northern tip of the island and turning south to travel along the east coast, the wind shifted. It started to blow out of the northeast, forcing the rough waves straight into the canoes. In seemingly the blink of an eye, the waves had grown to five or six feet and were tossing the canoes around as if they were toys. The six teams were pushed apart by the waves, one taking off in the lead, the others scrambling around to move away from the breaking waves on a narrow strip of shoals to the east. The water was icy cold as it sloshed around their feet at the bottom of the canoes. Men in the middle of the canoes abandoned their paddles to start bailing.

Suddenly Ken shouted out to the others, "We need help! We're sinking!"

A first wave had hit his boat broadside, sending water swirling around the ankles of Ken, LeSieutre, Hess, and Fredenburg. Before they'd had the chance to react, a second breaker followed the watery trail laid by the first, effectively swamping the canoe. The edge of the boat was nearly level with the lake's surface, and some of their gear was now bobbing freely in the water. Only the tapered points on the bow and the stern poked out above the surface of the lake. Everyone sat in three feet of icy water with their feet hooked under the gunwales to keep themselves from floating away. For each scoop of icy water the men were able to bail out, another wave pushed it all back in. To make matters worse, Hess was wearing a heavy plaster cast on one leg to protect his foot, which he'd broken only a week earlier when he slipped on some rocks. He'd continued in the canoes because there hadn't been any upcoming portages planned, and paddling didn't require much lower body movement. But now the cast had suddenly become a liability. Leaning back as far as possible to hold his leg above the water, Hess considered what would happen if their canoe sank beneath him or if they capsized. The cast was already starting to feel heavy as water soaked into it. If he fell in, there was no way he'd be able to swim back up to the surface. The cast would sponge up the water and he'd plummet like a rock to the bottom.

For the most part, Hess hadn't doubted his decision to come on the journey. He loved being outside with a group of friends, camping and canoeing every day. But until this point, his life had never been on the line. He'd had blisters and aches like everyone else, and there had been that minor eye injury after a piece of tinder flew into his face, and the stress fracture in his foot was a bit of a nuisance—not to mention it cemented his reputation for being accident prone—but nothing *serious* had happened. Nothing that might prevent him from returning home to a normal 20th-century life at the end of the expedition. Now he was contemplating his imminent mortality, in the form of drowning or hypothermia. Neither was very appealing.

"Hey! We're sinking!" Ken bellowed into the wind again, trying to get the attention of the other paddlers. Reid, redirecting his canoe to their assistance, instructed Kulick to start unlashing equipment from their boat in case they needed to jettison things to make room for more men if Ken's boat capsized. As Kulick was untying gear, DiFulvio in the rear maneuvered the canoe around to the left side of Ken's boat while Hobart's canoe pulled up on the right. Fialko's took the rear position while Stillwagon's raced ahead to shore to get a fire started.

"Yellow pants keeping you dry?" Cox joked as the four canoes inched toward shore, referring to the foul-weather gear some of the men wore under their outfits on rough weather days.

The four men in the submerged boat could hardly spare the energy to laugh. They continued bailing and paddling with grim determination. Hess lay almost flat on his back with his cast straight up in the air like a flag. It would've been comedic if the situation weren't so grave. The cold water soaked into their wool clothes and froze their limbs. If the men weren't warmed quickly, the first symptoms of hypothermia would set in. Once that happened, it would be much harder to get everyone safely to shore.

As the canoes made their way back to Washington Island, Ken started cracking jokes, trying to distract his crew from their shivering limbs and chattering teeth. His instincts kicked in as tension in the boat rose. Everyone needed a diversion from the miserable cold and the terrifying prospect of capsizing in the rough surf and freezing to death. As a trained actor, he knew he could provide that distraction, telling one joke after another.

After a brief but nerve-wracking struggle, the convoy of canoes made it to land, only a mile or two south of the point where they'd launched less than an hour ago. The waterlogged canoe bottomed out early because it had sunk so low and had to be dragged up to shore by a number of men. Hess was assisted out of the boat and hobbled up to land. His cast was probably ruined, but at least he wasn't at the bottom of the lake. Everyone who wasn't drenched and frozen rushed off to cut wood for the fires. For the first time since they'd started their journey, the fire was lit with matches from an emergency pouch. It was too risky to waste any time on authenticity now. Ken, Hess, Fredenburg, and LeSieutre stripped out of their heavy wool and linen clothes, peeling off each layer with trembling, numb fingers. Their skin was angry crimson red up to their chests, but none of them looked as if he had any frostbite. Naked but for their underwear, the men wrapped up in warm, dry blankets and huddled close to the fire. Marc Lieberman dug around his pack looking for a small bottle. Though they'd been given plenty of bottles of alcohol, he knew the momentary warmth from liquor would do more harm than good. Instead, he found a bottle of maple syrup and passed it around for everyone to take a sip. The liquid was like an elixir. Normally used with their break-fast foods, maple syrup (and other sugary liquids) could be a useful preventative against severe hypothermia. The sugars were a quick, easily digestible source of fuel that provided the body with a small boost of warmth. It wasn't until the crew had caught their breath and prepared to talk about their harrowing trip back to shore that someone realized there were only five canoes on the beach. The only canoe without an adult paddler had never returned to land.

⚓︎

Clif Wilson was having a good day. They were back out in their boats after a three-day hiatus, and he and his crew members had found their rhythm. Even the cold air and icy water couldn't bring down his mood. His curly blond hair was tucked under a wool toque, his fingers were warm beneath the double layer of mittens, and his toes were dry, despite the couple of inches of water that sloshed in the bottom of the boat, because he was still wearing the rubber waders he used for launching and landing the canoe. For once his boat was leading the pack, something that happened rarely. Most of the time they were lagging behind and causing delays for everyone else. He hated feeling as if the men in his boat weren't pulling their weight. As the avant, the man at the front of the canoe, Wilson watched for obstacles, set the paddling rhythm, and jumped in first upon landing. He felt no need to make apologies for his performance. It was the craziest position of the four. Always getting splashed by waves and keeping everyone else dry, always on the lookout for driftwood or dangerous rocks ahead. He felt he was living up to his duties. When there was a finger to point, he pointed it in another direction. He liked shouting at other people, telling them what to do and where they went wrong. He'd never gelled with the others in his canoe, and that only made their situation harder. Maybe that lack of camaraderie was why they never seemed to be in-sync on the water. But not today. Today their paddles cut such a steady path through the choppy water that they'd soon outpaced the other five canoes.

"Inside or outside?" Wilson shouted back to Bill Watts as they approached Hog Island, a tiny, rocky islet off to the east of Washington Island. As the gouvernail, Watts steered the canoe and made all decisions regarding obstacles and where they would land. They'd spoken about Hog Island earlier in the day with the rest of the group before heading out to the water. Its rocky shore made landing impossible, and the island itself didn't have much room for them—it was maybe one hundred yards across and covered in trees. At the morning debrief before they launched, Hobart told them they'd have to go inside the island or around it depending on the direction of the wind and waves. At this point, with no other boat ahead of them to advise any differently, it seemed like there would be more wind outside the island, but the waves might be smaller.

"We'll go outside," Watts said, using his paddle to steer through the water as the other three teenagers continued stroking forward. There was no second-guessing his decision. Watts had been chosen for the position for a reason. He was responsible and had plenty of wilderness experience as an Eagle Scout.

In less than five minutes, however, it became apparent that going around Hog Island had put the canoe at the mercy of strong waves. Whenever the weather was bad and the surf was strong, Wilson thought of the waves as having teeth—sharp teeth attached to powerful jaws that tugged at the boat and threatened to pull it under. Today the waves bit down on the canoe almost the instant they reached the far side of Hog Island, sending a flood of icy water into the boat.

"The others aren't following us," Watts said after a glance behind them. "They're heading back to shore. We need to turn around."

Just as the men maneuvered their paddles to turn the canoe around, a wave came pouring over the side on top of them. Jorge Garcia barely had time to pick up the bailer and start emptying the boat when a second wave doused them, pouring an even greater volume of water into the vessel. Before anyone could react or balk at how waterlogged their handmade breeches and woolen mittens were becoming, the boat flipped over.

Silence.

The first thing Wilson noticed after being fully submerged was the silence. The whistling wind was gone. No more sounds of water smacking the fiberglass hulls of the canoe, none of the soft vibrations of the paddles pulling through water. Along with the silence was the intense cold. The cold was so strong it was almost a sense of its own, like taste or smell. It burned and ached and would've made him gasp out in shock if he hadn't been trained to stifle the torso response that causes the body to increase oxygen intake when confronted with an abrupt drop in temperature. Not inhaling kept him from drowning, but his training had also taught him that they had only ten to fifteen minutes to get out of the water before their bodies started shutting down from hypothermia. If anyone passed out, he could say good-bye to any chance of survival. Randy Foster and Bill Watts were both muscular and stockier than Wilson and Garcia, but none of them could rely very long on extra body fat to keep them warm. Hundreds of miles of paddling and a rudimentary diet had taken care of most of their excess weight.

Time moved in strange bursts underwater, and in the instant after he moved past the miserable pain of the cold, Wilson realized he was still wearing his waders and they were filling with water, dragging him down to the bottom. He surfaced into the world of noise and oxygen and shouted to the others that he was sinking with the weight of the waders. Watts and Garcia came over to brace him as he kicked them off, his movements hindered by his bulky, heavy clothing and the numbness spreading across his body. After a brief struggle, he broke free of the rubber boots. All four checked with one another one more time to make sure they were all still there. They were shivering in the icy water, but so far everyone had managed to avoid drowning.

We're going to die, Wilson thought. He felt no panic, just resignation. Maybe his emotions were numbed by the cold like the rest of his body. *We're going to die, but we're not dead yet.* That was something, at least. His next thought was for the powdered hot cocoa packets he'd stashed away in his canvas sack, a contraband item. Although chocolate beverages were already popular in France by the time La Salle was tramping through the New World in the

1670s, his voyageurs wouldn't have had access to such luxuries while in the wild; and pretty much anything that the voyageurs couldn't have, the reenactors couldn't have. Lewis's rules. Not that they were always followed. And Wilson had really been looking forward to a clandestine mug of hot cocoa now that the weather was getting colder. So much for that. Ironically, he could've used it more than ever now that the first stages of hypothermia were setting in. As long as they were still conscious and able to swallow, hypothermia victims were supposed to be given warm, sugary drinks to help their bodies compensate for all the energy lost in staying warm.

"We need to cut all the gear away from the canoe," Watts instructed over the sound of the waves. Only a few minutes had passed, but with each minute they stayed in the water, their body temperatures would drop lower. Each teenager reached under the boat with the small knives they carried to cut away the gear that had been strapped down, releasing cast-iron cooking pots and food supplies and clothes, all the belongings they'd managed to keep with them until this point. Next, everyone linked hands over the boat, two on each side, and tried to keep their heads above the waves that kept breaking over them.

"Hey, if we wait till we're in between the waves, I can touch bottom without going under," Watts said. "Let's try to walk toward land. We'll use to boat to help us."

They waddled slowly through the waves, waiting for each trough so that they could bounce back up with the buoyant canoe. Every time a wave crashed over their heads, each person shouted out that he was still all right, still moving forward. The repeated dunking made them even colder, the heat leaching from their skulls. The body's initial response to submersion in freezing water is a constriction of surface blood vessels and an increased blood pressure and heart rate. The pulse, blood pressure, and respiration all decrease. After ten minutes or so, muscle function is limited and the body's core temperature drops. This is followed by gradual loss of mental abilities and, eventually, if the temperature falls low enough, unconsciousness.

By some stroke of luck, the young men had capsized only two hundred yards from shore. Had they been much farther from land, someone would've likely become unconscious from hypothermia before they reached solid ground. As it was, they struggled to keep moving. After a few agonizingly long minutes, they were submerged only up to their chests, then their waists. While they walked, they argued about what to do with the canoe, whether they should try to pull it in with them or let it go. The canoes were more than just the group's mode of transportation—they were works of art, constructed over the course of hundreds of hours using historical carpentry techniques. They were beautiful vessels, sleek and fast, and they'd carried the team all the way from Montreal. Releasing the canoe felt like betraying it, leaving it to the whim of the waves, but pulling it up could be dangerous since the shoreline was rocky and the surf was so rough. Plus, they weren't in any condition to lug the heavy vessel up safely. Even walking through the cold water required enormous exertion.

Eventually they decided to let the boat go after cutting away a waterproof bag that had been stowed in the bow. Garcia was slurring his words as they reached shore, barely able to move. He seemed to pull his limbs through the remaining inches of water with heavy, clumsy movements, and he acted confused, as if he were unable to comprehend what had happened. Watts was already trying to take the blame for the accident, the horror of the capsizing clear on his face. For once, Wilson had no desire to berate or lay blame on anyone's head. He quickly tried to reassure Watts that it wasn't his fault, that everything had turned out all right. Wilson and Foster, who were shivering but seemed less affected by hypothermia than the other two, half-carried Garcia up to the dry part of the shore, then helped to strip Watts and Garcia down to their underwear. Inside the waterproof bag were two sleeping bags and an emergency fire-starter kit with matches, which were never used on a daily basis. Flint would've been more useful after the capsizing, since the matches and tinder were soaked. At least the sleeping bags were dry. Wilson and Foster wrapped Watts and Garcia in the first one, their skin icy to the touch. Next, they stripped down to bare skin and wrapped themselves in the second sleeping bag, huddling closely together, shaking and numb.

After a few minutes of warming up, Foster volunteered to head to the opposite side of the tiny island to look for the rest of the crew. He was 195 pounds and mostly muscle and hadn't felt the effects of hypothermia nearly as severely as the others. Still shivering, he hurried through the trees and over the rocks to the other end of Hog Island. He peered out at the water and the distant shore of Washington Island. Nothing but white caps and steel gray water. All the other boats were gone. *They're all dead,* he thought in shock. *We had a hard time; we swamped. What about them?* The capsizing hadn't taken that long, so the boats couldn't have gone very far, but he saw no trace of them. He ran back to the others to get warm again and tell them what he'd seen.

Their canoe gone, unable to build a fire for themselves, the four could do nothing but pray the others hadn't capsized as well and that help was on the way in one form or another. But even in the uncertainty of what would happen next, even through the painful cold that bit into his limbs, into his bones, Wilson noticed a momentary burst of ecstasy at having survived a capsizing and a swim through thirty-nine-degree water. He was eighteen, he had traveled a thousand miles in a canoe that he helped build, and he could now say he'd bested drowning and, as long as someone came and built a fire for them within the next couple of hours, he'd beaten hypothermia, too. *This*, he thought, *is what it's like to be a god.*

❧

On Washington Island, confusion reigned. When they'd first landed, Lewis had walked to the nearest available phone to call Thor, their host, who was waiting with the liaison team at the site on the southern part of the island where the crew had planned to land. Now, faced with the second crisis of the morning, Lewis felt the beginnings of real panic. He asked the liaison team to reach out to the Coast Guard to see if there were any boats patrolling the area that could be sent to search for the four teenagers. When the word came back that the Coast Guard had already pulled all their boats out of the water for the winter and couldn't launch them again, Lewis and the crew's photographer, Bart Dean, went looking for someone who owned a boat and could give them a ride. They eventually found a skipper who offered his twenty-five-foot cabin cruiser as a search-and-rescue vessel.

From shore the lake looked deceptively calm. White caps were clearly visible, but otherwise the violence of the wind seemed to have abated. This illusion was quickly washed away as the cabin cruiser carrying Lewis and Dean left shore and began bouncing up and down on ten-foot waves. The boat's depth finder acted as if it were malfunctioning, giving a reading of ninety feet one minute, then five feet the next. The owner of the boat was pale with fear. He admitted he'd never been out in such rough water. There was no pattern to the chop, making the waves impossible to navigate.

"The bottom is real rocky here," the boat owner told Lewis and Dean when they asked about the depth finder. All three men were holding on for dear life, being tossed around the boat with each pounding wave. "Some of the rocks are the size of houses, they're so huge."

Almost as soon as the words left his mouth, a trough between two waves cut an opening in the lake to reveal an enormous rock that resembled the jagged pyramid tip of the Chrysler building in New York City. The skipper managed to keep the powerboat from crashing down on the boulder, but he was severely shaken.

"We're going in," he said over Lewis and Dean's protests. "There's no way we'll make Hog Island—we'll be lucky just to get back to shore alive."

The skipper turned the boat around, waves crashing over the stern and nearly swamping the small watercraft. As Lewis and Dean peered back at Hog Island, knuckles white from the force of their grip on the boat's rails, they noticed a helicopter flying along the coast. Using the powerboat's radio, Lewis hailed the Coast Guard, asking if they had decided to send it out to rescue the missing men. The Coast Guard officer responded in the negative, saying it was a Green Bay TV station, and they'd just reported seeing a smashed canoe drifting south of Hog Island. Lewis felt his heart sink. He asked the Coast Guard to radio the helicopter's pilot and request that they make a pass over Hog Island. Moments later the officer was back on the radio. The helicopter pilot had reported that the island appeared deserted.

Oh my God, Lewis thought in despair. *They've drowned. Four of my boys have drowned, and this is my fault.*

❦

Almost as soon as they'd realized a canoe was missing, John Fialko and the young men in his boat (Sid Bardwell, Steve Marr, and Doug Sohn) had hurried to their canoe to start the search. The missing canoe was the other half of their module, after all. Fialko was the only adult crew member between the two boats, and he felt a certain amount of responsibility for the teens. The paddlers on the two boats were supposed to look out for one another, so it only made sense that they be the first ones back on the water.

Hog Island, the spit of land the canoes had been closest to when they got separated, was a little less than a mile from the eastern shore of Washington Island, and it was the last place anyone had seen the teenagers. It seemed like the logical place to start looking. It wasn't long before Fialko's canoe was approaching the island, battling wind and waves, the surf crashing on the shallow shoals to the north. Every man scanned the island, trying to find some sign that the missing teenagers had landed there. But despite its size—probably no more than one hundred yards in any direction—the island was covered in a thick, dead jungle, the stubby trees packed so densely together that it was impossible to tell what might be hiding at the interior. Fialko directed the canoe to the southern tip of Hog Island in search of a protected cove, something that might keep them out of the waves and allow them to land. But there was nowhere safe, and they'd seen nothing of the men. Just as the boat was about to turn back, they caught sight of a canoe banging against the rocks and the crew huddled in sleeping bags on shore.

"We capsized, but we're all right. Don't try to land," Bill Watts yelled. His voice was anguished, filled with all the things that were impossible to convey with words: terror at what had happened, joy at the sight of the men, remorse and guilt for being the driver of the capsized vessel. The men in the canoe felt a similar combination of emotions, but above all else was relief. They hadn't lost anyone. But there wasn't time to allow any celebration just yet—they still needed to get the men back to the mainland.

Ignoring Watts's warning, Fialko steered the canoe around to the side of the island and tried to find a spot between the jutting rocks to land. A low promontory formed a sort of slip that the canoe could just squeeze into, and Fialko used it as a precarious landing spot while Doug Sohn jumped out and ran to his freezing crew members. After just a few minutes he came back with the report that everyone was all right, but they needed the emergency kit with matches and flares and more gear to get warm. As Sohn ran back and forth between the men and the canoe, the three remaining paddlers fought the waves to keep the canoe from being battered to kindling. Wave after wave poured into the boat and it was all Marr could do to bail out the water as fast as it came in.

But Fialko was more concerned for the boys on shore than he was with the state of his boat. He ordered Bardwell to head in and help Sohn get a fire going, then bring back whoever seemed to be in the worst shape. Bardwell shot out, forcing his way through the dense foliage and gathering sticks for a fire as he went along. There wasn't much ground to cover to reach the capsized crewmen, but the foliage was so thick on the island that it was impossible to follow the same path twice, and he was constantly crashing through the bracken. He found the four young men in two sleeping bags, all of them almost naked, their hair still wet. Bardwell stacked the lumber in a pile to start a fire, but the matches from his boat's emergency pack were wet. He and Sohn decided that the next best option was to use one of the flares to get the fire going, and soon a small pile of sticks was crackling, shedding heat on the grateful, frozen survivors of the capsizing. It was obvious that Garcia was coldest of all the men, so Bardwell bundled him up and led him out to Fialko's canoe. As soon as he saw the teenager, Fialko knew he was in no state to be carried back to Washington Island in a canoe half-full of icy water. He told Bardwell to keep Garcia by the fire and get him warmer and send along whoever seemed least affected instead. Randy Foster soon appeared and took Bardwell's spot in the boat. The canoe shoved away from the island, leaving Bardwell on shore with the others so that he could make sure they got as warm as possible and carry the gear they'd managed to salvage from the wreck to the shoreline.

All the while, Bardwell's mind hovered somewhere between terror and exhilaration. The adrenaline rush was like nothing he'd ever known before. Instead of panicking or feeling overwhelmed, he moved from one task to another quickly and efficiently, knowing that the lives of three other men depended on him and his ability to function. There was no time to question what might happen next or what might go wrong. He simply had to act and solve each problem that arose until everyone was finally safe.

Back on shore, the men waited impatiently to catch sight of Fialko's canoe. They passed around a pair of binoculars, hoping for a glimpse of the canoe or the missing men, but were unable to distinguish much of anything apart from the white-capped waves and the rough shoreline of Hog Island. After some time, one of the men finally sighted an overturned canoe floating away to the south and Fialko's canoe coming back. The sight of it was enough to spur them to action. If any of the teenagers were in the water, they'd need more than one boat to carry them back to shore. Dick Stillwagon and Terry Cox immediately decided they'd be far more useful on the water than staying on land, even if it meant putting more men at risk of capsizing. They put two more crews together and unloaded half the gear in the canoes they'd be taking so that there would be room for any extra men. Then it was back out into the gale to bring back the men on Hog Island.

As soon as Cox got into a canoe to help with the rescue mission, he realized he'd left his mittens on shore. His hands were already hardening up in the frigid wind. It wasn't that he minded the discomfort. Even before coming on the expedition, he'd been familiar with pain. It was a requirement for gymnasts. Training your body to do things it wouldn't normally do was by no means a painless process. He didn't like the cold weather and the effects it had on his body, but he could deal with it. He just couldn't believe he'd forgotten something so essential after three months of living as a voyageur.

Then again, everyone had been a little addled by the morning's events. Ken, wearing nothing but his soaking underwear and a blanket, had to be held back because he was so desperate to get back in a canoe and help the four teens who were still out on the water. His reaction could be chalked up to hypothermia, which sometimes robbed people of their senses to the point that they resist aid even when they're barely able to move. Or it could be something more inherent in his personality, the urge to help others no matter the cost to himself. Whatever the case, there was no way he could withstand the conditions on the water again after the soaking he and the other men in his canoe had received.

For his part, Cox was frightened but invigorated now that they had something to do. The waiting and not knowing had been far worse than the painful cold of being back on the water. It felt like every cell in his body had been set to maximum efficiency. All his senses were alive to the slightest change in the landscape. It was something between acute terror and crystalline lucidity. He would be a perfect machine until everyone was safe on land.

The wind was blowing thirty miles per hour now, up a bit from earlier in the morning. The waves were just as nasty as they had been half an hour ago when the five canoes came off the water. Before long, the two boats of paddlers could see that Fialko's boat was carrying a new passenger: Randy Foster, one of the missing teens. When the three boats approached one another, Fialko told them that everyone else was still on Hog Island. He didn't take the time to fill in the details; the water was too rough to spend much time talking. But even without all the details, the sense of relief that came with knowing the men were alive was enormous. None had drowned or been injured. Still, they did need fairly immediate assistance to prevent severe hypothermia from setting in. It was no time to feel complacent or victorious, not until everyone had been warmed up and transported back to the campsite.

Fialko's canoe continued on to Washington Island while the two other rescue vessels skirted the rocky shoreline, fighting against the waves to keep the canoes from being smashed on the jagged rocks. It was a terrible place for the fragile boats. When they reached Hog Island, Cox and the men in his vessel hung back about a hundred yards, watching while Stillwagon's men brought their canoe as close to shore as possible without causing any damage. There they waited for what felt like an eternity for the young men to arrive. Finally, Garcia emerged from the island, supported by Bardwell and Wilson. He was bundled in a sleeping bag and quickly ushered into Stillwagon's boat. Cox's heart surged. They were all going to survive. Cox's canoe took the place of Stillwagon's as the latter began paddling back to Washington Island, then Wilson hopped into Cox's boat and they too took off. Fialko's boat was already on its way back to retrieve the last of the stranded men, Watts and Bardwell, as well as all the gear the men had managed to salvage from their capsized canoe.

Cox tried to ignore the ache in his frozen hands as he paddled, listening to Wilson's version of what had happened. The teenager was happy to be alive, but also in shock, almost on the verge of tears. Whatever bliss he'd felt with the realization that he was going to survive the experience was now replaced by terror at how close they'd come to dying. "I've never been so scared in my life," he told everyone.

Cox and Wilson had started off the expedition as intractable adversaries. They probably had the worst relationship of any two on the team. Both were given to yelling, and Wilson's participation in the expedition had been questioned more than once by the adults. He was loud and bossy and had a temper. But Cox could outyell him and was unafraid of talking him down. Slowly, Wilson improved on his ability to work with the others in his boat, and Cox came to respect him for his hard work. They moved from dislike to begrudging respect to friendship. Though Cox had never doubted Wilson's stamina, he now had a new appreciation for the teen's ability to face adversity and overcome it with relish. Cox hoped like hell he'd never have to face such odds. What would his wife, Pam, say when he related the day's events? She'd been nothing but supportive since he'd convinced her of how much he wanted to participate in the expedition. But he'd never put himself in such risky situations before, never had to consider what might happen to her if he got injured, or worse. And now, four young men had barely escaped drowning and hypothermia.

Listening to the way the four teens had come together to survive, Cox felt immense pride in his team. He realized that in life-or-death situations, he could trust any one of the men to have his back.

The rest of the morning and early afternoon passed quickly. Foster, Wilson, Garcia, and Watts were reheated by a roaring fire and given large bowls of oatmeal to help warm up. When Lewis came back from the marina, tortured by the report of the wrecked canoe and the ensuing worst-case scenarios running through his mind, he was momentarily overcome when he saw that all the young men were alive. It was impossible to describe the immensity of his relief. If they hadn't survived, if anyone had been seriously injured or died, he would've been responsible. He had brought them here, put them through this type of weather, and seeing them now was staggering. It was joy and relief and pride—they'd done everything they'd been trained to do in just such a situation. Never before had their two years of training seemed more valuable. Their cold-water survival skills and capsize drills had both played a role in this horrible morning, and those lessons were the difference between living and dying. Once he'd ascertained that everyone was well and truly unharmed, if a little shaken, he set off to activate the phone chain that would let all the parents know the outcome of their accident.

Wilson and Garcia were interviewed by the local Channel 5 news station, hunched around the fire, cheeks finally regaining some color after their frigid swim earlier in the morning. They'd already dubbed themselves the "November Swimmers." Some of the adults speculated as to whether they might make national news because of the event, trying to put an optimistic spin on what had nearly been a tragedy. Publicity was hard to come by, and this capsizing could be proof of how well prepared they all were. The teenagers clearly thrived despite the trials they faced.

Of the four young men who'd been in the overturned canoe, Watts remained the most deeply upset by the accident. He'd been crying when his rescue canoe landed on Washington Island. No matter what anyone told him, he couldn't help feeling responsible for the accident.

"We got away from the group, which we shouldn't have done, stop," he said when the group held an official meeting away from the press and the public to discuss the capsizing. It had been his decision to paddle outside of Hog Island, and if he hadn't made such a terrible call, none of it would've happened. No matter what people told him about how well he'd done, he couldn't help feeling accountable for all the destruction the capsizing had caused: the canoe, which had been retrieved a few miles down the southern shore of Washington Island, was no longer seaworthy. There was a hole punched in one side, the bow was in shreds, a gunwale cap was torn off, and much of the lashing was gone. Ralph Frese, the blacksmith and canoeist back in Chicago who had helped design the boats, could help them fix it without too much trouble. But it would have to be driven down to Illinois. They'd be short a canoe for at least a week. Then there was the matter of all the gear they'd lost: two sleeping bags, a Dutch oven, a frying pan, a wooden mug, a copper mug, a three-gallon water bag, four pairs of mittens, fifty-five feet of rope, a pair of leggings, a pair of moccasins, a three-and-a-half-quart pot, and the handmade musket Watts had forged and welded with Fialko's assistance. Watts loved that musket. It was unique in the world since he'd made it, and now it was lost to the bottom of Lake Michigan.

Wilson, Garcia, and Foster were all in relatively good spirits after being warmed and fed. No one really wanted to rehash what had happened or dwell on the near miss. At one point, Foster, sitting alone, said to no one in particular, "That's enough thinking about death. I'm going to brush my hair." The entire crew felt good enough in the wake of the disaster that they decided to go forward with the show they'd planned for Washington Island students that evening. There were only a hundred students in the entire school system, but the crowd's enthusiasm matched that of a much larger audience.

That night the crew were treated to a fish boil by the residents of the island. Their hosts sold 115 tickets for the dinner at $3.50 each and donated all the proceeds to the expedition. To the crew the buttery fish, potatoes, onions, and slaw tasted like a gourmet meal by a Michelin-starred chef. Afterward the men tromped back to their camp to discuss what would happen next. Several people would have to take the battered canoe back to Chicago for repairs, a nearly three-hundred-mile drive that might take five or six hours depending on the traffic. Fialko immediately stepped forward since he was in charge of canoe maintenance, and Keith Gorse volunteered to accompany him even though it might mean missing several days of paddling. Everyone else would continue on the same schedule as before, just as soon as the weather broke. Until then they'd have to rely on the hospitality of the Washington Islanders just a little bit longer.

For three more days the crew waited for the strong winds and bad weather to break. Since they were falling behind on their presentation schedule, they took a ferry to Bailey's Harbor to perform their show at City Hall. The town was on the other side of Death's Door Passage, and the men marveled at the size of the waves slamming into the boat's hull. Those were waves they might've faced in their canoes if not for the perilous lesson they'd learned on the water days earlier. Every car on the ferry was coated in ice. During the performance at Bailey's Harbor the power cut out halfway through, and several people in the audience brought candles up to the foot of the stage, leaving the men to perform in the eerie flickering glow of candlelight. It created the perfect ambience, as if they really were apparitions from centuries earlier. The next day they were ferried back to Washington Island to do more sitting and waiting. The water was still too rough to make a safe crossing.

On November 8, more than a week after they'd first arrived, the wind finally died. Five canoes pushed off from the south shore of Washington Island to cross the treacherous strait. After thirty-five minutes of dogged paddling they reached their destination. Behind them, jagged waves were building over the shoals of Death's Door

Passage. They'd survived their experience going through one of the most dangerous spots on Lake Michigan, but only just. As one expert says of outdoor survival, "One of the things that kills us in the wilderness, in nature, is that we just don't understand the forces we engage. We don't understand the energy because we no longer have to live with it."[5] These modern voyageurs did have to live with it—they'd lived with nature's energy every day since August. Three months of constant practice had been enough for them to survive when the worst happened, but it hadn't been enough to keep them from avoiding disaster altogether. And as the air and water temperatures continued to decrease, the choices that meant the difference between a near miss and death would become less and less discernible.

Chapter Eight

"The Beginning of
Our Hardships"

Illinois Territory
December 1681

The harsh winters of New France came as something of a surprise to the Frenchmen who were accustomed to the weather patterns of their homeland. The Jesuit priests were among the first to travel into new regions of North America and they described their experiences of winter in much the same way they described other hazards: it was a matter of surviving the worst. One priest wrote of temperatures so cold they caused a tree to split in the woods and "make a noise like that of firearms."[1] Another wrote, "There are but few of us who do not bear marks of the weather, and one of the sailors has lost both his ears."[2]

With more than a decade of experience in North American winters under his belt, La Salle knew what to expect. He and his men learned to walk in snowshoes and abandoned their European style of dressing for the warmer gear worn by Native Americans. They wore several pairs of leather moccasins on their feet. Leather wraps called "mitasses" extended from their ankles up to their knees and were tied with laces to keep their legs warm and prevent their pants from getting snagged on briars. On their heads they wore toques, knitted wool hats made in bright colors that corresponded to different parts of the colony: those from Quebec wore blue, while men from Montreal preferred red.[3] Some men wore "Indian sunglasses" made of slitted pieces of wood, though La Salle always refused to wear the goggles and often wound up with snow blindness as a result.[4] The painful condition, known in the medical community as photokeratitis, is caused by an overexposure to ultraviolet rays—like a bad sunburn affecting the cornea and conjunctiva.

In addition to snow blindness, La Salle and his men faced starvation and frostbite each winter. On an earlier unsuccessful expedition in early 1681, La Salle and his troop returned to Fort Saint Joseph from a trek into the Illinois territory with cracked, bleeding lips and patches of skin on their faces that had turned black with frostbite. They had battled slushy terrain and thin ice on a jaunt down the Kankakee River, which the Native Americans called "a slow river flowing in a big swamp."[5] Suffice it to say, winter could pose a serious obstacle to an expedition down the Mississippi.

Sure enough, the rivers were freezing by the time La Salle reached Fort Saint Joseph in December 1681. It didn't help that five men from his crew, including a valued interpreter, had deserted the expedition "because they feared the hardships of the voyage," said Abbé Claude Bernou.[6] There was nothing La Salle could do to bring them back at this point. The best option was to keep moving forward with his remaining men and his Native American allies. The group made its way across the frozen landscape, trading their canoes for sleds when the Illinois River froze solid. The men pulled these sleds like oxen, wearing harnesses wrapped around their chests. It was backbreaking work, but at least they'd come prepared: they were well supplied with provisions and soon they'd be arriving at the Mississippi. The end was almost in sight.

<hr/>

Lake Forest, Illinois
November 29, 1976

Gary Braun, alias Jean du Lignon, crawled out of his shelter and was greeted by the frigid embrace of the air. Another freezing morning. The tents might not smell particularly good after a night of sleeping—a mixture of smokiness from the campfires and farts from the beans they all ate—but at least they were warm. As cook for his module, Braun had to be out of bed with breakfast ready before the group departed. Getting up was more of a challenge now that winter had set in. Both Braun and the fire starter, Chuck Campbell (a name no one but reporters used anymore; everyone on the crew just called him Roadkill or RK for short), wriggled out of their sleeping bags and into a damp layer of clothing, then set to building a fire and cooking the food as soon as they heard Lewis's wake-up call. Sometimes if RK wasn't able to get the fire started right away, he'd head over to Sam Hess and ask for a couple of coals from his module's fire. The method didn't matter to Braun, so long as the result was burning hot and steady so that he could get to work.

Being cook had its ups and downs. It was fun to experiment with recipes, and he could compare his results with his good friend Mark Fredenburg, who was cook for another module. Braun learned to make pancakes over an open fire and improvised new recipes whenever someone donated fresh fruit and vegetables or meat to supplement the crew's regular supply of flour, oats, beans, peas, and cornmeal. He came up with dishes such as apple cobbler and cheesesteaks with fried potatoes. But the job had its own set of challenges as well. He'd burned his hand on the Dutch oven while making sagamite, a thick corn porridge, and he always had to be up first thing in the morning. There was also the stress of preparing something that the six other men in his group would want to eat. He couldn't do much to make the peas and beans they ate each night for dinner in Georgian Bay more appetizing, and a good breakfast was dependent on good ingredients from the liaison team or generous communities. Most of the time they just had plain old oatmeal or cornmeal, both cooked with water and maybe a little sugar or raisins. Personally, he couldn't stomach oatmeal. Maybe it was the texture. He'd cook it for everyone else, but he always stuck to bannock on oatmeal mornings.

Breakfast was normally a fast affair, and today the crew had ten miles to cover to get from Waukegan to Lake Forest. The temperature was a good motivator for moving quickly onto and off of the lake: only seven degrees and a windchill of minus twenty-three. Braun was the avant for his canoe, sitting in front of Marc Lieberman and Dick Stillwagon. He was by far the shortest of the three—both Lieberman and Stillwagon were more than six feet tall—but that didn't stop him from being an effective wave blocker when the boat was pushing through chop. It was the catch-22 of being a bowman. All the avants had to be shorter or slighter than the other men in their boat to balance out the canoe, but their smaller stature also made them more susceptible to getting cold, and the avants usually got wetter than everyone else because of their position in the boat. Waves crashed over the bow or spray blew on them, and if they miraculously managed to stay dry all day, that would end when they jumped out of the canoe during landings. Getting doused hadn't been a problem when the sun was out and the temperature was above seventy. Annoying, but harmless. Now it was dangerous. No one wanted a repeat of the incident at Washington Island. The water had only gotten colder since then.

Curtains of steam rose from the lake as if the water were boiling as the crew set out for the day. The transfer of energy occurring between water and air was, in a sense, similar to a pot heating on a stove. At thirty-eight degrees, the surface of the lake was balmy compared to the air above it. The water turned into vapor in the cold air, resulting in steam fog. Clouds curled off the tops of waves like phantoms trailing their ragged cloaks across the smooth surface of the water. It was an eerie phenomenon and made it that much more difficult for the avants to keep an eye on the other canoes and any debris in the water ahead. And now there were more potential hazards than ever.

A lake in the process of freezing poses far more challenges than a warm one, and it comes with its own sets of rules to obey. On top of storms that can roar in without warning, there are snow squalls and steam devils. The latter had only been described four years earlier, in 1972, by two scientists out of Wisconsin. Walter Lyons and Steven Pease compared the whirling towers of steam to dust devils, which are significantly less powerful than tornadoes on land, just as steam devils are less powerful than waterspouts.[7] Nevertheless, the funnel clouds of steam were ominous to behold, even if they were probably less hazardous than a blizzard to the canoeists. The real threat to the integrity of the boats was ice. For now, the hardest ice with the sharpest edges was limited to the shoreline. It posed a problem only when the canoes set out or came back in. Out on the water the boats slid through skim ice, a thin layer of frazil crystals frozen together that couldn't yet form a thick, cohesive surface. The patches of slushy ice became strange sculptures in the rolling water. As waves broke the thin layer of ice, large pieces snapped against each other in the sloppy mess of surf. Each collision scraped off a less-than-solid edge, until the ice was round and rimmed like a lily pad. The discs were called "pancake ice." They'd been appearing in greater numbers lately, which could only mean the lake was getting closer to its freezing point.

Although the winter of 1976–1977 was proving to be colder than average for this time of the year, everyone on the crew had known they were going to be crossing the Midwest in the middle of winter and prepared accordingly. Their layers of wool clothing were warm and kept them comfortable even in the wet clouds of lake steam. Although some people questioned the expedition's decision to wear handmade period clothing instead of relying on newly developed synthetic fibers, wool was a tried-and-true insulator. The wool shirts, pants, scarves, and mittens had repeatedly proven their worth on the water. The men always wore two pairs of mittens when they were canoeing because the outermost pair was constantly getting splashed as they dipped the paddles in the water. Instead of soaking through to the skin, the water on the outside mitten froze and created another layer of insulation that kept their fingers warm and dry. The downside to this type of insulation was that the men had to chisel their hands off their paddles at the end of the day, since the ice fused the two together.

Wool is a hygroscopic insulator; it can soak up lots of moisture without feeling wet, a natural trick performed by the tiny pores on wool fibers that wick water away from the skin. At the same time the structure of the fibers, which are crimped instead of lying flat, create protected air pockets that prevent circulation. Wearing wool clothing helps trap body heat next to the skin, while

One of the crew's canoes in a display at the Chicago Canoe Marathon in 1976, shortly before the expedition. No glue or modern power tools were used in their construction, and each canoe took hundreds of hours to complete. *By the photographers of the La Salle: Expedition II.*

Randy Foster cooking for his module on August 7, 1976. The crew camped out in Quebec for several days before setting off on their voyage. *By the photographers of the La Salle: Expedition II.*

LEFT: Marc Lieberman as *Henri de Tonty* signs a document next to Reid Lewis (*La Salle*) on the day of their departure, August 11, 1976. The crew departed from a suburb of Montreal called LaSalle. *By the photographers of the La Salle: Expedition II.*

BELOW: Paddling into Beauharnois Lock while the rain pours down on August 13, 1976, near Valleyfield, Ontario. When it rained the men wore canvas ponchos that were more water-absorbent than water-resistant. *By the photographers of the La Salle: Expedition II.*

RIGHT: All six canoes together at the bottom of the Eisenhower Lock, accompanied by a tugboat on August 20, 1976. A large crowd gathered at the observation deck to watch the canoes go through the lock. *By the photographers of the La Salle: Expedition II.*

BELOW: George LeSieutre as the notary *Jacques de la Metairie* measures the declination of the sun in Alexandria Bay on August 22, 1976. LeSieutre used 17th-century tools to make a detailed map of the expedition. *By the photographers of the La Salle: Expedition II.*

ABOVE: Paddling past a limestone spire on Lake Ontario, August 26, 1976. The canoe at the front contains Rich Gross, Bob Kulick, Reid Lewis, and John DiFulvio. *By the photographers of the La Salle: Expedition II.*

LEFT: The group at a soggy campsite on Prince Edward Point, Lake Ontario, with Chuck Campbell starting a fire and Terry Cox watching, August 28, 1976. *By the photographers of the La Salle: Expedition II.*

ABOVE: The group at Sand Banks Provincial Park, triumphant after surviving high waves on Lake Ontario on August 30, 1976. *By the photographers of the La Salle: Expedition II.*

BELOW: Doug Sohn, Rich Gross, Sam Hess, and John Fialko give a musket salute on the deck of the *HMCS Haida* outside Toronto on September 8, 1976, while Reid Lewis as *La Salle* and Clif Wilson as *Sieur D'Autray* look on. The black powder muskets were made by hand and were used to fire blanks for performances. *By the photographers of the La Salle: Expedition II.*

ABOVE: The beginning of the Toronto Portage on Riverside Drive, September 10, 1976. The men walked more than 100 miles, doubling back multiple times to carry all their gear through the city. *By the photographers of the La Salle: Expedition II.*

BELOW: Carrying a canoe across a street in Toronto during the portage, which lasted from September 10 to September 21. The crew were often followed by kids and curious strangers. *By the photographers of the La Salle: Expedition II.*

The whole crew in a field off Weston Road near the end of the Toronto Portage, September 19, 1976. In the back row, left to right: Ken Lewis, Steve Marr, Marc Lieberman, Father Loran Fuchs, Sid Bardwell, Bill Watts, and Bob Kulick. In the second row: Rich Gross, Richard Stillwagon, Sam Hess, Mark Fredenburg, Keith Gorse, John Fialko, and Reid Lewis. In the front row: Jorge Garcia, Ron Hobart, Terry Cox, George LeSieutre, John DiFulvio, Chuck Campbell, Randy Foster, Gary Braun, Doug Sohn, and Clif Wilson. *By the photographers of the La Salle: Expedition II.*

ABOVE: Father Loran Fuchs says mass to the crew in a field of flowers off Weston Road, September 19, 1976. The priest traveled with communion wafers and wine to perform mass every Sunday. *By the photographers of the La Salle: Expedition II.*

BELOW: The liaison team. In the front row: Cathy Palmer, Sharon Baumgartner, and Barton Dean (the photographer). In the back row: Jan Lewis, Sid Bardwell (who eventually became a full-time member of the paddling crew), and Marlena Scavuzzo. *By the photographers of the La Salle: Expedition II.*

ABOVE: Ron Hobart next to his canoe looking out at Lake Michigan near Brevoort Lake on October 23, 1976. Upon entering Lake Michigan the group headed south for the first time after paddling hundreds of miles west. *By the photographers of the La Salle: Expedition II.*

BELOW: Paddling past a factory near Highland Park, Illinois, on November 30, 1976. In the canoe are Mark Fredenburg, Ken Lewis, Sam Hess, and George LeSieutre. *By the photographers of the La Salle: Expedition II.*

LEFT: Reid Lewis dressed in his full La Salle outfit at the Academy of Science in Chicago on December 9, 1976. *By the photographers of the La Salle: Expedition II.*

BELOW: A group of men carry their gear on tumplines through the U.S. Steel facility in Gary, Indiana, on December 19, 1976. *By the photographers of the La Salle: Expedition II.*

ABOVE: Gary Braun looks out at the ice and waves on Lake Michigan from Marquette Park, Indiana, on December 19, 1976. *By the photographers of the La Salle: Expedition II.*

BELOW: Bob Kulick, Keith Gorse, and Clif Wilson walk down a snowy road near the Indiana Dunes on December 20, 1976. *By the photographers of the La Salle: Expedition II.*

ABOVE: Mark Fredenburg tugs a canoe forward using a technique called "lining" on the banks of the Kankakee River. Below on the frozen river George LeSieutre and Ken Lewis push the boat. January 1, 1977. *By the photographers of the La Salle: Expedition II.*

BELOW: Trying to paddle down the half-frozen Kankakee River on January 5, 1977. At the front of the boat Doug Sohn uses an axe to chop through the ice while three men paddle through heavy snow behind him. *By the photographers of the La Salle: Expedition II.*

LEFT: Terry Cox takes a break and tries to get warm on the Kankakee River near Shelby, Indiana, on January 11, 1977. *By the photographers of the La Salle: Expedition II.*

BELOW: Men walk down the frozen Illinois River near Grafton, Illinois, on February 7, 1977. *By the photographers of the La Salle: Expedition II.*

ABOVE: Camped out just past New Madrid on February 21, 1977, on the Mississippi River. The men constructed their shelters using a canoe turned on its side, a canvas tarp stretched over the top, and three paddles to hold up the tarp. *By the photographers of the La Salle: Expedition II.*

BELOW: George LeSieutre, Sam Hess, and Mark Fredenburg fly through waves on the Mississippi River near Vicksburg, Mississippi, on March 22, 1977. *By the photographers of the La Salle: Expedition II.*

ABOVE: The crew at a presentation in Kenner, Louisiana, on April 2, 1977. In the front row: Ken Lewis, Steve Marr, George LeSieutre, Gary Braun, and Chuck Campbell; in the back row: Bob Kulick, Sid Bardwell, Marc Lieberman, and Keith Gorse. *By the photographers of the La Salle: Expedition II.*

BELOW: All six canoes stop for a paddle salute outside New Orleans on April 3, 1977, while a crowd and a fleet of powerboats look on. *By the photographers of the La Salle: Expedition II.*

At the Gulf of Mexico at the end of their voyage, Reid Lewis claims the territory for France next to a cross made of driftwood while the crew looks on, April 9, 1977. *By the photographers of the La Salle: Expedition II.*

pulling moisture away to keep the body warm and dry. There was nothing the men could do about the wind, though. Braun's canoe in particular had trouble in headwinds, since only three men were propelling the boat forward instead of four. Wind also increased the risk of hypothermia—when a strong wind came blowing into their faces, the men froze. The majority of the weather days the crew had taken thus far had been due to the wind. They called it being "windbound."

There was a slight breeze on this particular day's trip, but the crew was able to push their way through it. They covered ten miles in two short hours and landed in Lake Forest just before noon. From their landing site the men headed to the local elementary school for presentations and lunch. When they walked in, they were met by the stunned gazes of dozens of children. It was a reaction they'd grown accustomed to along with the winter weather. Their wool-clad limbs were covered in a veneer of ice that crackled and crumbled as they moved. Some had ice encrusted among the hairs of their beards. They walked slowly to avoid slipping on the wet floor in their leather moccasins. Wherever they went, they were sure to leave behind huge puddles as the ice melted off their clothes and leaked out of the wool fabric. It took a couple of hours to get the wool dried out by the fire every night. The process occasionally resulted in singed wool socks that reeked of burnt hair and sweaty feet.

From the awestruck elementary and junior high schools, the crew was taken in vans to Ferry Hall, a private boarding school. The large fireplaces and ornate chandeliers looked like they could've been pulled from Victorian England. Until recently, Ferry Hall had been a private girls' school. Two years earlier it merged with Lake Forest Academy, a local private boarding school for boys. The performance the crew gave that night was applauded by a huge audience of students, parents, and community members. It was always gratifying to see the number of people that turned out to see them and learn about the French voyageurs' exploration of North America, especially when the weather was terrible.

The evening indoors passed quickly and in relative comfort, although more than once crew members had been overcome by nausea after being inside for too long. Even if the air outside was biting, it was also fresh. Buildings felt small and confining after having spent so many days on the open water and so many nights with nothing but a thin layer of canvas between them and the sky.

Making the fresh air even better tonight was the slowly rising temperature. It was only twenty degrees, but that was a lot warmer than the seven degrees it had been in the morning. Since the crew had an excessive amount of firewood, they decided to build up one enormous bonfire at their campsite. Between the waves of heat that came wafting off the huge fire and the full moon and the rising temperature, three men convinced themselves it was warm enough to go for a swim.

Keith Gorse, George LeSieutre, and RK were all members of the "swim of the month club," an informal gathering of lake connoisseurs who had agreed to go for a dip in the water at least once every month. Though he was a close friend of LeSieutre and in the same module as Gorse and RK, Braun chose to stay back with the rest of the crew in the relative warmth of the night air. The crew watched as the teenagers stripped down to their underwear, bolted into the frigid water up to their heads, then promptly shot back out and ran up to the fire. Gorse slipped on the climb up and fell into a pebbly hill. The small, frozen rocks burned and clung to his wet skin until he got to the fire, where the rocks thawed and began falling back to the ground. The crew members who had watched this spectacle hooted at their lobster-red friends. It was an excellent way to end an enjoyable day. Even with all the new obstacles presented by the winter weather, the modern voyageurs wouldn't let the frigid temperatures and decreasing hours of daylight keep them down.

Belmont Harbor, Illinois
December 8, 1976

Seeing ice stretch out to the horizon at 5:00 A.M. after three hours of sleep wasn't the best way to start the day. The crew had been driven to their hometown of Elgin the day before to do a series of presentations in their high schools, a detour that allowed little time to visit with family and friends. At least they'd be in the Chicago area for almost a week and have the chance to visit more. The only downside was their exceptionally busy schedule, which meant no one would get as much sleep as they might like. This morning everyone was staring blearily at the iced shoreline anticipating a change to their original plans. The expedition was expected in Chicago in the afternoon. Canoe builder Ralph Frese had organized an outdoor banquet and welcome reception for them on the lawn in front of Adler Planetarium, complete with crystal glassware and china plates. The crew had planned to spend the day paddling the fourteen miles between Evanston and Adler, dodging ice floes and admiring the Chicago skyline. They would land at the 12th Street beach. But the thick layer of ice lining the shore meant that instead of making a triumphant entrance into the great city, courageous and proud beneath a layer of frost, icicles hanging from the gunwales of their handcrafted canoes, they'd have to be bussed in. Two dozen voyageurs climbing out of a bus didn't have nearly the same effect as a fleet of six boats coming over a steaming, icy lake. There just weren't any other options if they couldn't get past the ice. Put the boats directly in the ice and their hulls would be gouged to shreds by the jagged edges; try to walk the boats farther out and the men would risk breaking through thin spots in the ice and plunging into frigid water.

Never one to be daunted by the weather, Reid Lewis went with Stillwagon and some of the other adult crew members to scout the shoreline a few miles to the south . They came back around 10:00 A.M., just when most of the crew members had resigned themselves to a day of repairing moccasins and working on odd projects until they were driven to Chicago. The scouts had found a spot to the south along the shore where the ice wasn't too thick and didn't stretch out far into the lake.

"We're going to portage a mile and a half, then paddle the fourteen miles to Adler and arrive right on time at four," Lewis told the crew.

The men received the news with less enthusiasm than Lewis would've hoped. Braun was livid. In general, he was easygoing and rolled with the punches. He wasn't often ruffled by the decisions made by the expedition leaders. But setting out at 10:00 on an unplanned portage, then paddling fourteen miles through icy water and expecting to arrive by 4:00 P.M. was crazy. He guessed the portage would take at least three hours, loading the canoes for a paddle would take another hour, then the paddling itself would be at least three more hours, meaning they'd be landing at 5:00 P.M. or later, and in the dark. It was risky to be out on the water past sunset when the temperatures were this low and the water was filled with so many little icebergs. But what could he do, what could he say? His opinion wasn't going to change anything.

Disgruntled as they were, the men gathered their gear and set off down the shore through Northwestern University's campus. It was a disorganized mess, and it took almost four hours to travel the mile and a half to the open bit of shore. When they arrived, the beach was still full of jagged ice, but they were able to launch the boats without too much difficulty. At that point the sun was heading down the horizon and the cold was sinking into the men's bones. Spiky blocks of ice bobbed around them as they paddled. It was becoming rapidly apparent that they weren't going to make their welcome ceremony at Adler Planetarium and that staying on the water much longer was dangerous. The weather was just too cold for their clothes to keep them warm on a dark, frozen lake.

After two hours and about seven miles of paddling, the decision was made to find an appropriate landing site and make camp wherever they ended up. They were closest to Belmont Harbor, a sheltered marina near the Lincoln Park neighborhood of Chicago. There was nowhere to land but a five-foot break wall. The men made the landing and struggled to pull the boats out of the water without causing any damage from the rough surfaces. Lewis hurried off to the city to make phone calls and rearrange their schedule. He came back to tell them they'd missed the meal Frese had prepared for them, but they were on time for a cocktail reception at the National Bank of Paris. The crew shuffled off to a bus to make their appearance among the ritzy, glamorous attendants of the bank's party, feeling angry and exhausted. Guests at the event would later say the temperature in the room dropped when the men entered wearing their ice-covered woolen clothes with pink cheeks and frost in their beards.

When they returned to camp after sleepily schmoozing and dethawing in the well-heated bank, it was time for a crew meeting. The meetings were supposed to be a chance to make plans for the next day, as much as such things were possible with the ever-changing weather conditions. But lately they had devolved into unproductive shouting matches where everyone threw their conflict resolution training out the door. Tonight Cox let loose on

Lewis, shouting about the insanity of paddling in the dark, in the cold, without knowing if there would be anywhere safe to land. Were they going to put the schedule ahead of the crew's safety for the rest of the winter? Would they regularly be on the water past dark? Gradually the conversation became more constructive and the crew turned away from arguments to discuss what options they had besides continuing the slow paddle across the southern shore of Lake Michigan. Maybe they could follow the Chicago River to the Des Plaines. It would mean changing their schedule and canceling performances in towns in northern Indiana and southern Michigan along their published route, but it might save them a lot of trouble. For now, though, they'd give themselves some time to mull over the decision. The expedition wouldn't be moving anywhere until they were done with all their obligations in Chicago. In the next three days they'd be visiting the La Salle Bank and the Chicago Academy of Sciences, and giving numerous presentations and media appearances.

That night Braun went to bed in a temper. He counted the day among the worst so far on the expedition. What a difference a week made in his outlook on the winter, on the expedition as a whole! He didn't understand how decisions that put him in danger could be made without any input from the "student" crew members. They weren't students anymore, and the age difference between them and the adults had long ceased to make any difference in their day-to-day interactions, but they still weren't taken as seriously as the adults when it came to making important decisions. How much further would Lewis push them?

For his part, Lewis had no desire to see any of the men get hurt, and he knew traveling on the lake was risky. But the point of the expedition was to take risks, push themselves further every day, *show* people that modern man was capable of great deeds. It seemed like more and more crew members were willing to ease off now that the weather was colder. In Toronto, no one would quit, no matter how badly it hurt. Now, taking a day off when they weren't feeling up to their task had become the honorable thing to do. The phrase everyone used was, "Let's be considerate of ourselves."

The expedition wasn't a vacation or a summer camp outing—Lewis had always said it was going to be hard. He was disappointed to see the dwindling enthusiasm and was troubled by the divisions among the group. Just when he needed most to inspire his men, leadership seemed to be slipping away. Between trying to ameliorate the crew's relationship with the liaison team, coordinating with city officials, and making appearances as the public face of the expedition, he didn't have a lot of time to come up with heroic speeches urging his men "once more unto the breach." He sympathized with La Salle's struggle to maintain morale among his crew. Though the problems the two men faced were unique to their respective eras, the underlying issue was a similar one—how to unite a group of men under a common purpose when a number of impediments blocked the way. The obstacles they faced might be different, but their effects were the same: diminished morale and increased resistance against the expedition leader.

"Such is the lot of those men whom a mixture of great defects and great virtues draws from the common sphere," wrote Pierre-Francois-Xavier de Charlevoix in *History of New France*. "Their passions hurry them into faults; and if they do what others could not, their enterprises are not to the taste of all men. Their success excites the jealousy of those who remain in obscurity. They benefit some and injure others; the latter take their revenge by decrying them without moderation; the former exaggerate their merit. Hence the different portraits drawn of them, none of which are really true; but as hatred and the itching for slander always goes further than gratitude and friendship, and calumny finds more easy credence with the public than praise and eulogy, the enemies of the Sieur de La Salle disfigured his portrait more than his friends embellished it."[8]

East Chicago, Indiana
December 14, 1976

If the morning set the tone for the rest of the day, this Tuesday was shaping up to be a disaster. At the 6:00 A.M. wake-up call, the wind was blowing thirty-five miles per hour out of the south, the waves were sloshing up around the ice, and the thermometer was showing the same low temperatures it had been displaying for weeks now. Braun wished he could declare the avants to be on strike, but the men sent to scout conditions the day before had reported limited ice on shore and minimal slush ice farther out in the lake. They decided there wasn't enough of either to pose a real risk to the men's safety, and they only had a short distance to cover. These days they needed to take every opportunity that presented itself to move ahead.

Three days ago, Braun's parents had come down to the camp carrying five dozen donuts and milk for the crew. Yesterday he had woken early and enjoyed a hot shower at Crown Point High School and then had breakfast at Knoll restaurant. Today, on his 19th birthday, his only present would be heading out onto a wicked lake to paddle seven miles into a strong wind. A few people seemed uneasy about the decision, but the choice had been made. Braun anticipated a long, cold day. *Happy Birthday, Jean du Lignon*, he thought.

The first few miles weren't so bad. It was windy and a little wet, but Braun's three-man canoe was making forward progress. Then they came to Inland Steel. The company had built an artificial peninsula that jutted out into the lake, a massive complex of blast furnaces and roadways and landfills. The open-hearth mill was constructed at the turn of the 20th century and had dominated the area ever since then. In celebration of Indiana Day at Indiana Harbor in 1908, a writer penned some verses that captured the mill's impact on life in the area: "The skies are often dreary, and air is filled with smoke, in Northwest Indiana, from the gas and coal and coke; but we wouldn't be without it, for it's just the way we grow, in Northwest Indiana, where the furnace fires glow."[9] To reach their destination at Indiana Harbor Yacht Club, the men would be traveling past the scene penned by that early writer, hugging the ugly shoreline of Inland Steel.

When Braun's boat finished the trip two miles out into the lake and around the landfill, they continued parallel to the shore for several miles before making the turn back toward the south. It wasn't until they turned inland that they were blasted by the powerful wind. No matter how hard they paddled, they couldn't make progress. They'd gone four or five miles in the first three hours, and now they'd been paddling for what felt like ages without getting anywhere. The wind was too strong for the three men to overpower. They'd have to find somewhere to land and use a line to pull the canoe the rest of the way in, while the rest of the fleet made their way to the landing point by paddling.

The canoe approached a seven-foot break wall covered in ice. The boat bobbed up and down over waves that spilled over its edges, piling layer upon layer of ice on the gunwales. Braun would have to scramble up the wall with a line in hand, pulling the canoe alongside the wall for a mile or so while the others kept the canoe from scraping against it. It was probably less than a mile to their campsite, and lining a canoe was much easier than portaging it or fighting the wind all the way in. The only real problem would be getting up on top of the break wall.

Braun rose to his feet in the rocking boat, then balanced himself on the narrow, slippery gunwales and waited for a wave to nudge the boat up so that he could jump for the top of the bulwark. A little too far to the left or the right in any direction and he'd slip and fall. If he missed the top of the wall, he'd slip and fall. Either scenario ended the same way: him in the water, drowning or freezing to death. As Stillwagon had said at a crew meeting weeks earlier, at this point in the year it wouldn't matter how fast help arrived if a canoe capsized or a man fell in the water—they'd probably be dead of hypothermia or heart failure before anything could be done. That prospect was terrifying. Four days earlier, Braun had been one of the ten people who voted in favor of continuing on the lake instead of following the river system south. Thirteen people—a majority—voted to follow the rivers, but the vote was close enough that Lewis was allowed to make the decision and chose to continue on the lake. Look where Braun's vote had gotten him: he had made it to his 19th year on Earth, and now he wasn't sure he'd live to see the 20th.

A combination of dexterity, balance, and good luck allowed Braun to momentarily overcome gravity. He landed at the top of the break wall without slipping off the side. Relieved, he pulled the canoe into their campsite down the shore. But the incident had severely shaken him. For the first time he seriously questioned his decision to continue with the expedition. All the camping experience and wilderness survival training in the world hadn't prepared him to put his life on the line for a measly seven-mile day of paddling. What reason was there to think it would be getting any better in the coming months? They had at least ten or twelve weeks ahead of them before their route would take them far enough south to reach warmer weather.

Braun wasn't the only crew member who felt serious trepidation about continuing. Steve Marr, a teenager who had played the violin and been involved in theater before joining the expedition, was so upset about the decision to keep traveling along the lake that he went to Reid Lewis almost in tears. When he joined the expedition, he thought of it as being something momentous, an event that would have its own place in history. But he didn't want to be remembered for drowning in a lake in December. The point was to make it in one piece to the Gulf of Mexico. When Marr took Lewis aside to express his concerns, Ken edged in to lecture about not letting the shelf ice beat them. This only made Marr more upset. At that point, he was considering taking some time away from the expedition and going home for a few weeks. Nothing about paddling across a half-frozen lake appealed to him.

"I think you'll be upset if you go home," Lewis told him. He encouraged Marr to stick it out, to think about the integrity of the crew and what it would do to everyone else in his boat if he left. Marr was disappointed, but he accepted the logic in Lewis's argument. He decided to stay with the crew and hope for the best. That didn't make it any easier to face the lake, though.

The morning of December 15 unfolded bright and clear, a windless day with temperatures soaring into the fifties. After the last few weeks, it felt almost tropical. The main impediment to the crew's paddling—the wind—wouldn't be an issue on the lake today. If they left early enough, they could cover quite a lot of ground once they got past the ice. But instead of paddling, the men hopped on a bus and rode to Valparaiso and Michigan City, where they were expected for presentations all day long. Despite an agreement made at an earlier team meeting when Lewis said they would travel on the lake whenever possible, here they were stuck indoors when they could be making miles on the lake. Lewis simply felt, after considering the issue, that their obligation to the communities they'd promised to visit was just as important as making headway.

Without the support of these towns and the people who saw the voyageurs, there would be no expedition. One of the stated purposes was to educate the public. They couldn't just set off into the wilderness like the old explorers had done; they had performances and classroom visits and public appearances to make. When it came down to it, the voyageurs needed the public support. But that didn't make it any easier for the men to swallow when they were forced to give up a day of paddling in order to stay indoors and perform, especially now that every good-weather window was so precious. That night when the crew got back to camp after completing their presentations in Valparaiso and Michigan City, they learned that forecasters were predicting twelve- to twenty-mile-per-hour winds for the next day. The mood was mutinous.

On the 16th, a strong breeze was sending icy surf over a three-foot-high wall of ice along the shoreline. A scouting party including John Fialko was sent in the liaison-team vans to Burns Harbor, a small town about sixteen miles to the east. If the paddlers could get there in one trip, they'd have a good place to camp and an ice-free spot to land the canoes. But there were no safe places to disembark between Burns Harbor and Indiana Harbor, and with the wind blowing the way it was, there was no chance of leaving. The scouts called a predetermined number that Lewis was waiting at using one of the factory's phones. They told him to have the crew put the shelters back up, because there was no way they could go out. The men would have to spend the day mending and catching up on sleep. The simmering frustration from the day before seemed on the verge of boiling over.

Overnight the winds shifted to the southwest, then back to the northwest, remaining strong. The morning of the 17th presented a now-familiar prospect to the men sent to do reconnaissance on the ice levels: Burns Harbor had some slight openings, but there was ice spreading across the lake, and large sheets were piling up on top of one another. The scouts checked Michigan City, farther east, an Indiana town close to the Michigan border. The harbor there was also iced in. Out in the lake, frothing whitecaps lashed the icy shoreline. It was a scene reminiscent of the one they'd faced at Sand Banks on Lake Ontario. Going out to paddle was suicidal.

The crew gathered for a meeting in the afternoon, just as they'd done for the past several days. The uncertainty of what each new day would bring was chewing away at morale. Resentment over the decision to give performances instead of paddle on what now appeared to be one of the last nice days of the year hadn't yet abated. The options were laid out before the crew members, with a list of pros and cons attached to each. First, there was the lake. They could continue to sit and wait for an opening, then make the last jump across the lake on a nice day. This option would mean finding a new place to camp, getting behind on their schedule, and possibly waiting indefinitely. By the time the wind died down, extensive ice cover might prevent travel. Second, they could head back to the Des Plaines River, either by following the nearby Chicago River or shipping the canoes to Joliet, Illinois. From there, they'd paddle down the Des Plaines to the Illinois River and then the Mississippi. This option would mean cutting out all the visits they planned to make in Michigan and Indiana along the St. Joseph and Kankakee rivers, but it might also be safer and allow them to paddle farther. Finally, they could send the canoes ahead of them on their original route to the St. Joseph River and equip themselves with a minimal amount of gear to make the hundred-mile walk to the St. Joseph. They'd probably get to the river before Christmas, but it would mean walking all day every day, then being bussed to presentations at night.

In the end, the decision was made to walk. La Salle had occasionally abandoned his canoes when the weather grew too dangerous for paddling, so there was a historical precedent. And even if they got a little behind, at least they'd still be moving forward. The crew could make up time when they got back on the rivers. Even if the rivers were iced over, they would be far less treacherous than Lake Michigan. On a river you can always see the shore and land. You don't have to worry about the wind stirring up huge waves, and unlike on the St. Lawrence, a strong current wouldn't be a problem until they got to the Mississippi, and then it would be working in their favor. It would be a hard hike across the northern shore of Indiana and up into Michigan, but then it would be over. At least they'd made a decision.

A flurry of organization began after the meeting and lasted for a day and a half. They needed to find someone who could safely transport the canoes and most of their gear; winnow down their belongings to a thirty- to fifty-pound bag; organize the march through U.S. Steel in Gary, Indiana; and find a new way to construct shelters since they could no longer camp beneath the overturned canoes. The last of these tasks was quickly accomplished by a group of men who took some of the tarps to an open area and cobbled together a large shelter held up by paddles, stakes, and rope. The new tent was large enough for everyone to sleep under and was dubbed the "circus tent" for its resemblance to a three-ring affair. Unfortunately, after a few nights sleeping beneath it, the men discovered one problem with the new arrangement: while they slept, the humidity from their breath and any precipitation that fell overnight and leaked through the tarps formed miniature icicles that dangled above their heads. Whoever got up first in the morning was likely to send bits of ice showering down on everyone else.

The next week passed in a monotonous haze of snow and ice and pain. On the 19th the men clumped through U.S. Steel. That evening they were bussed ahead to Benton Harbor, Michigan, and attended Advent mass, where Father Loran addressed the audience.

"I'm sure the expedition didn't arrive as expected. But it arrived," he told the assembled congregation. "I'm sure Christ didn't arrive as expected—a great king. He arrived in a very humble way. It's appropriate for the fourth Sunday of Advent that the La Salle expedition arrive in a very humble way."[10]

On the 20th the group covered nineteen miles from Marquette Park in Gary to Michigan City, following Route 20 and Route 249. The snow came down in short-lived, sporadic blizzards, covering everyone in a layer of melting water and turning the landscape into a white wasteland. That night the men gave presentations to more than seven hundred people who braved snowy roads to see them at the St. Joseph Elks club and the Saint Joseph High School in South Bend. They returned to the circus tent shelter as always and slept as much as they could in the plunging temperatures. It was a constant struggle to get warm, between the freezing air and the icy ground that permeated the pads and sleeping bags they slept in. At least they were all in one space, so their combined body heat helped warm the shelter somewhat. Even so, sometimes at night the men woke up with their nostrils burning from inhaling the freezing air. They could pull their heads down beneath their sleeping bags, but after a short period of time that felt suffocating. Some, like Gorse, could sleep through anything, while others were lucky to get four or five restive hours of sleep at night. They made up for it by napping anywhere and everywhere.

The bright light at the end of the snowy tunnel was the prospect of putting the canoes back in the water on the St. Joseph. The approach of Christmas also brightened everyone's moods. They made it to Bridgman, Michigan, on Christmas Eve and spent the afternoon visiting nursing homes. In the evening they celebrated with the liaison team. Everyone put aside their hard feelings for the holidays. The ladies of the liaison team performed a parody of one of the crew's performances, then gave everyone gag gifts. For Sid Bardwell, a spelling book because his orthography was so horrendous; an eye patch for Sam Hess to remind him of his ocular injury; a book of travel mazes for George LeSieutre since he was drawing a map of the expedition using 17th-century tools. The crew and liaison team were all taken to the University of Notre Dame's Basilica of the Sacred Heart for midnight mass, where there were pews reserved for them at the front of the church. Everyone chuckled at the fact that they were allowed to bring rifles into a cathedral.

When the crew got back to their camp late that night, they were cheered by the sight of a Christmas tree the town of Bridgman had set up for them. They weren't at the best campsite—right outside a Texaco gas station—but at least they had bighearted hosts and a day of relaxation and family visits ahead of them. Saint Joseph High School was opened up to the crew on Christmas so that they could share a potluck meal with their families, away from the fans who flocked to them at the campgrounds, and away from members of the media. For a day they could take a break from being voyageurs and go back to being sons, brothers, and husbands. The festive mood was transitory. In the days following Christmas, the crew struggled to make any progress on the St. Joseph River. Although it rarely froze so early in the winter, the weather had already proven itself to be exceptional. Paddling through half-frozen water meant the avant had to chop away at the ice for the canoe to make any headway. More than one ax was lost when it slipped out of the avant's hands. The canoes were beaten up daily on the ice and patching them in the evenings was a full-time job for Fialko. When the crew arrived in Niles, Michigan, the decision was made to build sleds to carry the boats until they could permanently return to the waterways.

The crew spent an afternoon carving ladder-like sleds, paring down the runners with draw knives. The front ends of each of the runners were trimmed down to be narrower so that they could slope up and be strapped to the canoes. The six canoe sleds were augmented by two gear sleds that could transport whatever gear didn't fit in the canoes.

The continued kindness of communities and strangers along the expedition's route made what was starting to feel like a death march more bearable. As the men hiked through snowstorms, three people dragging each canoe sled at a sluggish pace, passersby stopped with coffee, hot chocolate, and encouragement. Local newspapers and TV stations tracked the men's progress and gave updates about their performances. After a particularly hard day of walking at the end of December, the men were invited to a private dinner at Tabor Hill Vineyard and Winery. The owner, Leonard Olson, took them on a tour of the winery to see the gleaming stainless steel vats and casks, then gave them a supper of corn and crab chowder and wine. Olsen was so impressed by the expedition that he offered to reserve a white wine, name it for the expedition, and donate a portion of the profits to them. After much food and more wine, the crew chose the name "Decidons demains"—*let's decide tomorrow*—to reflect the continued uncertainty and spirit of endurance that characterized their winter walk.

Apart from the difficulties posed by the weather and the ongoing frustrations with leadership and liaison-team miscommunication, fighting off modernity was the expedition's main challenge. They were doing everything they could to remain true to their stated goal of authentically re-creating the voyageurs' journey across North America, but the temptations of modern life were ubiquitous. Instead of camping outside every night, the men could have easily found rooms in a motel or taken advantage of the hospitality of locals and slept somewhere warm and dry. The option to quit or take a two-week break was tantalizing after a long day's hike across snowy fields and highways, especially now that colds and flus were becoming a more regular problem. La Salle hadn't had any other choice but to keep going when he was faced with bad weather. The modern voyageurs did have a choice, and they could see all the creature comforts they were missing.

Modern infrastructure worked against the men in other ways as well. When they were forced to walk on the road instead of through trails or over the frozen river (the latter was a hazardous undertaking since someone inevitably fell through the ice, sometimes up to his neck, and had to be fished out and warmed up before the expedition could continue), the rough, frozen concrete chewed up their moccasins and made their feet ache. It was like being on the portage through Toronto all over again, but this time there was no end in sight. And then there was the danger presented by modern vehicles. On January 3, one of the few days when the men were able to put their canoes in the water and inch slowly past the ice, a snowmobile came droning by. The driver was crossing a small bridge over the river when he got distracted by the sight of six canoes paddling through the ice floes and lost control of his vehicle. Snowmobile and driver went flying through the air, barely avoiding John Fialko's canoe as they plunged into the water. Had the snowmobile traveled a few feet farther or Fialko's canoe been paddling slightly slower, the men would've been crushed beneath the falling vehicle.

Fialko and his crew paddled over and got the snowmobiler out of the water while others went to call for help. The man had a concussion but was otherwise fine. None of the members of the expedition was hurt, though they were all a bit shaken. Funny as it was to see a snowmobile go flying over the river, it was also a warning: whatever clothes the crew wore or foods they ate, no matter how hard they tried to pretend otherwise, they were part of the 20th century and had to contend with its dangers.

Kankakee River, Indiana
January 11, 1977

After days of struggling to drag the canoe sleds through snow and paddling on rivers that were rapidly icing up, the decision was made to abandon the canoes for good. They'd be stored by the United Parcel Service, who offered to transport the canoes to wherever the expedition might need them. At this rate it might be weeks before the rivers were reliably water and not ice. Even parts of the Mississippi were frozen. The weather hadn't been so consistently, severely cold since the winter of 1917–1918,[11] and by all accounts, the winter of La Salle's journey down the Mississippi had been quite mild. Nature certainly wasn't cooperating to help them make a perfect re-creation of the original voyage. If the men left their moccasins or any article of clothing outside the shelter at night, it was sure to be frozen solid in the morning. Some nights the temperature was down to minus twenty-five degrees without factoring in windchill. On those nights, the air was so cold that their breath seemed to form a cloud that fell back down on them as they slept.

The first day of walking along the Kankakee was a brutal lumber through snow. The trees with their ice-coated branches were beautiful and the scene along the river held an undeniable serenity, but it didn't stop morale from slipping. When would they be warm again? When would they be back in the canoes? Just the other day, one of their last days paddling, someone had tossed a bag of oranges into one of the boats for the voyageurs to feast on. But by the time they stopped to eat them, the oranges were frozen solid.

Tonight there was one source of respite from the cold and the monotony of walking. The Fort Tassinong Muzzleloaders, a group of men who shot black-powder rifles and spent weekends pretending to live like 18th-century homesteaders, had erected three tipis and campfires for the expedition. The sight of the shelters already constructed and the warm fires waiting for them was a welcome one. The muzzleloaders were thrilled to be spending time with the famous voyageurs on their trek across the frozen Midwest. Although the voyageurs had to leave for a nearby performance, they came back to their camp later in the evening to enjoy the company of the muzzleloaders and share stories of their trials. Yes, the winter was a hard one—harder than most—and the men often grew dejected by the constant cold and pain. But every so often there were these moments of levity that brightened the gray days and made them feel as if they could carry on despite it all.

Chapter Nine

THE MOST DANGEROUS
PRODUCT THE INTELLECT
HAS CONCOCTED

Illinois River
January 1682

Since first setting out from Montreal in 1679, La Salle had undertaken two unsuccessful missions to reach the Mississippi. There was no knowing if he'd have more luck this third time around. The Frenchman's earlier expeditions into the wilderness had been nothing short of calamitous. Men deserted at every stop they made along the route, and the deserters often took food and valuable tools with them. La Salle wasn't taking any risks this time around. He decided to keep all his men together rather than sending small groups ahead to scout the area as he had in the past.

The Frenchmen paddling in La Salle's current and previous expeditions had a number of reasons for wanting to desert, not least of which was the likelihood of injury or death. But smaller grievances added up as well. The New World was filled with pests, beasts, and stranger creatures than those they knew in France. The mosquitoes alone were enough to drive a man mad. "I believe the Egyptian plague was not more cruel," wrote Father du Poisson in the *Jesuit Relations*. "[At night] we are eaten and devoured, they enter our mouths, our nostrils, our ears. They cover our faces, hands, and bodies . . . However adroitly you squirm under the canvas, there will always be two or three that enter with you, and it only takes two or three to make you spend a bad night."[1] La Salle and his men were safe from the bloodsuckers in the frozen north, but the farther south they traveled, the more they'd have to deal with them, even in winter.

There were also wolves, bears, and venomous snakes to worry about, as well as stampeding buffalo. For the men who hadn't been long in the territory, the buffalo must have made a striking impression. When they traveled in large herds, the drumming of their hooves resonated for miles. Years after La Salle and his men passed through the area, French writer Chateaubriand described the buffalo as having "the mane of a lion, the hump of a camel, the hide and hindquarters of a rhinoceros or a hippopotamus, and the horns and legs of a bull."[2] As befit their formidable appearance, buffalo had to be treated with caution. Even though they were herbivores, they had no qualms about trampling a man to death if he got in their way.

Apart from the weird and wild monsters the men encountered along their travels, they faced a number of other physical hardships. They could wander into inhabited territory and be killed by hostile Native Americans. The voyageurs could die of starvation, disease, or by drowning. It wasn't uncommon for men to be ejected from their canoes in rapids, and most of the voyageurs never learned how to swim. Many of their paddling songs memorialized those who had been killed in the wilderness. The canoes occasionally paddled past crosses erected on shore in memory of the dead.[3] If they managed to survive everything else, there was always exposure to the harsh climate. Winters were frigid and the only shelter the voyageurs could expect at night was the protection offered by their overturned canoes. Little surprise, then, that men in their twenties were considered old, and anyone who reached 40 was downright ancient, as well as incredibly lucky.

Fortunately for La Salle and his men, everything seemed to be working in their favor during this third expedition. They arrived at the Illinois River by mid-January. They hadn't encountered any warring tribes, and La Salle's plan to keep all of his men together was proving its worth—no one had deserted since a small number of men had departed this expedition several months earlier in the trip. Everything was falling into place so smoothly after years of misfortune that La Salle might have dared to hope his expedition would arrive at the mouth of the Mississippi by springtime.

Indiana Highway 2
January 12, 1977

The day began with a clear, azure sky, beautiful and deceptive. Bright sunlight glimmered on the frozen river and the snow-laden branches of trees, but the temperature was somewhere around fifteen below zero, with a windchill of minus forty. The men had spent a cozy night in the three tipis erected by the muzzleloaders, but that comfort was over now. There was walking to do. After eating breakfast and taking a few turns shooting the muzzleloaders' muskets (one of their members, Wild Bill Voyles, was a gunsmith), the voyageurs bid their comrades in historical reenactment farewell and set off.

The crew had been following the river system ever since they arrived at the St. Joseph River in Michigan, but a tortuous bend in the Kankakee River had them considering alternate routes this morning. The expedition was falling further and further behind its schedule. Every night after a bone-aching day of walking, a bus would pull into their camp to take the men to whichever town they were supposed to be performing in. They'd muster up whatever energy they had left, put on a show, eat a warm dinner, then head back to camp for another night of trying to sleep in temperatures that seemed to approximate the last Ice Age. It was an exhausting pace and any shortcuts were godsends. Hobart had compared their route down the Kankakee to nearby county roads and found they'd only have to travel eighteen miles along a road for what would amount to a fifty-mile walk on the meandering river. The decision was a no-brainer. Plus, it would save anyone else from plunging through weak spots on the ice. Almost everyone had gone up to their knees when they hit a weak patch of ice; Sam Hess had gone in up to his head just a few days ago. Luckily, he'd been attached by rope to someone else, or who knew how long it would've taken to fish him out, and if he would've survived the retrieval.

The men plodded down the road, packs balanced with the help of tumplines, their slow procession spreading out over a distance of a quarter mile or more. Some walked faster than others. Rich Gross was often one of the last ones into camp because he despised walking. He'd signed up for the expedition because he loved canoeing and being on the water. But somehow he found himself covering hundreds of miles on foot. It made his back and hips and legs ache, and he was desperate to be back in the boats. Some people walked alone, backs bent, eyes on the ground.

Others formed clusters to talk or silently commiserate. One such group included Keith Gorse, Bob Kulick, Marc Lieberman, and Clif Wilson. They called themselves the Frank Lloyd Wright Supper Club.

Walking all day with nothing to see but leafless trees, barren fields, and endless stretches of snow didn't require much brainpower. The muscles screamed, the joints ached, the skin chafed, but the mind was bored. It wandered in and out of bizarre worlds, settling on minutiae for amusement and looking for fellows to share in the experience. So began the Supper Club. The seed was planted in Michigan during the first hundred miles of walking, when the group passed a ramshackle building with a sign announcing it to be the Frank Lloyd Wright Inn. The thing was so incongruous it set off a flood of firing synapses that still hadn't stopped producing ridiculous fodder for entertainment. As the four teenagers walked, they came up with rules for and stories about their club. They debated which celebrities would be allowed entry, what each member's role would be, and what sort of initiation rituals they'd have (one included eating a twelve-course dinner in a phone booth). It was silly, but it distracted them from noticing the pain of putting one foot in front of the other. They tried to walk together as often as possible to keep the game going.

Breaks were the other anodyne for the weary walkers. Lunch was especially welcome. Today they had soup and hot cocoa from Stillwagon's wife, Rowena, and sandwiches from a conciliatory liaison team. The women had been threatening to quit after months of nothing but complaints and insults from the crew. Marlena had actually taken several weeks off in December and returned home, leaving Jan and her teenage helpers to muddle through on their own. All four were back at work now. However angry they might get about being taken for granted, they, too, wanted to see the expedition succeed. If only they could make it out of this endless winter. It put everyone in a temper.

Besides stopping for food, the men also came together for Argo breaks. Argo was the brand of cornstarch they carried, six big, yellow containers of it. The men weren't mixing the powder into food to make their soups thicker—it was used on the inner thighs to treat the rashes everyone had developed. The clothes they wore were made of wool and scratchy canvas, and all the walking they'd been doing caused the fabric to irritate the skin. Just another discomfort to deal with in addition to all the other winter ailments. The cornstarch soothed the burning rashes and led to ongoing jokes about "pulling down your pants and Argo-ing up."

When the men stopped for an Argo break shortly after lunch, Wilson was one of the last to get a box of cornstarch, and his friends were already heading back out to the road. He hesitated for a moment—run and catch up to them, or stay behind to apply some of the powder? He chose the latter. They wouldn't get too far ahead in five minutes. He'd have plenty of time to catch up.

After putting the Argo away and slipping back into his pack, Wilson took off down the road. He'd have to walk quickly to reach his friends, who were at the front of the line behind Hobart and Cox. The crystalline sky from the morning had long since disappeared behind a swath of gray clouds. Snow was blowing in streams across the road. The men had just come to the end of County Road 900 and turned south on State Road 2. They were a few miles south of the small town of Hebron, Indiana, and had an entire afternoon of walking before they could stop for the night. But they were making better time than they would have on the river. Traffic was sparse on the little two-lane roads they'd been following. Every once in a while a car would come rumbling by, spraying snow in the voyageurs' faces. They kept to the edge of the road to stay out of the way, but otherwise paid little attention to the cars. The struggle to keep moving was all consuming.

Bob Kulick was walking up near the front of the line with the other members of the Supper Club. Unlike the others, Kulick had his head up. He liked to brace his tumpline across his chest rather than on his forehead. It allowed him to look around at everything instead of just staring at the legs of whoever was directly in front of him. Today, this stance meant he was the first to see the semi truck. It was pulling into the left lane on the other side of the road from the walkers so that it could pass a white Chevrolet pickup whose driver had slowed to stare at the otherworldly members of the expedition. But the semi driver hadn't seen an oncoming car and was now trying to slide back into the right lane, the lane the men were walking alongside against the direction of the traffic.

He's never going to make it, Kulick thought.

"Get down! Everybody get down!" Kulick shouted to Lieberman and Gorse, trying to push them toward the ditch on the side of the road.

Behind them in line, Sid Bardwell felt a blast of air and heard a sharp beep, then the squealing of brakes, then the loud, distinctive crunch of metal on metal. Rich Gross saw the semi's trailer fly past him as it rammed into the Chevrolet.

Steve Marr looked up in time to see the rear tire of the pickup truck skidding toward him and tried to swivel out of the way, but his left leg moved a second too slowly.

Clif Wilson turned and caught only a glimpse of the Chevy's chrome jet hood ornament, exactly like the one that had been on his mom's station wagon when he was a kid. Then he was flying through the air.

Gary Braun and Jorge Garcia saw nothing but the dirty grille of the pickup truck, then muffled blackness and cold snow.

In moments of crisis, the mind seems to slow time to the point where the person experiencing the warp feels as if he can reach out and avert disaster the millisecond before it happens. This cruel illusion has nothing to do with a heightened ability to perceive the world. The brain is not operating at a higher rate like a camera with accelerated shutter speed. Instead, it's an effect of the amygdala becoming more active and laying down extra-dense memories. Adults feel as if time passes more quickly with old age than it did in childhood for much the same reason; their brains are not actively forming such vivid memories because none of the experiences are as new. A brain in emergency sees everything with a child's eyes again. *Remember this moment*, the brain is instructing itself. *It might later help you survive.* As the flood of information registers in the mind, the body must choose to give in to fear or use adrenaline as fuel for a fight.

Dick Stillwagon was the first to rush to the four men who had been mowed down by the truck and assess the how seriously they were injured. All the other men ran to their friends or scrambled to find some way to help. The semi truck was jack-knifed across part of the highway. Canvas packs and shredded clothes and sleeping bags were scattered across the embankment. Blood sprinkled the snow.

"My God, my God," Lewis said over and over again, his voice shaking.

The flurry of action was barely controlled chaos. After confirming that everyone was alive, the first thing the men could think to do was to make sure that those injured were warm. Marr was on the ground, half his body on the road and the other half on the shoulder. His left leg was horribly crooked. He seemed well enough, though, still smiling and just asking that no one try to move him. The shock and cold seemed to be dulling the pain. Braun had also managed to survive the incident relatively unharmed, despite being dragged for a short distance beneath the pickup. His sleeping pad had been torn completely apart by some sharp piece of metal under the truck, but it looked like the cooking pot he carried on his back might've saved him from being more seriously injured. The pickup truck's trajectory had continued for a ways past Braun, so he was on his stomach with some scrapes on his head that were bleeding, but he wouldn't need to be excavated from the truck. He had a sore arm and leg, but he said the worst of it was being forced to wait in the snow and frigid wind—Stillwagon had cautioned everyone not to move any of the injured men.

Wilson and Garcia were in much worse shape. After being thrown into the air, Wilson had landed heavily in a plowed corn-field. He was fortunate that there were several feet of snow on the ground. Had he skidded across the pavement, his injuries could have been far worse. As it was, he immediately sensed upon landing that he wasn't in any danger of dying, but the pain was excruciating. Gorse, Kulick, and several others asked if they could do anything to help.

"There's a rock under my back; get it out," he moaned. Blood dripped down a gash in his chin and his left wrist was throbbing.

"There's no rock," the others told him. It was agony to sit and watch him suffering without being able to do anything to help.

"Yes, there is, I can feel it," he said, starting to panic, trying to find a way to move and get comfortable.

Stillwagon looked Wilson in the eye. "Clif, there is no rock under your back, and we can't move you. Now I need you to calm down for me. Can you calm down?"

Wilson nodded and tried to take a deep breath. Later he learned from the doctors that what he felt digging against his back was probably a compressed vertebrae and part of his broken pelvis.

Garcia was in the worst condition of all. He'd rolled under the pickup truck and emerged on the other side like Braun, but unlike Braun he hadn't been protected by any of his gear. Blood leaked from his mouth, his nose, his eyes. His breath was coming in rasping gurgles. He seemed only semi-conscious and kept asking if he could go to sleep. Stillwagon told him no repeatedly. Sleep would be the worst thing. He suspected Garcia had some kind of internal injuries, and if they didn't get him to a hospital quickly, he would die. He called Ron Hobart over and asked him to stay with the teen to keep him from falling asleep while he made sure all the other injured men were being kept warm enough. Hobart crouched next to Garcia and alternated singing songs to him and asking the teenager to count the fingers he held up. He repeatedly reached down to brush melting snow out of the younger man's eyes.

While they waited for ambulances to arrive, the crew members who weren't with the injured redirected the cars that were trying to drive around the semi truck. Bardwell took four flares to mark the edges of the accident with Fialko. Hess, Kulick, and Gross were directing the cars away with no small amount of yelling and frustration. They all felt helpless and panicked. It was utterly unlike the capsizing on Washington Island. Then they'd known what to do. That was an accident they'd trained for. This wasn't. How much longer could the injured men survive outside in the brutal cold? Where were the ambulances? They seemed to be taking forever.

Finally one arrived from Valparaiso. Since both Braun and Marr seemed in stable condition, Garcia and Wilson were taken first, leaving the other injured men in the snow, fighting the pain of their injuries. Hobart accompanied those in the ambulance after Garcia asked him to stay with him. He prayed both the teenagers would survive the journey. It was another thirty minutes before the second ambulance arrived to whisk the two remaining injured men to Porter Memorial Hospital in Valparaiso.

The two truck drivers were doing their best to stay out of the way. Alvin Lilly, who had been driving the pickup truck, was uninjured, as was William Black, the semi driver. Although both felt terrible about the accident, neither received any citations from the police officers who arrived shortly afterward. The men on the expedition weren't supposed to be walking on the narrow, two-lane highway, the police told the two truck drivers.[4]

The liaison team got the call in their hotel room. Jan answered. It was a police officer, a stranger, who told them there'd been an accident. The officer didn't offer many details, but men had definitely been injured. As the team rushed to the small highway to find the men, all the women except Jan were crying. *Crying won't help anyone*, she thought. She had to stay calm. She had no idea whether her husband was among the injured, how serious the accident had been, and whether anyone was dead. As they neared the site of the accident, they were stopped by a police barricade.

"We need to get through; we're with the men," she told the officers. They were allowed to pass and drove on, where they were met by the sight of the wreckage. Some of the gear was still scattered around the pickup truck and there was blood in the snow. But none of the men were there anymore. Jan asked where the injured crew members had been taken and sped off to the Valparaiso hospital, fifteen miles away.

When they arrived, Jan caught sight of Reid on the phone, looking shaken. It was the first time she knew he was unharmed. One weight off her chest. The first bit of relief seeped into the numbness that she'd been operating under since the phone call.

But there were still the four young men who'd been injured, all of whom were undergoing evaluations at the hospital or, in Garcia's case, emergency surgery. She, too, began calling families and friends, using the phone tree they'd created before the start of the expedition so that loved ones could have quick access to news of the expedition. The goal now was to make them all aware of what had happened before the media started announcing the accident, and to get everyone who wanted to come to the hospital. Jan made it through nearly all the phone calls calmly, explaining what had happened and where the injured teenagers were now. Her composure lasted until she reached her mother. Then she was sobbing hysterically. No matter how professional and in control of the situation she'd wanted to be as head of the liaison team, talking to her mom made her feel like a child again, wondering how something so awful could have happened.

The ambulance ride to the hospital had been torture. Wilson had been strapped down on a backboard, in immense pain, listening to Garcia labor for every breath. It sounded like he was choking to death, drowning in his own blood. When they arrived at the hospital, they were both immediately rushed into the emergency room, Garcia for surgery and Wilson for tests to determine what was broken and if he had any internal injuries. As hospital staff were cutting off his clothes, Wilson was handed a phone to talk to his mom.

"I think I might have broken my wrist," he told her, trying to minimize the shock. He was right, but it was among the most minor of his injuries. He also had compressed vertebrae in his lower back, impact fractures in his femurs, a laceration on his chin from being hit by the hood ornament, and a crushed pelvis. No one had any hope that he or Garcia would be getting back in the canoes again, assuming Garcia survived.

A little later, after being put in casts and pumped full of pain medicine, Wilson was wheeled into a room with Marr, who was wearing a cast that stretched from his toes to his hip. The tibia and fibula of his left leg were broken. He'd be out of commission for weeks, if not months.

Braun alone had escaped relatively unscathed. He had shallow lacerations on his head, a contusion on his leg, and a dislocated collarbone. His left arm was up in a sling, and he was already wandering around the hospital in his voyageur getup, looking dazed and in shock. The doctors were releasing him. He'd have to stay with the liaison team for several days.

Lewis was stuck in a waiting room while Garcia was in the operation room. All the parents of the injured were now racing to the hospital. The drive from their hometowns in northern Illinois would take only about two hours. While Lewis waited for their arrival and the inevitable barrage of questions from them and from the media, he struggled to maintain the optimism he'd always had in the face of dilemmas. Lewis was familiar with the challenges of recovering from traumatic injuries. He'd been run over by a car his senior year of high school and spent the last few months of the school year at home in casts. It had been an incessant struggle not to be overwhelmed by the pain. He wouldn't wish the experience on anyone, but he had learned from it, learned to be patient during the healing process. But this was different. The lessons he'd learned would do no good to the men who were injured now.

Never far from Lewis's thoughts were several facts. First, he was responsible for the safety of each of these young men in a way that La Salle had never been for his crew members. Whether or not the crew members would have agreed with Lewis's assessment of his position was a moot point. Lewis *felt* the responsibility, so it was real. La Salle's voyageurs were paid for their troubles and were well aware of the dangers of paddling out into the unmapped wilderness. Lewis's students had been aware of the risks as well, and their parents had signed release forms, but none of them ever seriously considered the fact that they might die along the way.

The second thought that Lewis couldn't shake was that two of the four injured teenagers had, at one point, almost not been a part of the expedition. Braun was initially an alternate and joined the main group after another member had dropped out. If the other student hadn't left, Braun would've been with the liaison team the entire time, coordinating meetings and working safely behind the scenes. And then there was Wilson, who had come to Lewis early in the trip, when the weather was still warm and the air full of the droning of mosquitoes, to complain that he just couldn't get along with one of the other students in his canoe. Wilson wanted to quit because he knew he wouldn't last in such close quarters for the nine-month trip.

"If you quit, it's going to haunt you for the rest of your life," Lewis had told him. He suggested Wilson redirect the flame of his frustration into paddling, because his canoe had been lagging behind. The teenager agreed and never again mentioned leaving the expedition. But what if he had left? Could you compare those two regrets—not going through with the expedition and not being in hellish pain with numerous broken bones and a lengthy recovery ahead? Had Lewis made the right decision, or was the entire expedition as crazy as some people said?

"History is the most dangerous product the chemistry of the intellect has concocted . . . It produces dreams and drunkenness," wrote French essayist Paul Valéry. "It fills people with false memories, exaggerates their reactions, exacerbates old grievances, and encourages either a delirium of grandeur or a delusion of persecution."[5] Had the idea for the expedition been a delirium of grandeur? Had they all been too swept away by the possibility of living like La Salle? No matter how much humans hope to learn from history, how much they long to revel in its trappings and reanimate it in the present, the past is permanently lost. No amount of extravagant costumes or reenacted events can resurrect the precise social, political, economic, and personal conditions of an earlier era. But something in our nature seems to persuade us otherwise, to push us to strive for a connection with the people who have gone before us.

In tale upon tale of time travel into the past, travelers put themselves at risk of being discovered as outsiders, or killed by diseases that have been eradicated in their era, or forever lost to their family and friends—but that doesn't stop them from delighting in the experience. Time travel, with all its dangers, is still a coveted ability. But what of those travelers who go forward in time, who want to educate people of the future? What about men who purport to represent the 17th century and come for a visit in the late 20th? The future holds its own dangers. There were no cars, trucks, or roads in La Salle's time.

The tension between striving to live in the past and interacting with the present had never before been so poignant for the members of La Salle: Expedition II. It was chance that brought the pickup truck and the semi into a collision course, but it was the crew's determination to push forward despite everything, as the original voyageurs would have done, that brought them to the windy Indiana road where they became a distracting apparition for drivers. Who, if anyone, was to blame for what had happened?

After the second ambulance had arrived to pick up Braun and Marr, the uninjured men were shuttled to a nearby diner and plied with hot cocoa, tea, and pie on the house, while a stranger offered to buy them hamburgers. The food and warmth helped physically after spending so long in the bitter cold, but no one seemed able to mentally process the day's events. Grief and anger and confusion were starting to pervade the shock that they'd all felt in the first moments after the accident. Now they could do nothing to help. They simply had to wait. The adult crew members dazedly tried to organize the evening in a way that would allow the teenagers—and themselves—some time to reflect on the disaster away from a crowd of sympathizers and reporters. Stillwagon arranged for their gear to be stored in an empty classroom at the school just next door. Ken Lewis asked whether they should keep their commitment for a performance in the evening and was told in no uncertain terms that the crew could absolutely not be asked to perform, given the circumstances. He went to contact the community leaders who'd arranged the event to explain the situation and give his regrets that they couldn't be there. Cox asked around to find out if the crew could stay somewhere private with a phone, and they were ushered into an empty room in Hebron High School. Hanging over all of them was the knowledge that Garcia still might die, that he might already be dead and they just hadn't heard yet.

Once inside the high school, the men dispersed to talk in small groups or be alone with their thoughts. Hess went off into a corner by himself, imagining what his mom would've done if he'd been among the injured. He started crying as he thought of the men in the hospital, thanked God he was still alive and unharmed, then prayed that everyone would survive. Others contemplated the vagaries of chance. Randy Foster normally walked with Marr and

Garcia, but had been mad at them over something stupid in the morning and decided to walk ahead. If he'd been trekking with them as usual, he'd be in the hospital, too, maybe on the operating table like Garcia.

Lieberman and Kulick rehashed the incident, forcing themselves to relive what had happened like drawing poison from a wound. They'd received word that Wilson was in the clear, though pretty beat up. Apparently he was also annoyed that the doctors had shaved part of his beard off to stitch up the cut on his chin—a detail that reassured his friends that he was okay. Bill Watts said he saw the normally laid-back Doug Sohn approaching the truck "with fire in his eyes" before realizing he couldn't do anything with his anger and turning around.

Parents and family members poured in from Illinois to provide comfort and support. Surprisingly enough, everyone was unanimous in their insistence that the expedition had to continue. Even parents who had expressed reservations from the beginning believed the men should go on. They'd come too far and suffered too much to give up now. The real question was whether the men themselves would want to push on, knowing as they now did that their lives could be at stake.

Word finally came from the hospital that Garcia had survived surgery. His spleen had ruptured upon impact with the truck, a relatively common injury in car accidents. If he'd arrived at the hospital just a little later, he could easily have died. His spleen was removed in the operating room, and he had other injuries to contend with as well. His right arm and hand were badly broken. It would be an arduous convalescence, but the doctors were cautiously optimistic and listed him in stable condition on the critical list for the night. The relief everyone felt was palpable, and some of the tension leaked out of the gymnasium where all the men had gathered.

After everyone had had some time to be alone, a meeting was called to take a vote on where they would spend the night. Still-wagon suggested that they should stay indoors, violating one of the expedition's cardinal rules. It would be their first night indoors since their departure in August. But he didn't want the men to have to worry about staying warm and erecting a shelter on top of everything else. Most of the crew agreed with him: the vote was 16-1, Ken being the only dissenter.

Once the decision had been made, the muzzleloaders they'd stayed with the night before arrived to serve them bread and stew for dinner. Support from people who had followed the men's progress across North America was pouring in at an almost overwhelming rate. The phone rang nonstop with calls from all over the country. Someone even called from the Yukon Territory, having heard about the accident from Ralph Frese in Chicago. They wanted to know if they could help. The media was just as interested in talking to the crew about what had happened. Reporters from the *Chicago Tribune*, the Benton Harbor *Herald-Palladium*, and local radio stations called or visited to inquire about the men's condition. Within the next few days the expedition would appear on the front pages of a half-dozen newspapers and in numerous regional broadcasts. All the reporters and supporters of the expedition asked the same question: Would they continue? It was a question that would have to wait for the morning to be answered. For now they all needed rest and time to recover. Though they had chosen to spend the night in the high school gym, the men were uncomfortable and struggled to sleep in the heated room. It felt suffocating after so many nights outdoors. "No one had a very good sleep inside, the air felt dry and as though there wasn't enough of it," Kulick wrote in his journal the next day.

After breakfast the next morning, the men returned to Hebron High School for a crew meeting. There were students around now, giving the men curious looks as they traipsed through the hallway. The crew sealed themselves off in the auditorium for the meeting just as Braun arrived, his arm in a sling. He said he was okay, a little sore and tired from not getting any sleep during his night in a hotel room with the liaison team—it was hard to find a comfortable position when your collarbone was dislocated—but mostly he was just tired of answering questions.

With everyone assembled, Reid Lewis gave a report on the status of the injured men. Wilson and Marr were both being transferred to hospitals closer to home for ongoing care. They were both sad to be off the expedition for the time it took to heal, but hoped they might recover quickly enough to join back up before the end. Garcia had been taken off the critical list and was with his parents. He, too, would have to be transferred to a hospital in Illinois where his condition would continue to be monitored. Someone suggested creating a writing schedule, so the men could alternate sending letters to the injured crew members while they recovered. It would be a way of keeping them up to date with the expedition, of making them feel as if they were still part of it. The idea was ultimately rejected—it felt too much like forced sentiment. Those who wanted to write would write. Those who chose not to wouldn't be chastised. For all the relief they felt knowing that everyone would survive, the crew was still mentally recovering, still rebounding from the shock.

Every one of the injured men and their parents agreed the expedition should go on. No one wanted their injuries to be in vain—they needed the pain and suffering to mean something. It wasn't enough just to survive and recover; the injuries had to be framed as an obstacle they overcame, not the calamity that brought down the expedition. It was decided. The crew would continue on and leave the recovering men's positions open. When they could finally put the canoes back on the water it would mean some reshuffling—several boats would be a man short—but they could handle it.

The next order of business was to decide *how* to keep going. Everyone agreed that walking on the roads was out of the question.

"We're an attraction and a distraction to motorists," Stillwagon said. "I'm afraid of the 20th century."

"I don't want to end up as a hood ornament on some truck," Sohn added.

Reid Lewis and Fialko agreed. They couldn't take any more risks on the road, even if the route was shorter. The suggestion arose that they be bussed to the Illinois River. Everyone agreed that people would understand. No one would fault them for taking a bus to cover sixty miles after what they'd just been through. They'd already walked more than two hundred miles and paddled more than a thousand. It wasn't like sixty miles amounted to much in the grand scheme of things.

"We've paid our dues; we've had the worst winter on record," someone said.

"But it would disturb the continuity of the expedition," Ken Lewis said. He thought they should keep walking along the river, or get a police escort to follow them on the roads. That way they wouldn't have to worry about accidents. At the end of the expedition they could say they'd covered the entire route using nothing but manpower. But his idea was shot down as impractical and still potentially dangerous. They'd only get further behind in their schedule, and they'd never finish the expedition in the time they'd allotted for it.

When the vote was taken, everyone but Ken agreed that they should take a bus to Wilmington, Illinois, and plan on starting anew on the Illinois River. Even Reid agreed. He'd been uncharacteristically quiet at the meeting, perhaps still recovering from the shock of what had happened. Everyone was still feeling dismayed and despondent, but they all also felt a strengthening resolve. The expedition was suddenly deathly serious. The worst that could happen had almost happened. But everyone had survived, and all the injured voyageurs asked was that their teammates push on. Everyone was eager to honor that request.

Chapter Ten

✳

PARALLEL VOYAGES

Mississippi River
March 1682

When La Salle and his men finally found open water on the Illinois River, they swapped out their sleds for canoes and paddled on to the Mississippi. The expedition arrived at the Great River at the end of January 1682, but was forced to stop by the massive boulders of ice that came thundering down the Mississippi from the north. The river was choked with broken icebergs and drift ice, making it impenetrable. After waiting for another ten days for the ice to clear, the men finally set off down the serpentine pathway.

In all his travels, La Salle had become familiar with much of the flora, fauna, and indigenous peoples of North America. He had survived the rapids of the St. Lawrence River, learned native languages, and been the first explorer to ever sail across the Great Lakes. But the Mississippi River was an entirely new ecosystem and had given rise to vastly different cultures than those of the Midwest and Northeast. The tribes along the Mississippi lived in a fertile region with a milder climate, which allowed them to cultivate vast swathes of land and grow beans, squash, and maize. Because they had extra food and places to store it, permanent dwellings were built and societies grew more complex.[1] La Salle and his men met and feasted with members of the Acansa tribe, the Tinsa tribe, and the Natchez tribe, all of which lived in large villages with well-constructed lodges. They bartered for items like pearls and slaves, native men and women from other tribes who had been captured during warfare and were used for labor. The indigenous people were more successful in negotiating with other tribes along the river and finding food. La Salle and his men were also treated to ceremonial feasts of maize, beans, meat, and plums. When they reached the Tinsa village they were even given "figures of humans, bison, deer, alligators, and turkeys made from a paste of fruit,"—the native North American equivalent of marzipan candy figures.[2]

In addition to the food they were offered in villages, the Frenchmen found a plethora of things to eat along the river. They hunted deer, which appeared in abundance, as well as turkeys, swans, Canada geese, bears, and bison. The canoes paddled past flowering peach, plum, and walnut trees.[3] La Salle wrote of one surprisingly tasty dish made from macopins, a root that tasted like onions. "The Indians make a hole in the ground and into it put a layer of stones that are red from the fire, then a layer of leaves, then one of macopins, another of reddened stones, and so on to the top, which they cover with earth and let the roots sweat inside."[4] Even when the men ran out of provisions and were forced to fast, it wasn't long before they were able to find more food.

In some ways, the trip down the Mississippi River was proving to be easier than traveling across the Midwest. But there were still plenty of challenges. Despite a strong current, the Mississippi was a winding river. Sometimes after a full day of paddling, the men had made very little actual progress in terms of miles traveled south. The warm climate also meant more mosquitoes. The voyageurs often slept on elevated platforms to keep themselves away from the damp ground and buzzing bloodsuckers.

The most difficult of the crew's problems had little to do with the environment, however. First, voyageur Gabriel Barbier sustained a foot injury that would eventually leave him partially crippled. Next, the gunsmith Pierre Prudhomme got lost at the end of February while out on a hunting expedition. For ten days the crew searched for him high and low, fearing him captured or dead. Finally he appeared, floating down the river (in modern-day Tennessee) and barely able to hold onto the log that supported him. He was emaciated and exhausted, but alive. While La Salle's men had been searching for him, they'd built a small wooden fort for protection. In honor of the gunsmith's return, La Salle christened it Fort Prudhomme.

Apart from their short stays with various tribes and the time spent looking for Prudhomme, the men made good time down the Mississippi. At the beginning of April La Salle found brackish water. His search, it seemed, was nearly at an end.

Elsah, Illinois
February 7, 1977

"There are some parallels between La Salle's voyage(s) and ours that are interesting. The list can be expanded to include a lot of travel and equipment details." John Fialko made two columns in his notebook, one labeled "La Salle" and the other "La Salle II." The lists beneath the two were almost identical.

Money probs.—relatives	Money probs. —crew, friends, etc.
Relatives on voyage	Family involved at a different level—L-team
Morale—mutiny problem	Morale at times low
La Salle a pusher	R.L. (Reid Lewis) a pusher
La Salle didn't trust too many people	R.L. lets out just what people need to know to do their job

"I'm noticing some changes in Reid," Fialko added. "One of his more common statements is 'the expedition is falling apart.' I know we're not as together on some of the things we do. Not like we need to be."

After the truck accident, the men had been bussed to the Illinois River to make up for lost time. Since then the expedition had inched its way down the state of Illinois toward the Mississippi River. Despite their earnest commitment to moving forward in spite of the accident, every winter day felt like a grim repeat of the last. It was a struggle to keep moving over snow and ice, always putting one foot in front of the other, always a presentation to be bussed to at the end of the day and a night of restless sleep on the frozen ground to look forward to. Making each day all the more challenging was the threat of dehydration. Carrying water was impossible most days because it froze solid after a few hours. The men had to make do with drinks at lunchtime and ignore their thirst for the rest of the day, which left them irritable and even more exhausted.

In mid-January someone from the Army Corps of Engineers, a group with whom the men had been corresponding since they announced their plans to travel along the Mississippi River, told the men they'd probably have another six to eight weeks of walking before they could get back on the water. If the frigid temperatures eased up a little, that estimate might get moved back, but as January progressed it only got colder. The northern part of the Mississippi was frozen solid. The crew walked over frozen rivers and wind-swept lakes, through snowdrifts and backyards to avoid being on the road again. On January 28 around 2:30 in the morning their shelter was blown down by a sixty-mile-per-hour wind. The crew members awoke to a tangled bundle of canvas and sleeping bags. Snowflakes and straw that had been laid on the ground whipped around them in the blizzard as they hurried from their campsite into a nearby school, where they hunkered down for the rest of the night and the following day. With a windchill of minus seventy degrees, there was no way they could safely spend the day walking.

The effort required to stay warm leeched everyone's energies and depressed their moods. It had been mentally and emotionally taxing spending all day together when they were traveling across the Canadian-American border in the summertime; now the cold weather had them hemmed in like goats in a too-small pasture. Everyone's nerves were frayed, and there was no way to get any per-sonal space or time alone. As a last resort, some of the men turned to books and their journals to escape. Kurt Vonnegut's were popular choices and were passed around the group. Cox had been churning through Joseph Waumbaugh's cop novels. But the story that really resonated with multiple members of the crew was J. R. R. Tolk-ien's *The Lord of the Rings* trilogy. Sam and Frodo's journey across the wastelands to reach Mordor felt like the crew's endless march across the ice-covered Heartland. The epic fantasy was filled with all the same elements as their own expedition: unknown dangers, rifts between friends, hunger, cold, discomfort, and an important mission. Although saving Middle Earth from an all-powerful mon-ster was slightly more grandiose than educating Americans about

French explorers and the history of North America, that didn't prevent the books from feeling familiar and encouraging. "It's a dangerous business going out your door," Bilbo Baggins told his young cousin, Frodo. That had certainly been proven to be true time and again on this journey.

The only other escape from the daily grind of walking and being watched was getting sick. This was hardly an enticing option, and it was mostly out of everyone's control. Unfortunately, it was also unavoidable, since they were demanding much of their bodies and coming in regular contact with hordes of children when they did school visits. Men had to drop out for a few days because of severe colds, flus, and stress injuries to their knees. The sick and injured would get medicine from Stillwagon or visit a doctor, then spend a few days with the ladies of the liaison team, resting in climate-controlled hotel rooms and sleeping more than five or six hours at night. Dropping out for a few days, which had been unthinkable at the start of the expedition when everyone wanted to cross all thirty-three hundred miles with his own body providing the power, had become the acceptable and even the proper thing to do.

As the men slowly moved into the lower latitudes, another disheartening source of tension arose. They might not have known it from the temperature or the maps they followed, but the men had arrived in the South. On February 5, they crossed into Calhoun County, Illinois, and one of the members of the town welcomed them with the epithet, "Welcome to Hardin, boys, where the sun has never set on a nigger and never will."

The ugly sentiment was a reminder of just how dark the reality of 1977 could be. In Boston around the time of the bicentennial celebrations, a black man named Ted Landsmark was going to a City Hall meeting to discuss minority hiring practices when he was attacked by several white men. His assailants used the pole of an American flag to perpetrate the crime. In Chicago and New York, white homeowners bombed or burned the houses of blacks who moved into their neighborhoods.[5] When the teenagers of La Salle: Expedition II had graduated high school last summer, they left with memories of proms, football games, and race riots. Bob Kulick had once parked on the wrong side of the Elgin High School parking lot and was forced to dodge stones as he ran into the building. It had been a tense time, but all those issues seemed far behind them while they were paddling through the Great Lakes and tromping over mountains of snow in the Midwest. All the racial prejudices and silent judgments of the North would become more audible and visible in the South. They would soon be entering states where segregation had been the rule, not the exception, and lynchings—violent, traumatic acts of racial terror—had occurred for decades. For the first time there might be a black supervisor of two white cops on *Starsky and Hutch*, and President Carter might speak out about injustice and human rights violations in Czechoslovakia, Uganda, and the Soviet Union, but that didn't stop racism from thriving in many communities in the United States. Its roots were buried deep and stretched far across the country.

To everything else the reenactors had in common with the original expedition could be added this: both groups belonged to tumultuous, rapidly changing worlds. Those living in such eras have a choice—accept the change and let it sweep in a new world, or fight the current. For the voyageurs and their modern counterparts, the only option was to let the physical and metaphorical current carry them forward into an uncharted future, no matter how difficult that experience might be, or how much they themselves might be changed in the process.

Chester, Illinois
February 15, 1977

A procession of men carrying overturned canoes above their heads advanced down a slope that led to the Mississippi River, their colorful hats the only spots of color in the brown and white and gray landscape. Crusts of slushy ice and snow covered the rocky shoreline, making the walk more treacherous. A crisp wind whipped through layers of woolen clothing and covered the open water with small white ruffles of foam. Once the canoes had been gently set down at the river's edge, each boat's quartermaster organized the wooden chests and canvas sacks of supplies that had to be loaded in a Tetris-like configuration into the canoes. A tall towboat, painted in alternating stripes of red and white with its name, *Dixie Power*, in blocky capital letters, towered over the men as they worked.

Despite the wind and the clouds that muddled the sky, the crew's mood was jubilant. Only a few days earlier the Coast Guard had declared the river unsafe for boat travel due to ice and sunken branches clogging it downstream. Now, with temperatures finally starting to rise above freezing, the river was open. The six canoes of La Salle: Expedition II and the flotilla of towboats that acted as the nervous system for all kinds of industry on the river had permission to begin their collective voyage along the Great River.

A month had passed since the men had last sat in their canoes and attempted to navigate the jagged icebergs that bobbed along the Kankakee River. Two full months had gone by since the crew had consistently been in their boats and armed with their paddles. In that time, they'd covered 527 miles by foot, worked together to overcome a truck accident, and survived one of the coldest winters on record. Finally, *finally* they were returning to the waterways.

Now they could get back to their original goal of traversing the arteries of North America and enthralling audiences with their choreographed landings.

To celebrate being reunited with their beloved vessels, the crew held a second christening ceremony. The boats had made it through their winter storage looking no worse for the wear. Just the day before, Kulick, Gorse, Fialko, and Hess had driven fifty miles south to Cape Girardeau, Missouri, to retrieve the boats from their storage spot at the St. Vincent's Seminary. UPS had donated the use of one of its trucks to get the canoes back up to Chester, Illinois, on time for the launch. Bill Watts and George LeSieutre stood over the boats now with open bottles of champagne, letting the bubbly liquid splash onto the bows. Father Loran, looking austere in his black cape, gathered the group around for a short prayer. The men removed their woolen toques and bowed their heads as the priest blessed the voyage again. When all the benedictions, private prayers, and superstitious rituals were finished, the men hopped in their canoes and shoved off onto the mighty Mississippi.

A steady current sped the canoes on their way, helping them cover eight miles in an hour without much difficulty. They hoped to be in Grand Tower, Illinois, by the afternoon, a thirty-mile trip.

"That's two days of walking!" Rich Gross exclaimed to the other men in his canoe as they dug their paddles into the river.

As the fleet continued down the river, the cloudy sky cracked open and spilled its innards. Heavy snow pelted them in the face and was swirled away by the water. The combination of wind and snow chilled everyone, but the minor discomfort couldn't put a dent in their moods. Hopefully this would be the last snowstorm of the year, and if not, at least they weren't walking through it with heavy packs tugging at the weary muscles of their shoulders and backs.

Though spirits were high, ongoing personal problems still dogged the crew. The loss of Wilson, Garcia, and Marr didn't help, and it didn't look like the last two would be rejoining the group at any point, though Wilson was hopeful that he might still heal in time to paddle the last bit of the expedition. Braun, at least, had been back with the group for some time since his injuries had been the least severe. Several people were also out sick, including DiFulvio, which put Kulick in the position of gouvernail for the day. Such rearrangements had been made in nearly all the canoes to compensate for the missing paddlers.

The lingering disagreements between the adult crew members were also lying just beneath the surface of seemingly every conversation. But everyone was in agreement about the joy of being back on the water again. Whatever issues remained from the long winter were momentarily dispelled as the canoes arrived at their destination. The sun broke through the clouds as they landed at Grand Tower. There to meet them were members of the community and one of Reid Lewis's old friends, teacher Dean Campbell, who had participated in the Jolliet-Marquette expedition. Campbell had constructed a replica Iroquois longhouse along the river and invited the crew to stay in it for the night. The shelter had a frame made of sticks tied together with twine, which was covered by dark brown fabric. The rounded roof was high enough for some of the shorter crew members to stand up without hitting their heads, and a crackling fire inside the shelter made the air warm and smoky. The clouds that chased the men down the river during the day had dispersed by nightfall, and the sky was filled with gleaming stars. Outside the makeshift longhouse the canoes lay on their sides, waiting to carry their passengers farther down the river the next day.

New Madrid, Missouri
February 20, 1977

If the Great Lakes are the inland seas of North America, the Mississippi is its Nile River. It has enough superlatives to merit its Ojibwa name, *Misi-ziibi*, or "Great River." At 3,900 miles, the Mississippi is the fourth-longest river in the world, ranking behind only the Yangtze, the Amazon, and the Nile. It winds through ten states in the center of the country and its watershed stretches across more than 1.2 million square miles and thirty-one states—enough territory to fit France, Spain, Portugal, Germany, Austria, Poland, Italy, Greece, and Switzerland, with more than 250,000 square miles to spare. The river has shifted courses a number of times over many millennia, always following the path with the shortest and steepest gradient to reach its destination at the Gulf of Mexico. In its natural state the river sways from east to west and back again, like a monstrous serpent slowly undulating across a bog. At the start of the 20th century, the river was poised to change paths and join the Atchafalaya River to the west. It likely would have done so if not for the massive engineering efforts that went into forcing it to follow its current trajectory.

In 1879 Congress created the Mississippi River Commission to prevent floods, permanently fix the river's current path, and improve its navigability. The fight that ensued is still ongoing. Human engineers are holding their own against Mother Nature, but only just. The battle proved that throwing as much money as possible at a problem doesn't ensure its resolution.

In 1927 a violent flood tore the river valley apart and killed hundreds of people. The Flood Control Act of 1928 saw more than $300 million spent on rebuilding and fortifying the region against future floods—more than had been spent on Mississippi levees in all of colonial and American history combined. But less than half a century later, $500 million more was spent to repair another safety valve in the river system. A side channel called Old River was expected to be one of the main sites at which the Mississippi hopped over to join the Atchafalaya, so the Army Corps of Engineers built a floodgate system to regulate the amount of water leaving the Mississippi and entering the Atchafalaya. Like the handles of a faucet, the floodgates could be opened and closed according to the amount of water that needed to be bled off the Mississippi to prevent flooding. It seemed like a foolproof way to stymie the river's wayward behavior, but a flood in 1973 nearly succeeded in ruining the Old River Control System. The precipitation that caused the flooding was only 20 percent above normal for the time of year, hardly a one-hundred-year flood. But it was enough. That spring, two million cubic feet of water surged down the Mississippi *per second*. That's twenty times the amount of water that thunders over Niagara Falls. The Army Corps of Engineers scrambled to build an auxiliary system farther up the river to take some of the strain off the floodgates at Old River.[6]

As Mark Twain wrote in *Life on the Mississippi*, "One who knows the Mississippi will promptly aver . . . that ten thousand River Commissions, with the mines of the world at their back, cannot tame that lawless stream, cannot curb it or confine it, cannot say to it, 'Go here,' or 'Go there,' and make it obey; cannot bar its path with an obstruction which it will not tear down, dance over, and laugh at."

These were the forces La Salle: Expedition II would be coming up against in their voyage down the Mississippi. This wild, wily river could be dangerous at any time of year, but during the springtime all the melting snow from the north and rain from thunderstorms added to the churning mass of water. Huge trees were regularly sucked into the river and could destroy large ships without any trouble, to say nothing of birch-bark canoes. The ubiquitous trunks had their own names depending on how they were floating: those that stood up like spears in the riverbed were "planters" while the trunks that bobbed up and down in the current were "sawyers." Add to this the dozens of towboats pushing huge barges through the water and the thousands of wing dams that lined either side of the riverbank to reduce the need for dredging in the main channel, and the Mississippi was an extreme obstacle course for the canoes.

When Reid Lewis met with a member of the Coast Guard who worked on the Lower Mississippi before the expedition began, he explained that he'd already paddled much of the Mississippi during his earlier expedition. He was acquainted with the river and had a great deal of respect for it. Many of his crew members had knowledge of the river as well. John DiFulvio had passed numerous summers riding a speedboat down the Mississippi with his family and camping along its banks. Sid Bardwell spent a summer drifting down the river on a pontoon boat with one of his friends prior to joining the expedition. And by the point the men reached the Mississippi, Lewis reasoned, they would've already covered two thousand miles by canoe. The men would be experts at handling the boats. The Coast Guard officer gave his permission for the men to travel the river in the spring of 1977, but added, "If my son told me he was gonna go on the Mississippi in a canoe, I'd tell him he was out of his head."

Even with the reductions in their crew and the unique dangers posed by the Great River, the men felt hardly any trepidation. They'd survived windstorms on the Great Lakes and a capsizing in frigid Lake Michigan, weeks of paddling around icebergs, and two months of hiking through snow. Four men capsized and survived hypothermia, three more were injured, and one almost killed. They'd overcome every challenge thus far. Clif Wilson had even made a miraculous recovery and found a doctor who fitted him with a back brace so that he could get back in the boats and paddle again. The men didn't see the Mississippi River as a final hurdle, but as a clear path pushing them toward their destination with its rapid current.

The paddlers covered thirty-three miles in a relatively short amount of time on February 20. The water was choppy with a strong wind blowing out of the west—whenever they came to a horseshoe bend in the river they were paddling straight into the wind. Not the easiest day of work, but they were able to get where they needed to be. Since the men weren't due for a presentation until the following day in New Madrid, they landed on an empty stretch of shoreline in the late afternoon and set up the shelters for a relaxing evening. The crew members had different ways of entertaining themselves now that it was warm enough to wander away from the fires. Some read or wrote. Others went off for long walks to be alone with their thoughts, or to talk with friends, or to practice throwing the tomahawks they'd made. George LeSieutre was becoming particularly adept at eyeing a target then whipping the ax around at just the right angle so that the blade buried itself in the tree he'd aimed for.

Everyone returned to the three cooking fires when it came time for dinner. They had antelope steaks given to them by a stranger, one of the many supporters of the expedition who offered what they could to keep the men going. The meat was a good addition to their beans. They cooked the steaks like shish kabobs, skewered on sticks and held over the fire until the outer layer was grilled. They would eat the first cooked layer, then return the meat to the fire to roast the next layer, proceeding until it was gone. The fire emitted the occasional loud pop as the men sat around it, eating and talking. The air smelled of smoke and cooked meat, and the temperature was comfortably warm if they stayed close to the fire. In the woods around them, coyotes howled and yipped, calling out to one another and singing the songs of their nightly hunt. As the men relaxed in the evening air, enjoying the comfortable sensation of full stomachs, they could hear the honking of Canada geese. The sky was clear, with a bright, pearly moon that illuminated the birds as they flew through the darkness. The last time they'd seen geese was in Georgian Bay, when the birds were flying south. It was strange to realize they'd seen nature's cycle all the way through, from summer to fall to winter and now a return to spring. The voyage was drawing close to its end.

Memphis, Tennessee
March 3, 1977

The rain fell in an oppressive deluge, as if all the moisture in Earth's atmosphere had converged upon the Mississippi River at Memphis. Each canoe became a ghostly island in the downpour, almost invisible as the men struggled to peer through the nearly opaque curtain of water. For once the wind was helping them, blowing at their backs and providing a small amount of visibility. It also occasionally sent waves of dirty river water crashing into the sterns of their boats, which was less helpful. The rain soaked through the men's ponchos and clothes in minutes and shriveled the skin on their hands and feet. The huge droplets came down so hard and fast that their collision with the surface of the Mississippi made it almost impossible to distinguish where the rain ended and the river began. At least one man per boat had to dedicate his energy to bailing out the waves and rainwater that quickly accumulated in the bottom of the canoes. Though the air was relatively warm, the rain was icy. It drained the men's body heat as effectively as snow and ice, if not more so. Before long, half the crew was trembling.

Terry Cox felt more frozen than he'd ever been during the winter hike from hell, and Father Loran, who'd chosen that day for his return to the canoes after being absent since October, was shaking uncontrollably. They were all at risk for hypothermia if they didn't get warm and dry soon. The men had covered twenty-five miles despite the rainstorm; it was time to call it a day and find a campsite for the night.

The crew chose a soggy but easily accessible patch of earth to land. They hopped out of their boats, stumbling on limbs leaden with cold. The tempest had eased to a light drizzle, which made it possible to erect shelters that weren't leaking. Everyone stripped and hung their sodden clothes up to dry on trees and the ropes that held up the shelters, but unless the rain ceased completely, it seemed like they'd be paddling in damp clothes the next day as well. The gloomy weather kept the men from staying up after they'd eaten their dinner of hot dogs and macaroni and cheese. By 7:00 nearly everyone had retired to the shelters. They tried to ignore the water seeping into their sleeping pads. It was a dismal way to spend the night. And to think, just twenty-four hours earlier they'd been preparing for a party at the home of Memphis police lieutenant Edward Hudgens.

The five days the expedition had just spent in Memphis would set a pattern for the coming weeks. The men's schedule was stuffed full of nightly performances and daytime visits to schools and hospitals, leaving the men only the occasional evening or two away from crowds to blow off steam. Most of the extracurricular activities in Memphis had been organized by Lieutenant Hudgens, who went by the nickname "Hudge." The 53-year-old cop was in charge of escorting the members of the expedition around the city during their stay and helping with any issues that arose, including things like negotiating with the fire department after the voyageurs were told they couldn't build fires on their campsite in Tom Lee Park. Hudge and his officers spent several evenings with the crew, swapping stories about the police force for stories of paddling across the country. It was easier for the men to be frank about their experiences and the challenges of life on the water when they weren't being careful not to swear or presenting information in an educational, easily digestible format. Though the expedition's intended purpose was to educate the public, more and more crew members were avoiding visitors who came to their campsite armed with questions. Fialko was disappointed to see this response, but recognized the same unwillingness to engage with people in himself. With their busy schedule and lack of personal time, they all felt the strain of constant publicity. Adoration by crowds of young women hadn't lost its charm, but the visibility involved with being a minor celebrity was growing irksome.

For better or for worse, the expedition's reputation had only grown since the men had reached the Mississippi River. A film crew from an Arkansas news station had come to Memphis to start work on a documentary about the voyage. The cameramen planned to stay with the modern voyageurs until they reached the Gulf and planted a cross in the sand. The expedition was even followed by a reporter from *People* magazine, who watched several of their landing formations and took pictures that would be published to a national audience. The surge in publicity was welcome, but it also brought the men a degree of notoriety that they couldn't easily escape.

Fialko was happy to see the warm welcome the crew received in many of the towns they visited and especially appreciated the people who involved themselves in the spirit of the expedition. He was less pleased with how the crew members were treating one another. He tried to separate personal issues from the task at hand, but sometimes it felt like ongoing tension between crewmates overshadowed everything else.

In Memphis, there had been some hard feelings when the men wanted to cut loose for an evening and have drinks with Hudge, which made Reid Lewis uncomfortable. On the water, the paddlers were having trouble staying within sight of one another, those in the lead canoe forgetting to keep an eye on those who paddled behind them. They often found themselves bickering about where to land if a spot hadn't been arranged in advance. Wilson, who was a member of Fialko's module, contended Lewis was lying to the group about their schedule and protecting the liaison team from what he thought was valid criticism. In the teen's opinion, the women still weren't doing enough advance prep work or taking care of the essentials. Hobart no longer seemed to trust Lewis's decisions, and Cox sided with Hobart in criticizing every choice their La Salle made. If they all followed the psychological training they'd received before the expedition and delved to the root of the issue, maybe the problems would have been dealt with and dismissed instead of lingering and creating rifts. Instead, tension continually bubbled beneath the surface and every major decision Lewis made was resented or criticized.

"I think a lot of the criticism is unfounded, based on prejudice, mistrust, rumor, pressure, the tediousness of what we're doing," Fialko wrote in his journal. "I suppose I should talk to someone about this. Maybe I'm all mixed up. But tonight I feel good because of a telephone conversation I just had with Linda."

Two weeks later in March, Fialko had time to reflect on another aspect of the trip in which it seemed the crew wasn't meeting his expectations: their voyageur identities. It had been a short day on the river, only eight miles of paddling since they'd managed to cover fifty-five miles the day before, thanks to the strong current at their backs. For once the crew was complaining about Hobart instead of Lewis, who had directed them to a less-than-ideal campsite. In the morning the navigator told them they'd stop on the Louisiana shore not far from Vicksburg, Mississippi; but when it came time to get off the water, Hobart told them to head for a small island in the middle of the river because he thought it looked like a better campsite. The island was thick with grapevines and Virginia creeper, and the men had to spend time clearing vines off the ground in order to pitch the shelters. It wasn't the worst place they'd ever camped, but the extra work made everyone irritable. At least there was plenty of greenery all around them instead of the dead, brown plants they'd grown so accustomed to over the winter.

After a dinner of mixed vegetables, Fialko flipped back through a book he'd read before the expedition called *Interpreting Our Heritage*. Its author, Freeman Tilden, shared his experience in the National Park Service and offered advice on how best to ignite a spark of curiosity in audiences. "Through interpretation, understanding; through understanding, appreciation; through appreciation, protection," Tilden wrote.[7]

Fialko also looked through some letters sent to him by Bill Voyles, one of the muzzleloaders from Indiana. Voyles wrote that he and the other members of his group wouldn't want to appear with the voyageurs for fear of the unflattering light it would cast on them—the La Salle voyageurs were so dedicated to authenticity that most other historical interpretations looked shoddy by comparison. But Fialko wasn't convinced the men were staying true to their mission.

"When we began, we made a simple rule—everything that people saw would be authentic or appear to be so, or, where concessions were made, they would be covered. There was a time when we would duck into our shelter to eat a candy bar and plastic did not appear to exist . . . Now we eat or drink anything in public, with Coke cans appearing in camp and plastic jugs and other containers abounding . . . I thought everyone was going to be a voyageur for eight months. When someone visits our camp, for example, he should expect to see (and hear?) 17th-century voyageurs, an optimal interpretation. Last week in Rosedale, the visitors to our camp were treated to a football game, paperback novels, and modern songs.

"I can make an excuse and say the length of the trip is getting to everyone, that we can't be true voyageurs because we have a 20th-century schedule, or a number of other excuses, but for my part they are all weak excuses," he continued. "When, in the final evaluation of any project, it is asked, did you do the job? Can we answer yes, or mostly, or sometimes? Has our pride lessened?"

Wrapped up in the desire for a perfect reproduction were both modern and timeless fears. The fear that the future would sweep away all remnants of the past in its rough current, the fear that no matter how well they performed their role as voyageurs, the act would be forgotten as soon as the curtain fell, the fear that all their work and suffering was ultimately meaningless. The world was changing so rapidly, from technological innovations (Apple was founded by Steve Jobs and Steve Wozniak in 1976) to societal expectations (women and men were starting to regularly live together outside of wedlock), that clinging to the past felt like one of the only ways to exert control on the present. The tension of a society struggling to recognize itself was palpable. Only a few years earlier French president Valery Giscard d'Estaing stated, "The world is unhappy. It is unhappy because it does not know where it is going and because it senses that if it knew, it would discover it was heading for disaster." What could a crew of men paddling down the Mississippi River in strange costumes really do to help the world, to keep it from catastrophe? Who would remember their journey in five years or ten years or twenty?

But by the next morning, Fialko had come around once again. A quiet night of sleep on the river seemed to have calmed his crisis of faith in the expedition. Maybe he held himself and others to an unattainably high standard. "The editorial of last night I think is the result of my wanting us to be perfect," he wrote. "We are voyageurs—but 20th-century voyageurs. People still respect what we are doing and are satisfied by what they see."

Natchez, Mississippi
March 23, 1977

Dozens of girls in colorful hoop dresses and tight bodices emphasizing narrow waists spun around the dance floor with their partners. An audience that included two dozen grubby voyageurs looked on in delight. The crowd rose to its feet when the Confederate flag was brought out and joined in the singing when "America the Beautiful" was played. Reid Lewis had been singled out among the crew members and was asked to join the dancing. In his formal red jacket and black hat with a sword buckled at his hip, he looked the part of a dashing general. But he was a reluctant participant, Jan thought as she watched. Her husband wasn't nearly as comfortable on a dance floor as he was in a canoe. He did well enough despite his embarrassment, spinning around with his partner. It was an incongruous pairing: a French voyageur with a Southern belle.

Sometime after February 15, the expedition had crossed the boundary between the "apparent South" (places north of the Mason–Dixon line but with some of the same cultural beliefs as the states below the line) and entered the "real South," a land replete with antebellum mansions, twangy accents, and stories of the "War of Northern Aggression." The air was warm, the mosquitoes had reappeared, and some of their Southern hosts joked about the voyageurs' funny northern accents.

While the men were in Vicksburg on March 20, they visited the Old Warren County Court House Museum and went on a tour of the infamous Vicksburg battleground with a guide named Gordon Cotton, who was a member of the Warren County Historical Society. He liked to refer to the Civil War in terms of "us vs. them," interspersing his account of the battle with statements like, "We fought hard but they outnumbered us." Lewis mentioned that he'd once known a Southerner who was 17 before he learned "damn Yankee" was two words instead of one. As Civil War historian Shelby Foote, who was born in Mississippi, once pronounced, "Southerners are very strange about that war."

Whatever beliefs the locals may have held about the war fought a century earlier, no one could say the expedition wasn't benefiting from plenty of Southern hospitality. On the river they were cheered on by the captains of tugboats, who shouted from their megaphones things like, "History in the making!" and "You're never gonna get out to the Gulf if you don't get up and get after it," when the crew was sleeping in late. They received large meals from 4-H clubs and restaurants in every town, a canoe escort out of Vicksburg, visits to antebellum mansions, and free mint juleps during their tour of the *Mississippi Queen*, the largest paddle wheel steamboat ever built. The magnificent ship was like a floating hotel, with 206 state rooms and a carrying capacity of 412 guests plus 157 crew. The ship had been on the Mississippi for less than a year and traveled 170 miles each way between Natchez and New Orleans, with a day of travel costing anywhere from $100 to $200.

Much as the men enjoyed the warmer weather and the friendliness of the locals, everyone was ready for the trip to be over. They were past the seven-month mark and well into the one-month countdown. In early April they'd arrive in New Orleans for celebrations with family, friends, and followers. From there it was a few hundred more miles down the river to the Gulf of Mexico. Some of the men were already antsy and ready to be done, while others weren't quite ready to say good-bye to their voyageur lives.

"Most of the crew is hanging on pretty good," Fialko wrote in his journal one evening outside Baton Rouge. "I think the attitude of most of the crew is 'let's get it over with.' I wonder if we'll look back at this and think of mostly the good times, or will the negative stuff come back to haunt us?"

Chapter Eleven

THE GREEN BUOY

Gulf of Mexico
April 9, 1682

The question of when exactly La Salle reached the end of the Mississippi River is difficult to answer. In one account, Henri de Tonty recorded that the party separated into two groups to follow a fork in the river on April 7 and on April 8 they reunited, having successfully found the Gulf of Mexico.[1] The official account recorded by Jacques de La Metairie, the expedition's notary, says April 9 was the date when a cross and a leaden plate engraved with the arms of France were placed on shore at the edge of the ocean. A third account, this one written by Nicholas de la Salle (no relation to La Salle), establishes April 22 as the date on which La Salle claimed the Mississippi River and the territory covered by its watershed for France.[2] While the exact date surely held some importance for La Salle and his men, it is of slightly less concern for the armchair traveler. The goal in highlighting the discrepancies here is not to argue in favor of the veracity of one account over another but to illustrate how much is lost in the passage of time. Even something as seemingly straightforward as the date of an event can be subject to debate. History is a series of events that have been recorded by a limited few but experienced by many. The tale is often altered in the retelling, and varies from one person's perspective to another's.

On whichever date La Salle arrived at the Gulf of Mexico, he followed the protocol required of all French explorers. He displayed the king's arms along with the Latin inscription "Louis the Great reigns. Robert Cavelier, with the Lord Tonty as Lieutenant, R. P. Zenobe Membré Recollet, and twenty Frenchmen, first navigated this stream from the country of the Illinois and also passed through its mouth on the 9th day of April, 1692." He also prepared a *procès-verbal*, a document that served as a title for the "discovered" land. As a final nod to the Christian God who had lead them there safely, La Salle had his men erect a cross and sing the national hymn "God Save the King" in Latin.[3] He named the territory La Louisiane for the king.

Whether or not La Salle realized the scope of his claim in North America, it's certain that King Louis XIV didn't. An ocean and a world away, the Sun King was busy with the removal of the court to the Palace of Versailles and a campaign to take control of Luxembourg. For most of its history under France, the Louisiana territory would be overlooked and underfunded. In 1803, the United States, a fledgling country, purchased the territory from France for $15 million without France ever realizing what exactly she had been in possession of for 120 years.

As for La Salle, his dream of establishing a French colony where the Mississippi emptied into the Gulf of Mexico slowly disintegrated. When La Salle's ally, Governor Frontenac, was replaced by Joseph-Antoine de La Barre, La Salle had no choice but to return to France and present his case before the Court, since La Barre refused to offer his support the way Frontenac had. In France, La Salle argued that the mouth of the Mississippi held strategic importance and deserved to be the site of a new French colony. He was given command of three ships and more than three hundred crew members and colonists to sail for the Gulf of Mexico, but the voyage was plagued with problems as soon as they set sail. One ship was lost to privateers and another sank in Matagorda Bay. When La Salle's ship landed in December 1684 with far fewer colonists than he'd anticipated having, La Salle believed they were near the Mississippi and instructed the men to construct a fort. But a navigational error had actually placed them close to modern-day Matagorda, Texas, some four hundred miles west of the Mississippi. Over the course of two years, more than 140 of the 180 colonists who lived in the colony La Salle created died in their struggle against the wilderness, local tribes, and lack of supplies. La Salle set out on multiple occasions to search for the Mississippi River in hopes of contacting the French forts farther up the Mississippi to request aid. Growing increasingly desperate, he made a final attempt with a group of men early in 1687.

One day in March, La Salle sent out a small hunting party that included his nephew, Colin Crevel; his servant; and their Indian guide, Nika. After an argument broke out between members of the hunting party, the three men were murdered by their compatriots. On March 19, 1687, La Salle went to investigate the hunting party's delay and was lured into an ambush and killed, perhaps because the men no longer trusted his leadership, or perhaps for personal reasons. Seven men survived the mutiny and eventually made their way up the Mississippi River to report La Salle's death.[4] His body was never recovered. His legacy gradually faded into the relative obscurity of high school history books, his name becoming one of those familiar but meaningless placeholders that adorn street signs and townships.

Donaldsonville to the *Delta Queen*
March 31, 1977

The paddleboat appeared around a sharp bend in the river, its four white decks stacked one on top of the other like a delicately iced layer cake. All the levels were filled with people watching for the expedition's arrival. As the canoes pulled closer to the vessel, the men raised their water-worn paddles to salute the assembled crowd. From this distance they could read the ship's name printed in white block letters on a black stern: *Delta Queen*.

The voyageurs were welcomed to shore by the captain, dressed in a black jacket with two rows of golden buttons running down the front, and a small marching band complete with trumpet, trombone, and drum. One by one the crew walked up the red-carpeted gangplank and stepped onto the historic vessel. Unlike their small canoes, the *Delta Queen* herself barely shifted with the weight of the young men as they boarded. At 285 feet long and 58 feet wide, the paddleboat weighed 1,650 tons before any passengers stepped aboard. She was the oldest paddleboat still operating on the Mississippi River and had a reputation that stretched across the entire country. Originally the *Delta Queen* operated on the Sacramento River between San Francisco and Sacramento. In World War II she reported for duty in San Francisco Bay. After surviving the war, she was brought through the Panama Canal up to the Ohio River and traveled between New Orleans and Cincinnati. In 1970, nearly fifty years into her faithful service, the old ship was added to the list of National Register of

Historic Places. It was onto this physical vestige of history that the voyageurs now stepped.

The captain directed the men to the Mark Twain room for their presentation. The enclosed space was dark compared to the bright, open river, despite the windows that lined either side of the room. A large audience crowded into padded chairs and behind rows of tables to listen to the presentation. The men went through the normal round of songs and skits, educating their audience on the history of the voyageurs and French exploration of the Mississippi Valley before eventually coming to one of their a cappella numbers, "À la Claire Fontaine." The love song was used to explain the voyageurs' connection to the people they left behind whenever they set out for the wilderness, and it rarely failed to evoke similar feelings of homesickness in its performers, especially now that they were so close to completing their expedition.

The day before, ten miles up the river in Donaldsonville, some of the men had ended their family phone conversations with "See you Saturday." Only two days away. Three days from now they'd make their grand entrance in New Orleans, and in ten days the voyage would be over. It had been 233 days since they had set off from Montreal, a group of recently graduated high school students and their teachers wearing funny costumes on a mission for God and country—well, at least for country. They'd been awkward time travelers then, unaccustomed to the rigors of paddling all day and the discomfort of sleeping outdoors in all weather. Now they were confident voyageurs who could paddle canoes in their sleep (literally—some crew members were known for dozing while they paddled) and navigate the contours of the nation's waterways. In ten days that lifestyle would end. The self-made time machine would be disassembled, one artifact at a time, until they were regular young men again, preparing to start the early years of their adult lives. But for now, the mixture of nervousness and unbearable eagerness for the end of the trip had to be pushed aside. The next ten days were going to be overflowing with engagements.

After their presentation in the Mark Twain room, the voyageurs were escorted around the rest of the ship. The captain invited them into the pilothouse, demonstrating the wheels and levers that propelled the paddleboat at a leisurely pace up and down the river. Outside the pilothouse he showed them the ship's calliope. The instrument looked similar to an organ, with its wooden frame painted red. But instead of moving wind through pipes to produce sound, the calliope, which was made from large whistles sometimes pulled from old locomotives, used steam to produce its shrill music. This calliope was used to great effect when the *Delta Queen* entered or departed a harbor. Since the volume of a calliope couldn't be controlled, the loud songs could be heard near and far.

From the *Delta Queen* the men were escorted into another era of the past, this time to the Antebellum South. Not far from where the *Delta Queen* was docked at Burnside lay the Houmas House. The magnificent Greek revival mansion was built in 1840 and named for the members of the Native American tribe who sold the land to its original French owners. The entrance to the mansion was an oak alley, the gnarled tree branches crisscrossed like manmade arches over a covered path. The mansion itself was enormous, surrounded by columns and topped with a belvedere that overlooked the manicured terrain. Waiting at the front of the mansion among the columns was a small group of Southern belles wearing hoop skirts, one in lilac, one in powder blue, one in navy blue, all with knitted shawls wrapped around their shoulders. The women chatted with the men as they went through their tour of the mansion, the two groups perhaps comparing the relative authenticity of their costumes and their knowledge of the period they were representing.

The mansion was beautiful and seemed thick with ghosts of the pre–Civil War past. It was perfectly convincing except for one jarring absence: there were no slaves. That was the problem with re-creating the past—it was easy to get caught up in the grandeur of the illusion, immersing oneself in the minutiae of replicable details and avoiding the human tragedies that accompanied such lifestyles.

Both the visit to the *Delta Queen* and the Houmas House passed quickly. By 4:00 the men were back in their canoes, returned to the familiar era of the French voyageurs. They paddled for another hour before pulling off to look for a campsite in a field strewn with cow patties. It was easy work compared to the previous day, when they'd paddled sixty miles and arrived after dark on a black river illuminated by the lights of towns and industrial facilities. With the end of the expedition approaching, many of the crew members had grown more introspective in their nighttime musings. Just a few days ago, Bob Kulick had been ruminating on the Elton John song "Goodbye Yellow Brick Road." There was college to think about now, and a move to Connecticut since his parents no longer lived in Illinois. What would happen next?

"I thought how nice it must be to have 'finally decided my future life beyond the yellow brick road,'" Kulick wrote in his journal, quoting a line from the song. "Because I'm coming to the end of my 'yellow brick road' and I realize that the apprehension I feel about returning to the 20th century stems from the fact that I have not yet gotten a grasp on what my 'future life beyond the yellow brick road' is going to be. This trip has been my 'yellow brick road' in that it has held security. Maybe the freedom that I've been saying I've had in this past year is a false sense. All the rules have been outlined and I've known what is to happen more or less each day. Now that the road is ending, maybe this is when I'll find my freedom. I guess only time will really tell."

New Orleans, Louisiana
April 3, 1977

The bow of the canoe shot a foot out of the water as it crested a wave and landed with a splash. The strong southern wind chased gray clouds across the sky and turned the river into a choppy froth, like egg whites whipped into stiff peaks. If not for the warm temperature, it would've been an absolutely miserable paddle. The men were battling both wind and waves, getting doused repeatedly and having to bail the boats out, which made for sluggish progress. But they had a 2:00 arrival time for New Orleans, and nothing was going to delay them, short of the total destruction of one of the boats by an angry river monster. Towboat pilots *had* warned them about the wampus cats, but in addition to being mythical animals, it seemed unlikely the cougar hybrids were aquatic.

As the six canoes drew closer to their destination at Audubon Park, a small fleet of powerboats materialized, bobbing around on the chop. A powerboat with a wooden sign proclaiming REGATTA PATROL carried Jorge Garcia, whose right arm was still wrapped in a sling. Neither he nor Steve Marr had been able to rejoin the expedition—Garcia due to his lengthy recovery and healing arm and Marr because the cast that stretched from his toes to his hip would be too much of a liability, not to mention that it limited his range of motion. But both were able to travel in the vans with the liaison team, and they joined the evening presentations. Marr had even found crutches made from uncarved branches to make him look like a historically authentic invalid.

A New Orleans fireboat joined the assembled fleet and fired its water cannons as the canoes came into view. Jets of water arced high above them, glinting in the patchy sunlight and splashing down into the river. On shore a crowd of over one thousand people cheered as the voyageurs arrived in formation. The viewers lined the shore and observation deck, spilling out over the rocky slope down to the river. Cameras flashed and memorialized the moment. Three hundred years earlier La Salle had passed this spot without any fanfare. The land was all marshes and swamps, dense with mosquitoes and alligators. The improbable city of New Orleans hadn't yet been dreamed up.

The men pulled their canoes ashore with some difficulty, given the density of the crowd. As soon as they had enough space cleared from the crowd, Lewis unsheathed his sword, thrust it into the air, and claimed the land for France. Again. Wearing a ruffled blue shirt, George LeSieutre unfurled a white sheet of paper with the words of La Salle's original declaration printed across it. Lewis read the speech in front of a tall wooden cross they planted in the ground while the crew members and a huge audience gathered around him. When all the speeches and ceremonies were completed (the men were made honorary citizens of New Orleans, gifted framed copies of a speech made in the U.S. House of Representatives congratulating them on their expedition, and informed that the Illinois Legislature had declared La Salle: Expedition II a Historic Landmark in Illinois), family members and reporters surged forward. The voyageurs were conspicuous in the crowd of men and women wearing T-shirts and jeans and sunglasses. Many of the young men had left their shirts off after arriving; their skin was tanned and pocked with bug bites. Mark Fredenburg wore a skunk hat over his curly brown hair and a necklace of shells. Others had unruly beards and headbands holding back their long hair. Whatever transformation had been anticipated at the start of the voyage now appeared complete. The parents of the voyageurs beamed at their sons' achievement.

Lewis, always the first to be cornered by a reporter with a microphone, was explaining all the additional trials his crew had faced compared to the original expedition. La Salle never dealt with barge and tanker traffic or water pollution. He hadn't needed to dodge wing dams and carry water casks between stops. Granted, the men on the modern expedition never had to worry about starvation or attacks from hostile Native Americans like the earlier men had, and they relied on accurate maps to chart their course. They still had their own difficulties to overcome in the "civilized" world of the 20th century.

"I think we have mixed emotions about how things have changed," Lewis told a reporter from the Associated Press. "In some ways we have made magnificent progress, in other ways we have painfully regressed." The latter half of this statement was a reference to the environment, which Lewis saw as becoming hopelessly degraded and polluted since La Salle's era.

Elsewhere in the crowd, reporters had their microphones pointed toward other crew members, asking about the difficulties of the journey and the long winter. Ralph Frese, the amateur historian who had in some ways inspired the voyage, answered questions about the men's use of wool during the long winter and described Lewis's mission to bring a living history museum to people all over the country. It was a chaotic, cacophonous gathering, the culmination of a goal the crew had striven to meet for seven months. It almost didn't matter that they still had more than one hundred miles to paddle to reach the Gulf. They'd made it this far. A few more days of work was nothing in comparison to how far they'd come.

That was, in effect, what Lewis had told Father Loran Fuchs a few days earlier while Lewis was standing on the riverbank, enjoying the peacefulness of the water.

"Do you regret having done this?" the priest asked.

"The time for regret was way farther north," Lewis responded. Now was time for celebration. Now was time for reveling in their successes. For the past three years, Lewis had dedicated his entire life to the realization of this dream, and now it was almost at a close. Despite all the hardships, the arguments, the badmouthing and gossiping, despite the pain and suffering and privations, despite the doubts about the capability of the leadership and the rupture between the crew and the liaison team, they had made it. Overcoming all the tests tossed at them by nature had been a challenge—nearly deadly at times—but equally difficult was surmounting personal disputes and working as a team. And then there were all the other obstacles, the daily quandaries and problems. How many times had Lewis worried for the integrity of the expedition, worried about the debt they were accumulating, worried about the lasting effect of injuries his crew members had suffered? Now they had almost reached their final goal. New Orleans was the penultimate event before the grand finale at the Gulf of Mexico. The final difficulty would be resisting the intoxicating attractions of the Crescent City and, unlike Odysseus's men, not succumbing to the spell of the lotus-eaters.

Two members of the group were, unfortunately, forced to leave the festivities in New Orleans instead of accompanying the group to its final destination. Bart Dean, who had paddled with them, camped with them, and photographed their lives for the past eight months, was headed out to Los Angeles to live with his girlfriend and get going on his career as a screenwriter. To thank him for his work and his companionship, the crew signed one of their spare paddles and gave it to him. Cathy Palmer, a member of the liaison team, had been surprised by her parents and brothers by the announcement that the whole family was taking a trip to the amusement park in Florida that had opened only a few years earlier—Disney World. It was a huge deal that the whole family would be going, but instead of feeling excitement at the prospect,

Palmer was devastated. She'd come all this way with the men, and now she wouldn't be seeing them to the end.

The other members of the liaison team, though they planned on staying till the Gulf of Mexico, seemed to have mentally checked out months ago. Sharon Baumgartner, who'd managed to stay optimistic for much of the trip, struggled to keep her focus as the end neared. She was frustrated with Jan and Marlena, having overheard the two older women dismissing her as "still young." Back home she'd been nominated as a candidate for the Miss Elgin beauty pageant, and her head was full of ideas for her hair and makeup and what talent she'd present. Jan and Marlena had struggled with the crew members' complaints since the start of the voyage, and it hadn't grown any easier to deal with the criticism. Now more than ever they wanted to see the expedition come to an end and return to their lives in the classroom.

As for the rest of the crew, New Orleans presented some of the most tempting opportunities for carousing that they'd seen since departing from Montreal. Bourbon Street called with its easy access to alcohol, and several of the young men got in trouble with Lewis when they tried to go out in their civilian clothes so as to attract less attention. Lewis admonished them for acting like the expedition was over—they had dinners to attend in New Orleans that were being hosted by the French and Canadian consular offices, schools to visit, performances to complete. Yes, there was some downtime to spend with their families, but that didn't mean they were done being voyageurs. The end, he reminded them, was still a week away.

Pilottown to the Gulf
April 9, 1977

For the first time since they'd departed Montreal, John Fialko had butterflies in his stomach. Fitting, really, to be nervous for the first and last day. He'd eaten a candy bar and an apple for breakfast when they woke up at 5:00, then busied himself with breaking down the campsite and loading the canoes. By 6:10 all the canoes were gliding down a calm river flanked by a small support team— the powerboats held friends and family members. The dense mass of industrial machinery and huge vessels that had dominated the riverbanks since Baton Rouge had given way to vast tracts of forest and marshes. Wispy branches of water hickory and pond cypress drooped over the river as the scattered houses of Pilottown disappeared behind the boats.

The village was inhabited by only thirty people. It had one bar, a school where four students studied, and no stores. The town had no roads and was inaccessible by car—visitors could arrive only by boats and small planes. Strangest of all was the town's layout. Everything, including the sidewalks, was on stilts. The Mississippi rose and fell every year during flood season and any houses built on the swampy ground would've been repeatedly washed away. This far south the Mississippi was constantly remaking itself, and that variation was what brought about the creation of Pilottown in the first place. The houses were mostly occupied by barge and freighter pilots who navigated the ever-changing channels of the river. They hopped on boats in the Gulf, captained them north through difficult passages, then returned control to the ships' pilots. Or they transported boats in the opposite direction, from New Orleans to the Gulf. Either way, the job required them to have an intimate familiarity with the river. This knowledge made many of the captains dubious of the expedition's ability to return from the Gulf, which was a necessary post-finale journey unless the men wanted to be stranded on a sandbar outside the Mississippi River.

"Those headbands on your heads don't make you Indians," one of the pilots told the crew. Paddling down the river would be easy enough, sure. The little canoes wouldn't have to worry about shallow spots or sand banks. But turning back north would mean fighting against a strong current. Too strong to be overpowered by muscle strength and force of will, in the pilots' minds. They gave the expedition a radio to take with them just in case they needed a lift back. One pilot was so certain the expedition would be stymied by the current that he bet them a bottle of whisky that they wouldn't make it. The crew was less concerned. It was like the St. Lawrence River all over again. Many had claimed that the current was too strong for canoeists, yet they'd conquered it in the earliest days of the voyage. Now they were at their peak of physical fitness. It might take a while to make the fifteen miles back to Pilottown, but no one on the crew had any doubts that they could do it.

In addition to their skepticism, the pilots provided useful information on which branch of the river to take out to the ocean. Of the four channels, the pilots recommended the canoes follow South Pass. Loutre Pass to the east and Southwest Pass to the west were both longer routes, while Main Pass was north of their starting point. It was a beautiful day for paddling, with no wind to speak of and a gleaming blue sky—maybe it was Mother Nature rewarding the men at last for all the grief she'd put them through over the winter.

After two hours of paddling, the canoes were nearly at the Gulf. Farther ahead they could see the line of trees fall away and the water opening up to the ocean. In the distance a buoy was visible on the blue water. This was the mythical end point they'd heard about since before the trip began. The green buoy was a marker to guide tankers into the Mississippi. It indicated the start—and end—of America's largest river system, its most vital artery.

"As we approached the gulf and actually saw salt water, I thought of the time, the hassles, the hardships, mental and physical, and they all came together for that one instant when we passed the bell buoy and turned north," Ron Hobart would later write of the experience. "Three years of work and sacrifice have paid off to the highest degree."

The buoy grew larger as the canoes drew closer. They formed a line and the men pulled furiously at the water with their oars. From the back of his canoe Mark Fredenburg paused to fire his musket, and the group let out a tremendous volley of whoops. The land that had enclosed them on the river for so long opened up to the immensity of the ocean, the dirty brown sediment–laden river water fanning out into the gulf and sinking beneath the cerulean expanse of salt water. Less than a mile out from the mouth of the Mississippi was the green buoy with its flashing green lantern. Here the boats came to a stop.

One by one, each crew member reached his paddle through the metal structure and beat the bell that hung from the top of the buoy. It rang out again and again, everyone cheering and turning to shake hands with their crewmates and open bottles of wine that had been given to them earlier in the expedition. When Clif Wilson got to the bell, he was overwhelmed with emotion. He'd been pretty certain he was going to die in the capsizing off Washington Island, and he'd been seriously injured in the truck accident. And now, despite all that, he was unwaveringly and unmistakably *there*. The thrill he felt was almost painfully powerful. He never expected to play professional football, but he imagined that the feeling bursting inside him was something akin to winning the Super Bowl.

From the buoy the canoes turned back to the nearby sandy beach. Waiting for them there were the wives, parents, and friends who had supported them throughout the voyage. As they paddled, Terry Cox pulled off his moccasins and cast them into the ocean. The leather slippers had survived everything since the Toronto portage. It was time to return to modern footwear. As soon as they landed, the crew ran straight into the ocean, splashing and tackling and hugging one another. Steve Marr followed behind on his crutches to get his cast wet, and Jorge Garcia waded in. Even Lewis, in his white ruffled La Salle costume, joined the gaiety. Father Loran watched the merriment from shore. He looked somber in his black robe and scraggly gray beard. Whatever he may have been pondering—the significance of their accomplishment, the mirth of a God watching the culmination of a historic canoe voyage for a second time—he suddenly seemed to snap out of his reverie. He raced down to the water, his momentum carrying him in up to the waist. He jumped forward to fully submerge himself, but sank hardly more than a foot. There was a sandbar directly in his path. Those who saw him watched as he emerged, sandy, waterlogged, and laughing.

It was only fitting that the liaison team be thanked for their hard work by being thrown in the ocean as well, so the men formed small groups to carry the women to the water. Baumgartner, in a short-sleeved blouse and long skirt, was dropped onto her back into the waves, grinning from ear to ear the entire time. Jan and Marlena were slightly more reluctant, but submitted to the ritual dousing. They'd survived the trip, too, after all. In some ways, it had been as much a struggle for them as it had been for the crew. They'd had to deal with arguments and logistics and the ravages of the winter. The vans weren't even equipped with heaters, so they froze while driving over snow and ice. And here they were at the end, on a beach in Louisiana facing the boundless ocean.

After an hour of playing, it was time to get down to business. Randy Foster constructed a tall cross of driftwood and buried it in the sand. For the second time Lewis drew his sword and read the declaration that would turn the Mississippi Valley into French territory. The crew filled the air with shouts of *"Vive le roi!"* at the end of the proclamation and helped bury a plaque in the ground beneath the cross, a replica of the plaque La Salle carried with him that named King Louis XIV the ruler of the region.

For all the similarities between the original voyage and La Salle: Expedition II, there were ways in which the expeditions were hard to compare. The original voyageurs really were the first Europeans to travel all the way down the Mississippi River and see the delta spreading out like an enormous aquatic fan. Being the first to do any great thing is always remarkable. They were visitors to an already inhabited land, living in a world that would have been hard for their relatives in France to fathom. Their achievement continues to be memorialized today. The name of the state in which the Mississippi River ends was bestowed by La Salle: Louisiana, the land of King Louis. Maybe those voyageurs were brave men or foolhardy men or desperate men. History can't tell us how they reacted upon completion of their voyage. Did they run shouting into the ocean, hugging one another? Did they think about their wives or parents or the enormity of the unknown world? It's impossible to say. Metal plaques and the written procès-verbal say nothing about who these people were, their likes and dislikes, their quarrels and quirks.

As for the modern reenactors, personality was everything. It was what divided them and brought them together again, what kept them moving forward when others would have stopped. Would they be remembered for all they'd done? Would states and cities and schools and streets be named for their accomplishments? No. As the years went by, fewer and fewer people would remember the journey of the last voyageurs. But the men themselves would have the voyage permanently etched in their skin and bones. One can't embark on an odyssey and return unchanged.

It took another four hours of paddling for the men to reach Pilottown again. The current pushed hard against them as they made their way north, just as the pilots had warned. But it wasn't strong enough to stop them, especially after their grand success. When they pulled into the little stilted city, they were met with incredulous looks from the pilots and a bottle of whisky in the bar. The man who'd made the bet was too embarrassed to show his face.

Pilottown to Venice, Louisiana
April 10, 1977

The morning after the end was surreal. It was a Sunday, so Father Loran held mass as he usually did. It was the first time in years the people of Pilottown had mass performed in their village, and they were grateful for it. The pilots shared a breakfast with the voyageurs, complete with eggs, grits, sausage, and French toast. Then it was time for a last day of paddling, retracing their path for the second day in a row. They had no choice but to follow their earlier route once more and head back up the river to reach Venice. It was the closest town accessible by road, and they needed cars to carry their gear and themselves back to their homes in Illinois and trailers to cart the canoes back with them.

Even against the current, it was a short paddle. Only two and a half hours on the river. No audience waiting for them or their shows, no potlucks to attend or schools to visit. Only their 20th-century lives to get back to. It was chaos trying to unload the canoes for good and organize the five thousand pounds of gear in the trunks of cars. Everyone was rushing, most of them eager to leave. Ken Lewis was thinking about his celebratory visit to New Orleans and the bottle of bourbon and box of Cuban cigars he had planned to buy. He'd decided to forgo those vices. It hadn't been an easy eight months going clean, but why break his streak now?

He could treat himself with a greasy, sugary beignet from Café du Monde instead, and maybe a cream puff from another patisserie, and a lavish dinner at a nice restaurant. He could still take the hot bath, and it would still feel superb. Then, when he got back home, he'd join Alcoholics Anonymous and keep himself away from beer and liquor forever.

Gary Braun seemed to be one of the few who felt disappointed by the abrupt ending. It felt so . . . unceremonious. They'd done a final paddle salute on the Mississippi River, planted the cross yet again, and Lewis had thanked all the crew members for their hard work, then that was it. Braun didn't know what he wanted in place of the disorganized jubilation. Something that would provide more closure. Something that would say, "This is the very last day of your life as a voyageur. You're about to reenter the real world." Instead everyone just changed out of their voyageur clothing and into their civvies. Lots of guys had trouble fitting into their old clothing. Some had lost weight, others had gained it, and all of them had increased their muscle mass. Their thighs were larger and their shoulders wider. Normal clothes felt strange. Packing the five thousand pounds of gear they'd carried across the country in canoes and on their backs felt strange. Getting into cars and vans and boarding planes felt even stranger. They were walking out of the past into the present, a world that had existed all along right before their eyes and to which they now unquestionably belonged again. It was an uncomfortably abrupt transition. Braun knew they'd all be meeting up as a group in a month's time to assemble their notes and put on a few final performances. But by then everything would be different—they'd be 20th-century men again who just happened to know quite a lot about the lives of those who lived three hundred years earlier. Right now there seemed to be no acknowledgment of all that they'd been through. Everyone just wanted to get home. They wanted to say their good-byes and forget about the 17th century for a while.

Sid Bardwell hopped into one of the liaison team vans once more to transport a couple of men to the airport before driving the van back up to Illinois on his own. He appreciated the quietness of the drive after so many months of being surrounded by other people. After only a day away from the crew, the whole expedition felt like a vibrant, fantastic dream. It had lasted seemingly forever and now it was suddenly done. His alter ego Nika, La Salle's Indian guide, died a fast death on that car ride home, left behind somewhere in the Louisiana bayous. But the person who exited the van in Illinois wasn't the same person who'd first driven it to Montreal last summer. Like all the others, Bardwell had changed.

"I think the question usually asked is how was it, which is impossible to answer," he wrote in his journal when he got home. "Hell it was good and it was bad, it was hot, it was cold, it was one hell of a lot of fun and it was a real bitch, but I am glad I lived it. Then if the person who asked the question in the first place is still there, they ask, What next? or, Would you do it again? Yes, if I had never done it before, but having done it, it's been done."

EPILOGUE

For only the second time in three and a half decades, the crew of La Salle: Expedition II had gathered together for a reunion. Those who'd grown to be close friends over the course of the journey had kept in touch throughout the years, but it wasn't until 2012 that they'd all made a concerted effort to reunite with everyone. That first gathering was held in New Orleans, and there were four generations present for the celebration: parents of the voyageurs, the now middle-aged crew members, their children, and even a few grandchildren.

It had been a minor shock for those who hadn't seen one another in more than thirty years. Gone were the wild beards, the long hair, and the well-defined muscles of their canoeing days. Now most had gray hair or none at all. Some had beer bellies and wore glasses, while others had suffered illnesses or gone under the knife for injuries old and new. The men who had been teenagers when they were last together had jobs, wives, and children. They were lawyers, accountants, construction workers, park rangers, business owners, managers, and teachers. But underneath the new skins they'd acquired with age and experience, they retained much of what made them voyageurs.

The second reunion in Wisconsin required much less reacquainting. They'd seen one another only two years ago and already had plans for another reunion, this one to be held in Toronto in 2016 for the expedition's 40th anniversary. There were discussions of family life and careers, the problems and conveniences of the 21st century. But as always, the conversations held around a crackling bonfire eventually turned to their one shared experience and the ways it continued to shape them.

"I'm afraid there's a lot I don't remember," George LeSieutre said of the voyage. He sat next to his wife, Annie, both of them with graying hair, George's thick and in disarray. He was still thin and fit despite the passage of years: he liked to run marathons and the occasional ultra-marathon.

"Join the club. It's the forgetful club. The forty-year club," Randy Foster said.

"You hear the story and it's like, do I know that? Or have I just heard the story so many times?" Chuck Campbell said. He still wore a beard and had the same soft voice he'd had on the trip.

"Should I know that? Was I there?" LeSieutre concluded. Why was it so difficult to reconstruct something they'd all lived?

Part of the problem in creating a coherent narrative was that they were twenty-three individuals, all with different perspectives, different memories, different responses to what they'd undergone. The expedition had never been one story. It was the accumulated experiences of twenty-three young men living through something extreme and unique that tested their fortitude and their ability to see past one another's flaws. Little wonder that it was so hard to remember everything or understand what precisely had happened after nearly forty years had passed.

There, too, was the lack of organization of the surviving physical mementos. At the end of the expedition, everyone had taken home their canoe paddles, voyageur clothing, personal journals, and a collection of photos. Normal life resumed, with most going to college, others to work. Some of the crew members had scrapbooks created by family members that were filled with yellowing newspaper clips about the expedition. A few copies of the vinyl LPs the men had made during a short recording session at a studio in Chicago at the end of the expedition were still floating around eBay and used record shops, and were occasionally purchased by those who wanted to hear the songs of the voyageurs.

Reid Lewis himself had old promotional materials and documents from his La Salle: Expedition II presentation, which he created at the conclusion of the expedition as a way of paying off the debts he still owed. But the professional film footage of the men in canoes was gone. The boxes of notes from their nineteen interdisciplinary projects had vanished. No lesson plans were created. No studies were undertaken. The notes and recordings were lost in the chaos of trying to pay off debts in the aftermath of the expedition, and Lewis himself had been busy crafting the presentation he gave to hundreds of schools and businesses across the country and around the world in his new role as a motivational speaker. Years later, the letters from students and executives who saw his presentation were what mattered most. Their stories of using Lewis's advice to overcome personal hardships were the tangible result of the successful reenactment voyage. They were proof that the same spirit of adventure that had motivated him to organize the expedition could still be shared with and utilized by people of all ages.

But apart from those people who saw the post-trip presentations, La Salle: Expedition II became a mostly forgotten reenactment that happened during a brief, feverish period when America was obsessed with examining its historical roots. Whatever significance the voyage was supposed to have in the larger national narrative had long since been buried by a new discourse—terrorism and technology and social media and climate calamities. What then, was the point? Did any of it matter?

Perhaps the expedition's real value was unmeasurable, existing in the memories and abilities of all those who were touched by it. It was the hundreds of fires the men cooked and ate from for eight months and the stories they told one another each night. It was the children and adults who saw the lengths the men would go to in order to reach their destination. It was the courage and determination they showed in the face of so many hardships, major and minor, along the way. It was the self-confidence each of the participants earned by completing such a strenuous journey, the generosity they were shown by strangers, the friendships they formed. Each of the crew members carried all of these things inside them throughout their lives, thanks to the improbable vision of one man: Reid Lewis.

Whatever their relationship with him may have been on the expedition, all the crew members agreed that Lewis was the driving force behind the expedition's completion. Lewis, on the other hand, insisted that the expedition didn't belong to him, even though he was its creator. "It was our expedition," he said decades later. "Everyone played an important role, including all the thousands of people along the way." He credited his wife and the other members of the liaison team and everyone on the crew and all their supporters with the expedition's success. No matter how much or little a person had done to support the voyage, all of it mattered. They all provided the manpower for his original idea.

Though Lewis and his men had set out to create a replica of a much earlier journey, the end result was something else, unique and wholly new. It was a wild jump into the natural world, a Thoreauvian rejection of modernity and its easy comforts. La Salle embraced the world he lived in; the members of La Salle: Expedition II rejected it. But instead of making the men unfit for a life with electricity and indoor plumbing and the communication and information capacities of the Internet, living like voyageurs gave them the courage to overcome obstacles that have haunted humans since the dawning of self-awareness—uncertainty and doubt. More valuable than the increased muscle mass or the knowledge of obscure 17th-century names and events was the confidence the crew members gained in completing their odyssey. As Lewis likes to say, "You don't cross a canyon in two jumps. You either go for it or you don't." At numerous points along their route the modern voyageurs encountered gaping chasms, valleys so wide and obviously uncrossable that most sane people would have turned back. But they never did. They always chose to jump.

ENDNOTES

CHAPTER ONE: MAKE NO LITTLE PLANS

1   Mark Kurlansky, *Cod: A Biography of the Fish That Changed the World* (New York: Walker and Company, 1997).

2   Claiborne Skinner, *The Upper Country: French Enterprise in the Colonial Great Lakes* (Baltimore, Md.: Johns Hopkins University Press, 2008).

3   Donald Johnson, *La Salle: A Perilous Odyssey from Canada to the Gulf of Mexico*, 1st ed. (New York: Cooper Square Press, 2002).

4   Chilton Williamson, Jr., "They Almost Stole the Bicentennial," *National Review*, 8/20/1976.

5   Ibid.

6   "The U.S. Begins Its Birthday Bash," *Time*, 4/21/1975.

7   "Bicentennial Times," American Revolution Bicentennial Administration, April 1975.

8   "The Birthday Spirit," *Time*, July 5, 1976.

CHAPTER TWO: RECONSTRUCTING THE PAST

1   Anka Muhlstein, *La Salle: Explorer of the North American Frontier*, trans. from French by Willard Wood (New York: Arcade Publishing, 1994).

2   Claiborne Skinner, *The Upper Country: French Enterprise in the Colonial Great Lakes* (Baltimore, Md.: Johns Hopkins University Press, 2008).

3   "Letters Patent Granted by the King of France to the Sieur de La Salle on the 12th of May, 1678," *Collections of the Illinois State Historical Library*, vol. 1., ed. H. W. Beckwith (Springfield: H. W. Rokker Co., 1903).

4   William Henry Atherton, *Under the French Regime, 1535–1760* (Chicago: S. J. Clarke, 1914).

5   "Letters Patent Granted by the King of France to the Sieur de La Salle on the 12th of May, 1678," *Collections of the Illinois State Historical Library*, vol. 1., ed. H. W. Beckwith (Springfield: H. W. Rokker Co., 1903).

6   National Center for Education Statistics, http://nces.ed.gov/programs/digest/d07/tables/dt07_075.asp

7   Jon Van, "Teens to Put Safety First in Reliving Canoe Trek," *Chicago Tribune*, March 14, 1976. This quote and the following quotes are taken from this article.
8   Karen Blecha, "Reliving the Past," *The Daily Herald* (Chicago), July 17, 1976.
9   "Hooray for That Old RWB," *Time*, July 5, 1976.

CHAPTER THREE: THE LIFE OF A VOYAGEUR
1   Anka Muhlstein, *La Salle: Explorer of the North American Frontier* (New York: Arcade Publishing, 2013).
2   Using http://freepages.genealogy.rootsweb.ancestry.com/~unclefred/MONETARY.htm and http://www.bls.gov/data/inflation_calculator.htm to calculate inflation
3   Sophie White, *Wild Frenchmen and Frenchified Indians: Material Culture and Race in Colonial Louisiana* (Philadelphia: University of Pennsylvania Press, 2013).
4   Robert Cavelier Sieur de La Salle, *Relation of the Discoveries and Voyages of Cavelier de la Salle from 1679 to 1681*, trans. Melville B. Anderson (Chicago: The Caxton Club, 1901).
5   Henri de Tonty, *Relation of Henri de Tonty Concerning the Explorations of La Salle from 1678 to 1683*, trans. Melville Anderson (Chicago: The Caxton Club, 1898).
6   Claire Puccia Parham, *The St. Lawrence Seaway and Power Project: An Oral History of the Greatest Construction Show on Earth* (Syracuse, N.Y.: Syracuse University Press, 2009).
7   David Lowenthal, *The Past Is a Foreign Country* (Cambridge: Cambridge University Press, 1985).

CHAPTER FOUR: THE BONDS OF BROTHERHOOD
1   John Upton Terrell, *La Salle: The Life and Times of an Explorer* (New York: Weybright & Talley, 1968).
2   James E. Bruseth and Toni S. Turner, *From a Watery Grave: The Discovery and Expedition of La Salle's Shipwreck, La Belle* (College Station: Texas A&M University Press, 2005).
3   Carolyn Podruchny, *Making the Voyageur World*. (Lincoln: University of Nebraska Press, 2006).
4   Ibid.
5   Martin Cleary, "Flaming to Finish," *The Saturday Citizen*, July 26, 1976.

CHAPTER FIVE: STUCK BETWEEN TWO WORLDS
1   John McPhee, *The Survival of the Bark Canoe* (New York: Farrar, Straus and Giroux, 1982).
2   Charles Patrick Labadie, *Minnesota's Lake Superior Shipwrecks (A.D. 1650–1945)* (St. Paul: Minnesota Historical Society, 1990).
3   Carolyn Podruchny, *Making the Voyageur World* (Lincoln: University of Nebraska Press, 2006).
4   Ibid.
5   William C. Foster, ed., *The La Salle Expedition on the Mississippi River: A Lost Manuscript of Nicholas de la Salle, 1682*. (Austin: Texas State Historical Association, 2003).
6   Anka Muhlstein, *La Salle: Explorer of the North American Frontier* (New York: Arcade Publishing, 2013).

7   Dr. Ron Williamson, director of archaeological master plan of Toronto. http://heritagetoronto.org/its-not-the-trail-its-the-land-it-crosses/

8   Grace Lee Nute, *The Voyageur* (St. Paul: Minnesota Historical Society Press, 1987).

CHAPTER SIX: NO TRAILS BUT THE WATERWAYS THEMSELVES

1   "Henri de Tonty's Memoir of 1693," *Collections of the Illinois State Historical Library*, vol. 1., ed. H. W. Beckwith, (Springfield, Ill.: H. W. Rokker Co., 1903).

2   Ray, C. Claiborne, "Mighty Acorns," *New York Times*, Oct. 19, 2009.

3   Carolyn Podruchny, *Making the Voyageur World* (Lincoln: University of Nebraska Press, 2006).

4   Colin G. Galloway, *New Worlds for All: Indians, Europeans, and the Remaking of Early America* (Baltimore, Md.: Johns Hopkins University Press, 1997).

5   Shelley J. Pearen, *Exploring Manitoulin*, 3rd ed. (Toronto: University of Toronto Press, 1992).

6   Sigurd Olson, *The Singing Wilderness* (New York: Alfred A. Knopf, 1981).

7   Ibid.

CHAPTER SEVEN: TRAPPED AT DEATH'S DOOR

1   Toby Lester, *The Fourth Part of the World: An Astonishing Epic of Global Discovery, Imperial Ambition, and the Birth of America* (New York: Free Press, 2009).

2   Conan Bryant Eaton, *Death's Door: The Pursuit of a Legend* (Jackson Harbor Press, 1996).

3   Mark Thompson, *Graveyard of the Lakes* (Detroit: Wayne State University Press, 2000).

4   Michael Schumacher, *November's Fury: The Deadly Great Lakes Hurricane of 1913* (Minneapolis: University of Minnesota Press, 2013).

5   Laurence Gonzales, *Deep Survival: Who Lives, Who Dies, and Why* (New York: W. W. Norton and Co., 2003).

CHAPTER EIGHT: "THE BEGINNING OF OUR HARDSHIPS"

1   Paul LeJeune, *Jesuit Relations*, vol. 5 (1632).

2   Gabriel Marest, "Letter from Gabriel Marest to Father de Lamberville," *Jesuit Relations*, vol. 66 (1702).

3   William Bennet Munro, *Crusaders of New France*, vol. 4, The Chronicles of America, ed. Allen Johnson (New Haven, Conn.: Yale University Press, 1920).

4   Anka Muhlstein, *La Salle: Explorer of the North American Frontier* (New York: Arcade Publishing, 2013).

5   Ibid.

6   Ibid.

7   See http://docs.lib.noaa.gov/rescue/mwr/100/mwr-100-03-0235.pdf

8   Donald S. Johnson, *La Salle: A Perilous Odyssey from Canada to the Gulf of Mexico* (New York: Cooper Square Press, 2002).

9   Jeff Manes, "Clearing the Air Would Be a Start," *Chicago Tribune*, Nov. 18, 2014. http://posttrib.chicagotribune.com/news/manes/30991557-452/manes-clearing-the-air-would-be-a-start.html#.VMaZgC7F94F

10   Ralph Lutz, "La Salle Voyageurs Arrive in Berrien," *The News-Palladium* (Michigan), Dec. 20, 1976.

11 A. James Wagner, "The Severe Winter of 1976–77: Precursors and Precedents," http://www.nwas.org/digest/papers/1977/Vol02No4/1977v002no04-Wagner.pdf

CHAPTER NINE: THE MOST DANGEROUS PRODUCT THE INTELLECT HAS CONCOCTED

1 Père du Poisson, *Jesuit Relations*, vol. 67.
2 Anka Muhlstein, *La Salle: Explorer of the North American Frontier* (New York: Arcade Publishing, 2013).
3 Carolyn Podruchny, *Making the Voyageur World* (Lincoln: University of Nebraska Press, 2006).
4 "La Salle Voyageurs Hit by Truck in Indiana," *Chicago Tribune*, Jan. 13, 1977.
5 Paul Valéry, *Selected Writings of Paul Valéry* (New York: New Directions Publishing, 1950).

CHAPTER TEN: PARALLEL VOYAGES

1 William C. Foster, ed., *The La Salle Expedition on the Mississippi River: A Lost Manuscript of Nicholas de la Salle, 1682* (Austin: Texas State Historical Association, 2003).
2 Ibid.
3 Ibid.
4 Pierre Margry, *Découvertes et établissements des Français dans l'Ouest et dans le Sud de l'Amérique Septentrionale, 1614–1754*, vol. 2 (Paris: D. Jouaust), p. 173.
5 "The Bicentennial Blues," *Ebony*, June 1, 1976.
6 John McPhee, "Atchafalaya," *The Control of Nature* (New York: Farrar, Straus, Giroux, 1989).
7 Freeman Tilden, *Interpreting Our Heritage* (Chapel Hill: University of North Carolina Press, 1957).

CHAPTER ELEVEN: THE GREEN BUOY

1 Henri de Tonty, "La Salle's Voyage Down the Mississippi," *Collections of the Illinois State Historical Library*, vol. 1., ed. H. W. Beckwith (Springfield, Ill.: H. W. Rokker Co., 1903).
2 William C. Foster, *The La Salle Expedition on the Mississippi River: A Lost Manuscript of Nicholas de la Salle, 1682* (Austin: Texas State Historical Association, 2003).
3 Henri de Tonty, "La Salle's Voyage Down the Mississippi," *Collections of the Illinois State Historical Library*, vol. 1, ed. H. W. Beckwith (Springfield, Ill.: H. W. Rokker Co., 1903).
4 Robert S. Weddle, "La Salle's Survivors," *The Southwestern Historical Quarterly* 75, no. 4 (April 1972).